REA

MAIN LIBR **FRIENDS**
OF ACPL

P9-EGM-565

110 Sa3d   7107245
SALLIS, JOHN, 1938-
DELIMITATIONS, PHENOMENOLOGY
 AND THE END OF METAPHYSICS

110 Sa3d   7107245
SALLIS, JOHN, 1938-
DELIMITATIONS, PHENOMENOLOGY
 AND THE END OF METAPHYSICS

ALLEN COUNTY PUBLIC LIBRARY

FORT WAYNE, INDIANA 46802

You may return this book to any agency, branch,
or bookmobile of the Allen County Public Library.

MAIN LIBRA.

DELIMITATIONS

Studies in Phenomenology and Existential Philosophy

GENERAL EDITOR
JAMES M. EDIE

CONSULTING EDITORS

David Carr
Edward S. Casey
Stanley Cavell
Roderick M. Chisholm
Hubert L. Dreyfus
William Earle
J. N. Findlay
Dagfinn Føllesdal
Marjorie Grene
Dieter Henrich
Don Ihde
Emmanuel Levinas
Alphonso Lingis

William L. McBride
J. N. Mohanty
Maurice Natanson
Frederick Olafson
Paul Ricoeur
John Sallis
George Schrader
Calvin O. Schrag
Robert Sokolowski
Herbert Spiegelberg
Charles Taylor
Samuel J. Todes
Bruce W. Wilshire

DELIMITATIONS

Phenomenology and the End of Metaphysics

JOHN SALLIS

Indiana University Press

Bloomington & Indianapolis

Allen County Public Library
Ft. Wayne, Indiana

© 1986 by John Sallis
All rights reserved

No part of this book may be reproduced or utilized in any form or by any
means, electronic or mechanical, including photocopying and recording, or by
any information storage and retrieval system, without permission in writing
from the publisher. The Association of American University Presses'
Resolution on Permissions constitutes the only exception to this prohibition.

Manufactured in the United States of America

Library of Congress Cataloging-in-Publication Data
Sallis, John, 1938–
Delimitations—phenomenology and the end of metaphysics
(Studies in phenomenology and existential philosophy)
Bibliography: p.
Includes index.
1. Metaphysics—Addresses, essays, lectures.
2. Phenomenology—Addresses, essays, lectures.
I. Title. II. Series.
BD111.S27 1986   110   85-45700
ISBN 0-253-31691-X
1 2 3 4 5 90 89 88 87 86

Contents
7107245

Die Grenze (πέρας), griechisch gedacht,
ist aber nicht das, wobei etwas aufhört,
sondern das, worein es entsteht, indem es
darinnensteht als demjenigen, was das
Entstandene so und so »gestaltet«,
d. h. in einer Gestalt stehen und das
Ständige anwesen lässt.

Martin Heidegger, Parmenides

Acknowledgments

Because these texts are linked to various particular occasions, settings, and projects, there are many people—more than I could name—to whom I owe gratitude in connection with them. Especially I would like to express my thanks to the following: Robert Bernasconi, Parvis Emad, Michel Haar, David Krell, Kenneth Maly, E. W. Orth, Thomas Sheehan, and David Wood. Many of the issues taken up in these texts were subjects of seminars and discussions in which I participated at the Collegium Phaenomenologicum in Perugia, Italy; I am grateful, especially to Guiseppina Moneta, for having had those opportunities. For help especially during production of this book, I am thankful to Kelly Mink, to my daughter, Kathryn, and to my wife, Jerry.

Chicago
April 1986

Ὁρισμός

Delimitations—of metaphysics. Delimitations by which metaphysics would be determined, not only in its positive constitution but, most decisively, at its limit, in its limit. Thus, it is a matter—quite literally—of defining metaphysics, a matter of thinking it from its end, a matter of what is called—all too carelessly nowadays—the *end* of metaphysics, even the end of philosophy as such; or, a matter of what, more recently, has come to be called the *closure* of metaphysics, even though Derrida himself has repeatedly indicated how thoroughly such a representation remains itself metaphysical, attached to metaphysics' self-representation in the figure of the circle.[1] But of course there can be no question of simply breaking with the circle any more than there can be one of simply breaking out of the circle.

It is a matter, then, of marking the *limit* of metaphysics. What is the shape of this limit? What kind of figure is it? It is not a point at which metaphysics would cease, not a terminal point on the line of metaphysics. For metaphysics does not cease, not even today, indeed least of all today, when, though perhaps still most concealedly, it begins—the words are Heidegger's—"its unconditional rule in beings themselves."[2] Neither is the limit simply an encircling line marking a boundary at which metaphysics would cease. In the first instance, it is much less a matter of cessation than of unfolding:

> A limit [*Grenze*] is not that at which something ceases but, as the Greeks recognized, a limit is that from which something *begins its essential unfolding* [*sein Wesen beginnt*]. Therefore the concept is: ὁρισμός, i.e., limit.[3]

It is a matter of the limit by which metaphysics would be delimited, the limit from which its constitution would unfold, the limit which its constitution would unfold, the limit which, enclosing metaphysics, inaccessible to it as such, would also grant and preserve it.

All the texts assembled here are engaged in marking this limit, this end that would be also the origin of metaphysics. More precisely, they are engaged in marking the operation of the limit, the delimitation in which metaphysics unfolds from the limit, constituted by and yet withheld from the limit, withheld by its very constitution, constituted by its very being withheld. And yet, to mark the limit is to broach a transgression of it; it is to evade somehow the controlling operation of the limit, to displace oneself from it, venturing thus a series of transgressive delimitations. Delimitations—of the delimitation of metaphysics.

Polyphonic delimitations. Texts in which various, dispersed voices speak from the limit, tracing different lines around that horizon. It is not only that the texts were written for—and in several instances read aloud at—different occasions, different kinds of occasions, over a period of several years; but also that they are situated at the limit in very different ways, speaking from it, accordingly, with very different voices.

Certain of the texts mark directly the limit and its transgression. The limit is addressed as closure, as a configuration of completion and termination, as the place—in Heidegger's formulation—where metaphysics is gathered into its most extreme possibilities. Transgression is broached as an opening of imagination and as an abysmal operation.

In others the voices resound from within metaphysics, though never without a certain decisive discord. They resume its appeal to τὸ πρᾶγμα αὐτό, its opening to the things themselves, resume it at that point where it is made to determine the very concept of rigor, in the work of Hegel and of Husserl, that is, in phenomenology. Here it is a matter of retracing—at two points ever so close to those at which a final inversion exhibits the exhaustion of the possibilities open to metaphysics (Marx and Nietzsche)—the completion of metaphysics, its drawing into closure, of retracing it in order again, but now more exclusively from within, to broach the transgressive question, to broach it now as that of the displacement of the things themselves, to broach it by beginning to puncture the enclosure from within, releasing an imaging within the very things themselves. It is a matter of preparing a displacement of phenomenology from within, a displacement by the very force of its appeal to the things themselves, hence a displacement that would be at the same time a radicalizing of phenomenology itself.

Opening to the things themselves, opening as the rigorous renewal of metaphysics in phenomenology, turns, then, into closure; and yet, in that very turning it broaches an opening beyond, the opening of the space in which those things themselves to which phenomenology would attend can show themselves, the clearing in which they can shine forth. Hence, another voice, not without a certain dispersion in itself, speaks almost in the name of Heidegger, whose texts have elaborated what is called clearing (*Lichtung*). Here it is a question of the meaning of Being, that is, of the horizon within which (the limit from which) the self-showing of Being/beings can take place, a question initially of world, then of temporality, then of truth, then of clearing—throughout, a question of limit, of the delimitation of Being, a question of ὁρισμός. It is a matter of opening beyond Being (ἐπέκεινα τῆς οὐσίας), beyond *die Sachen selbst,* or rather, of redetermining *die Sache des Denkens* as clearing; it is, as it were, a matter of translating—quite literally—*die Sache selbst.*

The final word is had by a voice speaking from the darkness, from another closure, not the closure in which metaphysics is completed or exhausted, but rather a closure at the very heart of that opening that is called clearing, concealment at the opening of unconcealment, withdrawal in which the voice must be drawn along if it is to speak from it. A limit; what one would call limitedness as such, were not its very operation a disruption of the very schema of the as such; a horizon that would no longer mark the seam where the sky is joined to the terrestrial surface; a ὁρισμός still more unseen. No longer just the darkness of night with its promise of dawn, but the darkness of enclosure, a darkness in which everything dies away and even heroes become mere shades. The Greeks called it Hades.

I.
CLOSURE OF
METAPHYSICS

ONE

Imagination and Metaphysics

As a way of broaching the question with which this lecture will be concerned, I would like to adopt a little flight of fancy that Kant inscribes near the beginning of the *Critique of Pure Reason*.[1] I shall adopt it in a way that may itself appear a bit fanciful. The flight is that of a dove. The dove, cleaving the air in its flight and feeling the resistance, ventures out toward empty space, upward toward the heavens, supposing that there its flight would be still easier and freer. The dove is an image of metaphysics, and its flight represents the ascent that metaphysics would enact, the ascent out beyond the world of the senses, the ascent into the beyond. The question concerns the power of flight: Does the dove ascend on the wings of imagination?

Metaphysics has never given an unqualifiedly affirmative answer to this question, has never been—or at least has never taken itself to be—a flight of fancy. In metaphysical discourse there is nothing comparable to that discourse that Shakespeare, referring to the poet, put into the mouth of Theseus in *A Midsummer Night's Dream*:

> The poet's eye, in a fine frenzy rolling,
> Doth glance from heaven to earth, from earth to heaven;
> And as imagination bodies forth
> The forms of things unknown, the poet's pen
> Turns them to shapes, and gives to airy nothing
> A local habitation and a name.[2]

Metaphysics, on the contrary, would have nothing to do with airy nothing; it wants to know nothing about the nothing. Nor would it have anything to do with such illicit trafficking back and forth between heaven and earth.

Accordingly, metaphysics has always been suspicious of imagination. Recall the case of Descartes, of those strategies by which he would protect properly metaphysical understanding from the corruptive intru-

---

Text of inaugural lecture presented as Arthur J. Schmitt Professor of Philosophy at Loyola University of Chicago on 6 December 1983.

sion of imagination, for example, his resolve that in the search for the true self there is to be no reliance whatsoever upon imagination:

> And thus I know manifestly that nothing of all that I can understand by means of the imagination is pertinent to the knowledge which I have of myself, and that I must remember this and prevent my mind from thinking in this fashion, in order that it may clearly perceive its own nature.[3]

Much the same suspicion of imagination is expressed, more imaginatively, by Samuel Johnson:

> Imagination, a licentious and vagrant faculty, unsusceptible of limitations, and impatient of restraint, has always endeavored to baffle the logician, to perplex the confines of distinction, and burst the inclosures of regularity.[4]

Or again, it is expressed in Dryden's warning that

> Imagination . . . is a faculty so Wild and Lawless, that, like an high-ranging Spaniel it must have Cloggs tied to it, least it out-run the Judgment.[5]

Or finally, Shakespeare, again through the mouth of Theseus:

> Such tricks hath strong imagination,
> That, if it would but apprehend some joy,
> It comprehends some bringer of that joy;
> Or in the night, imagining some fear
> How easy is a bush supposed a bear![6]

The operation of this suspicion is not, however, simply an operation at a distance. The suspicion does not operate simply by setting imagination once and for all at a distance, by excluding it from the project of metaphysics as something simply opposed to that project. It will be recalled that even Descartes has, in the end, to summon imagination to the aid of that very understanding that he would protect from it. It is, then, precisely the impossibility of any simple exclusion that renders the suspicion so radical, that makes it necessary for it to be exercised ever anew, that binds it so closely to metaphysics. Imagination can be neither simply excluded from nor simply appropriated by metaphysics.

In this lecture I shall undertake to investigate the dynamics of this relation between imagination and metaphysics. It will be, at least initially, a matter of tracing the double gesture by which metaphysics both appropriates imagination and yet excludes it, sets it at a distance. By investigating this strange dynamics, this gesture bordering on contradiction, I hope to venture a few steps in the direction of a question responsive to our time: What becomes of imagination at the end of metaphysics? Is imagination—that is, the word, the concept, perhaps even the thing itself (if I may use, provisionally, this very classical schema)—entangled in the web of metaphysics in such a way that it too cannot but fall prey to a deconstruction that today would dislodge all metaphysical securities? Is the closure of metaphysics also the closure of imagination and of its field of play? Or, on the contrary, does the closure of metaphysics perhaps serve precisely to free imagination and to open fully its field? Is it perhaps even on the wings of imagination that one can effectively transgress metaphysics and station oneself at the limit, hovering there without security?

But let me be more specific about how, this side of such questions, I shall proceed. I shall focus on certain pivotal texts from the history of metaphysics and shall attempt to show how the dynamics of the relation between imagination and metaphysics is traced in those texts. First of all, I shall consider certain Platonic texts. Here it will be a matter of observing how the relation between imagination and metaphysics takes shape, how its dynamics are constituted, with the very inception of metaphysics. The second text to be examined is Pico della Mirandola's treatise "On the Imagination." This text, standing at the threshold of modern thought, at the same time gathers up virtually the entire ancient and medieval reflection on imagination. The third text, Kant's *Critique of Pure Reason*, is a pivot on which modern thought turns perhaps most decisively. In it the question of imagination and metaphysics is vigorously renewed.

Before I proceed, some preliminary points need to be mentioned for the sake of clarity. It is especially important to call attention to the way in which metaphysics, the nature of metaphysics, is to be understood here, a way which is rooted in Continental philosophy since Hegel and which I cannot adequately develop here. Suffice it to mention two points in this regard. First, metaphysics is taken to have a history that is not simply extrinsic to it—that is, it is taken as something which was founded, which has run a certain course, and which since Hegel has come to a kind of end, as something which cannot be defined independently of this history. And yet, though I cannot deal with the issue here, clearly one could not indefinitely postpone taking some account of the torsion already installed within such a concept of metaphysics as historical, the torsion resulting from the fact that metaphysics is also constituted as a turning away from history. Second, metaphysics is to be understood here not so much as a particular discipline alongside others within philosophy as a whole but rather as the execution and elaboration of the fundamental movement or gesture which first opens up philosophy as a whole, which founds it—as, to take an example that I shall have to deal with later in some detail, the Socratic turn from sensible to intelligible opens up the very space in which philosophy moves. But here again one must be careful not to construe matters too straightforwardly, for this example is, of course, not really an example at all but, on the contrary, first con-

stitutes the very field of oppositions in which there can be anything like
an example.

Finally, it is important to note that, formally considered, the relation
between imagination and metaphysics has a certain twofold character.
This twofoldness is indicated perhaps most clearly by the grammatically
twofold genitive: metaphysics *of* imagination. The phrase refers both to a
metaphysical theory about imagination and to a metaphysics in the very
accomplishing of which imagination would play a major role, a metaphysics which would be the work—or, perhaps better, the play—of
imagination. It will be important to observe how these two sides of the
relation are interwoven in the history of metaphysics.

It is in the *Phaedo* that Socrates, recounting his own history, tells of that
decisive turn by which he was set once and for all on his way. According
to his account, that turn came only after he had repeatedly experienced
failure in his efforts to investigate things by the method of his pre-
decessors, namely, that direct method of investigation which would proceed to explain certain things by referring them directly to other things.
Socrates relates that as a result of this experience he came eventually to
have recourse to a kind of indirect way of investigating things, a way
which he describes as analogous to the procedure of studying things in
an image rather than looking at them directly. He says: "So I thought I
must have recourse to λόγοι and examine in them the truth of beings."[7]
This recourse he describes as a matter of "placing something under," as
one might place a foundation under an infirm structure. What is thus
placed under he calls a ὑπόθεσις; he mentions the beautiful itself, the
good, the great. In other words—words which are, however, decisive for
the entire history of metaphysics—the recourse is a matter of positing
explicitly certain εἴδη that are already tacitly posited, expressed, in λόγος. Thus, in the recourse certain εἴδη are posited over against the
sensibly present things, posited as "standing under" those things, as their
foundation. Hence, the Socratic turn consists in the opening of the
difference between immediately, sensibly present things and those εἴδη
that would be their foundation—or, more precisely and literally, those
εἴδη in which the sheer unobstructed look of things would be had. Note
especially the remark that Socrates is careful to add: Though his turn is
analogous to the procedure of turning from things (i.e., originals) to
images (of those things), it is ultimately quite distinct from such a procedure. It is ultimately even an inversion of that procedure, a turn not
from original to image but, conversely, from immediately present things
(recognized as images) to their originals. The Socratic turn thus differen-
tiates between things in their immediate, sensible presence and those
things in their original truth, in their originary presence; and it shifts
away from immediately, sensibly present things, away from the fragmented presence of the immediate and sensible—shifts away in order to

prepare a reappropriation of those things in their originary presence. By marking this difference between τὸ νοητόν and τὸ αἰσθητόν, the Socratic turn poses the task of mediating this difference and in posing this task founds metaphysics. More precisely, the Socratic turn constitutes the field of metaphysics as a field of presence and metaphysics itself as the drive to presence.

In the Platonic dialogues there are many representations of this difference, this field—for example, that line which is drawn and divided near the center of the *Republic*. The schema of image-original is explicit in Socrates' description of the relation between the two segments which represent the divisions of the sensible as a whole: In the transition it is a matter of εἰκασία, of apprehending images (εἰκών) *as* images in such a way that one sees through them to the originals which they image. It is, for example, a matter of apprehending the shadow of an artifact as a shadow and hence as disclosing the artifact itself, a matter of that kind of apprehending that comes to be exercised by the exceptional one among those cave-dwellers described in that image at the very center of the *Republic*. But it is not only underground, not only within the sensible, that the schema of image-original is in play. For when, emerging from the cave into the open space above, the escaped prisoner prepares to lift his gaze from the earth to the heavens, he makes his preparation by gazing at things as they are *imaged*, as they are, for example, reflected in pools of water. This schema determines the entire course represented by the cave and the line. It constitutes the structure within which the metaphysical reappropriation of presence would be played out. The field of metaphysics, the field of presence, is structured by the dyadic relation between image and original; it is structured by the indeterminate dyad.

In this sense, then, one may say that metaphysics is a matter of imagination, provided, of course, that imagination is distinguished from mere fancy. It is a matter of eikastic imagination, not of phantastic imagination. Granted this limitation, the two sides of the genitive, the two senses of metaphysics *of* imagination, become perfectly complementary: The metaphysical theory regarding imagination would be simply the self-understanding of a metaphysics accomplished by imagination.

And yet, the Platonic Socrates incessantly sets imagination, even eikastic imagination, at a distance. The poets, the painters, the sophists, all those who deal in images are ferreted out, distinguished from the philosopher, and banished from the city. One would, of course, need to insist on the subtlety and irony of the Socratic criticisms of the image-makers; and one would need to take account of the massive self-reference of these criticisms, to take account, for example, of the fact that an image stands at the beginning, the middle, and the end of the very dialogue in which image-making is most explicitly condemned, viz., the *Republic*—indeed, not just an image but the image of images, the image

of a realm in which all would be mere images, mere shades.[8] Nevertheless, the taking of distance from imagination belongs structurally to the
metaphysical project no less than does the appropriation of imagination.
For though the schema of image-original structures the field of metaphysics in such a way that the drive to presence can be oriented and
carried out, it also, on the other hand, serves to inhibit that drive and to
divert it into a play of presence and absence. Insofar as the structure
remains in force, every original remains withdrawn, concealed, behind
its image, glimpsed only through that image, not in its originary presence. And if indeed one did succeed in traversing the distance from
image to original, one would do so only at the cost of opening up another
such space behind what would then prove not to have been truly original.

Such is, in briefest outline, the dynamics that governs the relation
between imagination and metaphysics in the Platonic texts: Imagination
both empowers and inhibits the metaphysical drive to presence, and
metaphysics must, accordingly, both appropriate and take distance from
imagination. The metaphysical theory regarding imagination is not only
a matter of metaphysical self-understanding but also one of distinguishing metaphysics from an other from which, as from the sophist, it can
never free itself once and for all.

During the period of nearly two millennia that separates the Platonic
texts from Pico's treatise of 1500 "On the Imagination," several shifts
occur which affect the relation between imagination and metaphysics
and the dynamics of that relation. The most significant shift occurs in the
conception of imagination; it is a shift from εἰκασία to φαντασία, from
eikastic imagination to phantastic imagination, and it is marked lin-
guistically by the fact that both Latin words *imaginatio* and *phantasia* are
translations of forms of the Greek φαντασία.[9] Remarkably, εἰκασία goes
virtually untranslated. This shift prescribes a whole series of realign-
ments in the relation between imagination and metaphysics, and one of
the virtues of Pico's treatise is the transparency with which these realign-
ments are presented.

The shift is announced at the very outset of Pico's text: He identifies
his theme as that power of the soul which the Greeks call φαντασία and
which in Latin is called *imaginatio*. It is so called in Latin, he notes,
because of those images which it forms in itself, images which are linked
to those likenesses of things that are conveyed through the exterior
senses. Deferring the explanation of that link of imagination to sense,
Pico focuses momentarily on those things themselves:

> For whatever the object of sensation, and that means everything corporeal
> which can be perceived or felt by any sense, the object produces, insofar as it
> can, a likeness and image of itself, in imitation of incorporeal and spiritual

nature. This spiritual nature communicates its powers to the inferior world in imitation of God himself, who in his infinite goodness, spread far and wide, has established and preserves the universe.[10]

The passage is remarkable, for it broaches on both a horizontal and a vertical axis that schema of image-original which according to the Platonic texts structures the field of metaphysics and corresponds to eikastic imagination. Objects, such as the senses can present, produce images of themselves; they are image-makers of themselves, originals necessarily distinct from those images of themselves which they produce in the soul. Furthermore, on the vertical axis, this image-making accomplished by objects is an imitation, an image, of that superior image-making practiced by the soul insofar as it impresses its form on the inferior, corporeal world, e.g., in the practice of an art in the classical sense. In turn, and finally, the soul's image-making is an imitation, a moving image, of that absolutely original image-making practiced by the creator. This utterly Platonic beginning is even identified as such: Plato's name is mentioned, and a reference is made to the *Timaeus*. But then, as though it might otherwise displace the discussion of φαντασία that has been promised, Pico abruptly sets the entire eikastic structure aside: "But enough of such reflections, since here is not the place for them." Pico's text has begun by reenacting the shift away from εἰκασία.

A new, more controlled beginning is made, and now the authority of Aristotle is explicitly invoked. Now the constitution of the field of metaphysics, its structuring, hardly comes into question. Instead, the investigation centers on imagination—phantastic imagination—as a power of the soul. As such, imagination proves to be essential to all knowledge, an ally that must come to the aid of all other human powers if they are not to fail in the function bestowed upon them by nature. As Pico writes, actually shifting at this point in his text to the word *phantasia*: "Nor could the soul, fettered as it is to the body, opine, know, or comprehend at all, if phantasy were not constantly to supply it with the images themselves."[11] Imagination is the great mediator: It receives the impressions of objects from the senses, retains them within itself, and renders them purer before passing them on to the higher powers of the soul. As in the Platonic texts, imagination mediates the ascent from the sensible, though now it is a mediation withdrawn into the soul rather than one that draws the soul into a dyadically structured field of presence.

However, Pico's text is by no means written to celebrate the mediating role which imagination plays in the soul's ascent. On the contrary, almost from the beginning—the new, more controlled beginning—Pico stresses that "imagination is for the most part vain and wandering."[12] As he proceeds, the condemnation becomes more and more severe, and an entire chapter—chapter 7, entitled "On the numerous Evils which come from the Imagination"—is devoted to enumerating the charges. Imagination is identified as the mother and nurse of ambition. Cruelty, wrath, and passion are said to be born from and nourished by imagination; likewise with the insatiable thirst for gold and the ardor of lust. Imagination is also charged with bringing about "all monstrous opinions and the defects of all judgment"; it is at the origin of most sins and is the source of those heresies that pervert the Christian faith. However, more significant than any of these charges is the one made in defense of philosophy:

> And if we turn our attention to the functions of the philosophic life, we shall see that no lesser disadvantage has accrued to it from false phantasies. Indeed, when I consider the source of the shifting, the manifold, differences in opinion that have come down even to our time from those great philosophers, Thales, Democritus, Empedocles, Zeno, Pythagoras, and the others, nothing strikes me as more reasonable than that we should pass sentence upon the treacherous imagination.[13]

Philosophy itself, empowered by imagination, is also corrupted by it, by its vanity and its wanderings. Thus, Pico writes his treatise not to celebrate imagination, nor even just to understand it, but to condemn it:

> But imagination is for the most part vain and wandering; for the sake of proving this to be so I have assumed the present task of demonstration.[14]

Above all, Pico writes his treatise in order to condemn the corruption with which imagination threatens philosophy; or, rather, since it cannot be a matter of simply excluding imagination, his task is to set imagination at a distance from philosophy, to render its threat ineffective by developing a theory of imagination in which that threat is exposed. And yet, even this kind of defense is limited; for imagination, empowering knowledge, is always already in play in that very knowledge, that theory of imagination, by which it would be exposed and set at a distance. Indeed, Pico explicitly marks this limit: "Since the imagination itself is midway between incorporeal and corporeal nature and is the medium through which they are joined, it is difficult to grasp its nature through philosophy. . . ."[15] The dynamics of the relation between philosophy, i.e., metaphysics, and imagination is such that appropriation and distancing are mutually limiting.

Pico stresses the need for distancing. His metaphysics of imagination, i.e., his metaphysical theory regarding the nature of imagination, belongs to metaphysics, to metaphysics as empowered by imagination, belongs to it not so much as positive self-understanding but as a necessarily limited taking of distance from imagination and thus from the threat which it poses to metaphysics. Nevertheless, it is only a matter of stress within a dynamics which, despite the shift from εἰχαστία to φαντασία, remains essentially the same as that traced in the Platonic texts.

In the *Critique of Pure Reason,* written nearly three centuries after Pico's treatise, there remains scarcely a trace of eikastic imagination. On the other hand, the conception of phantastic imagination is greatly enriched and expanded, and its various forms are differentiated. Correspondingly, Kant's conception centers on imagination not just as a power of the soul but rather as the fundamental synthetic power of the subject, the synthetic power necessary for the constitution of an object for the subject.

The sense of this shift in the conception of imagination is closely linked to another, more extensive shift, the shift which makes the *Critique of Pure Reason* such a pivotal text in the history of metaphysics. This text announces a radical shift in metaphysics as such, announces it through the very form assumed by the text, the form of critique, announces it by giving voice to the need to institute a tribunal by which the claims of metaphysics can be decided. What are the claims that require such critical judgment? The claim to purely intellectual knowledge, to knowledge through pure concepts. What is the decision rendered by the tribunal of pure reason? On its negative side, the decision is that metaphysics has no legitimate claim to a knowledge of purely intelligible being, of things as they would be independently of their way of appearing to human sensibility. On its positive side, however, the tribunal upholds the claim that metaphysics makes to purely intellectual knowledge of objects as they appear to human sensibility; it upholds this claim by demonstrating that those purely intellectual determinations, those pure concepts, those categories, are at work in the very constituting of the sensible object, to which they must then subsequently have objective application.

The primary shift is thus a kind of closure, a shift of the intelligible into the sensible. More precisely, insofar as the intelligible is to the slightest degree accessible to human knowledge, it is no longer to be simply contrasted with the sensible but rather is regarded as merely a dimension within the sensible, its categorial determination. The difference originally opened by the Socratic turn, the difference between sensible and intelligible, is now, in Kantian critique, opened within the sensible itself—or, if you will, confined within the sensible. Such is the shift which metaphysics thus undergoes, a shift, a relocation, a confinement, of its very field.[16]

In the constitution of this field, thus shifted, the role played by imagination is no less fundamental than in the classical instance. Now it is a matter of the constitution of the sensible object as such, specifically, of the mediation between the poles of the new field, between the intuitive and the conceptual or categorial. To perform this mediation is the role of imagination, a role which it plays, not (as in the classical instance) by moving eikastically through image to original, but rather by bringing into play its power of synthesis. And yet, even in this decisively modern conception of imagination and of its function, one can still discern a trace of the dynamics that governed the Platonic conception in its relation to metaphysics and to the field of metaphysics. For, in Kant's words, "*imagination* is the faculty of representing in intuition an object that is *not itself present*"[17]—that is, it is the faculty by which one brings to presence something which is not present, or, more precisely, the faculty by which one brings to presence something which remains in another regard absent. To the same degree as eikastic vision through image to original, imagination as redetermined in Kantian critique both empowers and inhibits the metaphysical drive to presence. The difference is, however, that Kantian critique installs imagination within a field which has itself been displaced, a field which is no longer simply governed by the drive to presence, a field which is reconstituted this side of the purely intelligible, this side of the thing-in-itself, this side of that originary presence that provides classical metaphysics with its τέλος. The field of metaphysics as reconstituted in the *Critique of Pure Reason* is a field in which the play of presence and absence, the play of self-revelation and self-withholding, the play of imagination, is released from that repression that would subordinate it in the end to the ideal of sheer revelation, of pure presence.

Thus, imagination and metaphysics, as redetermined in the *Critique of Pure Reason*, are utterly appropriate to one another—so much so that the Kantian theory of the nature of imagination is wholly continuous with critique as such, which provides metaphysics with that self-understanding requisite for delimiting its possibilities and its limits, i.e., its field. Such delimitation is sufficient, and there is no need to supplement it with an indictment of imagination such as Pico found it necessary to provide in his treatise. Now, with the *Critique of Pure Reason*, there is no need to set imagination at a distance from metaphysics. This utter appropriation gets expressed most transparently two decades later, when Schelling, in his *System of Transcendental Idealism*, comes to identify theoretical reason as such with imagination.[18] This identity, this appropriation, is echoed by the great English Romantic poets—for example, by Coleridge's account of imagination as that power that "urges us up the ascent of Being,"[19] by Wordsworth's identification of imagination as "reason in her most exalted mood."[20]

And yet, this appropriation of imagination to metaphysics is not un-

limited. On the contrary, it is most decisively limited by the most fundamental division within reason itself and, correspondingly, within critique, viz., by the division between theoretical and practical reason,
between the *Critique of Pure Reason* and the *Critique of Practical Reason.*
However much imagination, extending between sensible and intelligible,
can empower theoretical reason and make it possible to delimit a metaphysics of nature, imagination is, on the other hand, that power which,
perhaps most of all, must be rigorously excluded from the domain of
reason's practical employment. Practical reason must be *pure* practical
reason, unmixed with elements of sense such as would otherwise be
drawn into it by imagination. It is a matter of a determination, a self-
determination, unmediated by imagination.[21] It is a matter of a pure,
practical presence to self, unmediated by that play of sense and imagination that contaminates that cognitive presence to self that is based on
inner intuition. However much imagination is appropriated to theoretical reason, to the metaphysics of nature, it is with equal rigor excluded,
distanced, from practical reason, from the metaphysics of morals. For
critical metaphysics as a whole the dynamics of the relation between
imagination and metaphysics remains essentially the same as that traced
in the texts of Plato and of Pico.

And yet, there remains another moment of the metaphysical project
that I have quite deliberately avoided making explicit up to this point. It
is a moment that supervenes upon that dynamic relation between metaphysics and imagination that has now been outlined in texts of Plato, of
Pico, and of Kant.

One can perhaps discern this moment most distinctly, most thoroughly separated, in reference to the specific form which the dynamics
assumes in critique. In the Kantian conception of practical reason there
is operative not only a distancing of metaphysics from imagination but
also a rigorous stabilizing of that distance, a setting of practical reason in
a domain in which it would be essentially free of imagination. In other
words, it is a matter of establishing a certain refuge beyond the play of
imagination, a refuge in which, delivered from that play of presence and
absence, reason could be self-determining, genuinely one with itself,
present to itself in an originary way. The *Critique of Practical Reason* in
effect compensates for that shift which the field of metaphysics under-
went in the first *Critique*, compensates by positing a new intelligible
order: "If freedom is attributed to us, it transfers us into an intelligible
order of things."[22]

That moment of the metaphysical project that I want now to make
explicit can thus be characterized as a certain stabilizing of the otherwise
dynamic relation between imagination and metaphysics. It is a matter of
positing a refuge beyond the play of imagination, a refuge in which pure

presence would be protected from the threat of imagination. It is a matter of decisively limiting the dynamic relation between imagination and metaphysics by means of a repression of imagination.

This moment is constantly in force in Pico's text and is precisely what allows him to pass so lightly over the positive role which imagination plays in metaphysics. He can pass beyond this role because metaphysics itself is genuinely realized, is genuinely metaphysics itself, only in that domain in which imagination is repressed. Pico outlines this domain in his conception of *intellectus,* that highest power of the soul, the power by which one can contemplate those purely intelligible things that are absolutely removed from the region of sense. Within this domain of intellectual contemplation, one is able, in Pico's telling phrase, to "dominate phantasy." He continues: "When the soul has withdrawn itself into the intellect, there, as in its own protected palace and enclosed citadel, it reposes and is perfected."[23]

This movement of repression is also in force in the Platonic texts—or, rather, one might say, at *play* in them, since it is rarely traced in those texts without being set within a dialogical play of the utmost subtlety and irony. Within the *Republic* the discussion at the end of Book VI is exemplary, especially if read along with its resumption in Book VII. I am referring to the discussion in which Socrates speaks with Glaucon about that segment of the divided line that represents dialectic, that is, the uppermost of the four segments, if, for convenience, I may assume the usual vertical representation. Socrates describes this final stage of the soul's ascent by contrasting it with the kind of movement in which the soul engages at its penultimate stage, represented by the third, the next-to-highest, segment of the line. At its penultimate stage the soul continues, as at the lower stages, to make use of images, but now, as Socrates explains, "using as images the things that were previously imitated."[24] It proceeds, then, upon hypotheses, that is, originals posited for what now show themselves to be images. Thus, the penultimate stage preserves the dyadic structure—that is, this stage is constituted by shifting to another, more original level the image-original structure that is most manifestly operative at those stages represented by the lower segments of the line. It is precisely this dyadic structure that would finally be left behind—or, if you will, repressed—at the level of dialectic. Socrates says that in its ultimate ascent the soul, proceeding now without images, would move away from hypotheses toward an ἀρχή, a beginning or ground, that would be aloof from the dispersive play of imagination.

Glaucon is moved by what Socrates says about dialectic; and after Socrates has, in Book VII, gone through the penultimate stage in its full articulation from arithmetic to harmony, Glaucon is eager to move on to dialectic and to go through it in the same way so as to reach that place that would be, in his words, "a haven from the road." Socrates' response is most remarkable:

> You will no longer be able to follow, my dear Glaucon, . . . although there wouldn't be any lack of eagerness on my part. But you would no longer be seeing an image of what we are saying, but rather the truth itself, at least as it looks to me.[25]

It would be a matter of seeing the truth itself instead of an image, a matter of seeing the original truth, the true original—at least, Socrates says, *as it looks to me,* that is, in that appearance that it offers to me, the *image* that it casts in my direction. Need it be said that Socrates reintroduces here the play of subtlety and irony that had almost been lost as the discourse became more and more single-mindedly oriented to what Glaucon calls the end of the journey, the haven from the road?

In the discourse woven by the history of metaphysics, however, such subtlety and irony tend to disappear more irrevocably, to disappear in favor of a massive repression of imagination. It is a matter of stabilizing the otherwise dynamic relation between imagination and metaphysics, of positing a refuge, a haven, aloof from the play of imagination. This moment makes of metaphysics an unqualified drive to presence by subordinating it to a τέλος of pure presence, the end of the journey, the place of the true original whose presence is undivided by any casting of images. This τέλος is equally ἀρχή, the original which grounds. The concept of ground is thus put in force and metaphysics is made a drive to ground.

But let me no longer pretend that this moment is something added to metaphysics, something that would alter an already constituted field and the orientation within that field. On the contrary, this moment belongs to the very constitution of metaphysics as such, i.e., as it runs through its great orbit from Aristotle (metaphysics as knowledge of origins and first causes) to Hegel (metaphysics as the arrival at absolute self-presence). Metaphysics as such is drive to presence, drive to ground, and the repression of imagination belongs integrally to it.

And yet, I have deliberately kept this moment detached from a certain field, the field in which obtains the dynamic relation between imagination and metaphysics. I have kept it detached because it is precisely the moment that gets detached at the end of metaphysics, in that closure of metaphysics announced most forcefully by Nietzsche and analyzed most thoroughly in recent Continental thought. In this end, this closure, that strategy by which the dynamic relation between imagination and metaphysics was stabilized, that strategy by which imagination was finally repressed, comes to show itself precisely *as a strategy.* The closure of metaphysics is precisely the emptying of every refuge in which pure intelligibility might find protection from the threat of imagination.

The end of metaphysics is, then, the release of imagination into the entire field, the return of the repressed. And yet, the field does not remain the same; it is not, as I pretended earlier, merely the field of metaphysics without its final moment. For that final moment, the τέλος of originary presence, is precisely what orients the field of metaphysics. Once that moment is detached, the field is no longer simply a field of presence, a field oriented to presence.

And yet, as a field of eikastic imagination, it must be an oriented field, a field in which certain lines of directionality mark the difference between image and original, prescribing the movement in the field. But it must be also a field of indeterminate and irreducible duality, a field in which the movement of imagination never comes to rest in an absolute original aloof from the field and the play.

Let me recall some words of that author to whom Nietzsche was referring when in the 1880s he wrote, perhaps exorbitantly, that "the author who has been richest in ideas [*gedankenreichste*] in this century so far has been an American."[26] Nietzsche's reference is to Emerson, and it is from Emerson's essay "Circles" that I cite these words:

> Our life is an apprenticeship to the truth, that around every circle another can be drawn; that there is no end in nature, but every end is a beginning; that there is always another dawn risen on mid-noon, and under every deep a lower deep opens.[27]

It would be a matter of a field that would compound the way up and the way down, a field upon which two suns might cast shadows and beneath which the caverns might open endlessly. It would be a matter of joining end and beginning, of bending the line around into a circle, and of redrawing that circle indefinitely.

More precisely (perhaps), it would be a matter of taking the directional, oriented character and the reiterably dyadic character of the field as traces or residues of what metaphysics began by calling λόγος and εἰκασία and ended by calling reason and imagination. It would be a matter of venturing, beyond the closure of metaphysics, to reassemble these moments which metaphysics from its beginning has set apart. Writing under erasure, attending to the subtlety and risk of the move, one might then broach the demands of a logic of imagination.

Let me recall the flight of fancy, the flight of the dove. The dove of metaphysics soars off into the heavens, ventures out into empty space where nothing any longer offers support, where flight becomes finally impossible. The dove may then realight upon the ground in search of security; it may even seek refuge, a haven, by creeping down into those caverns which open endlessly, inching along through them, molelike. But just as the emptiness above is an absolute absence which precisely as such is the promise of full presence grown silent, so the ground below is equally compromised by those endlessly opening caverns in which, as in Hades, there are only shades, only images. What the dove must learn is to *hover* between heaven and earth, drifting a bit with the currents, resisting the lure of the emptiness above and the illusion of fullness below.

TWO

The End of Metaphysics

Closure and Transgression

I could have begun, most appropriately perhaps, by withdrawing the title "The End of Metaphysics." Then, having first announced it only to withdraw it, I would at least have approximated in speech to what one does in writing by erasing or crossing out, producing a text in which both what was written and its effacement can be read. Why such a beginning? Why might it have been most appropriate? Because, in the first place, the title is simply misleading, indicating almost nothing of the immense complexity of that phenomenon that it pretends to name, most notably the complex of senses, the multiplicity of determinations, of the end of metaphysics. But there is also a more radical reason for setting the beginning under erasure: a kind of self-effacement intrinsic to the very question of the end of metaphysics. Here I can only allude to this peculiar reflexivity, allude to it by pointing to the metaphysical origins of those concepts, those senses, of "end" to which any discourse on the end of metaphysics would have recourse. In other words, any such discourse makes use of certain developed senses of "end," senses that have come to be developed precisely within the history of metaphysics; it is metaphysics that has rigorously determined the senses of "end" as τέλος, as πέρας, as *terminus*, etc. But then, it must be expected that the end of metaphysics will bring radically into question these metaphysically determined senses of "end." The end of metaphysics brings the very sense of end—hence, its *own* sense—into question.

And so, in this lecture—this attempt at a discourse on the end of metaphysics—a certain vigilance will need to be exercised, an attentiveness both to the multiplicity of senses and to a certain effacement, erosion, or slippage of those senses. Specifically, I shall distinguish four primary senses in which metaphysics has been proclaimed to be at its end. I shall suggest also how these senses slide, as it were, into the sense of end as closure. Accordingly, if one takes the situation of thought in

---

Lecture presented at Loyola University-New Orleans on 5 April 1984.

our time to be determined by the end of metaphysics, then that situation—the situation in which we would venture to think today—would be most appropriately represented by the figure of closure. The task of thought in the contemporary situation would be, then, somehow to disrupt closure; to think at the end of metaphysics would be to transgress closure. And so, having distinguished the various senses of end, having then gathered them into end as closure, I shall finally attempt to outline a series of strategies of transgression.

The lecture is thus divided into two parts, the titles of which constitute the subtitle of the lecture as a whole, "Closure and Transgression," it too calling for reservations hardly less stringent than those I have expressed regarding "The End of Metaphysics."

(A) CLOSURE

It is Nietzsche who most forcefully proclaims that metaphysics is at its end. These proclamations are among his most scandalous: his proclamation that God is dead, that being is a fallacy and a vapor, the last smoke of evaporating reality; or, again, his story, in *The Twilight of the Idols*, of how the true world finally became a fable.[1] What Nietzsche announces in nearly all his texts is the effacement of what always, from the beginning, has constituted the object of metaphysics: the effacement of that God who would be the highest, most perfect, being, the effacement also of that which would determine every being simply insofar as it is, the effacement of being qua being. With the effacement of its object, metaphysics comes, then, to a kind of termination, to an end in the sense of termination. Nietzsche would proclaim this termination of metaphysics, would proclaim simply: Metaphysics is no more!

And yet, metaphysics cannot *simply* terminate. It cannot simply disappear, leaving everything else intact. Nietzsche's recognition that the sense of end as termination is not simply a matter of utter termination is most explicit in the final episode in the story of how the true world finally became a fable. The complexity of the sense of end as termination is presented in terms of the metaphysical opposition around which the entire story is organized, the opposition between the true world, i.e., the intelligible, and the apparent world, i.e., the sensible:

> The true world—we have abolished. What world has remained? The apparent one perhaps? But no! *With the true world we have also abolished the apparent one.*[2]

Nietzsche's point is that the effacement of the intelligible does not simply leave the sensible unaffected in its basic determination. The sensible does not simply remain intact, because it has always been understood precisely *in opposition to* the intelligible. The effacement of the true world is the effacement of the very opposition and hence of the determination of the apparent world in terms of that opposition, an effacement of its very determination as apparent, as sensible. Even beyond its termination metaphysics continues to cast its shadow; and one who would proclaim the end of metaphysics would be called to engage in new struggles— such as those to which Nietzsche refers in that section of *The Gay Science* which is entitled "New Struggles" and which reads:

> After Buddha was dead, his shadow was still shown for centuries in a cave— a tremendous, gruesome shadow. God is dead; but given the ways of men, there may still be caves for thousands of years in which his shadow will be shown.—And we—we still have to vanquish his shadow too.[3]

Such is, then, the first sense that I want to distinguish: the end of metaphysics as its termination—a termination so complex, however, that it casts its shadow over all previously established determinations, setting all sense in motion, calling not just for new determinations but for a renewal of the very possibility of determination.

Another kind of ending of metaphysics had, however, already been proclaimed long before Nietzsche. The approach of such an end—and the hope for it—is announced in the last sentence of the *Critique of Pure Reason*:

> If the reader has had the courtesy and patience to accompany me along this path, he may now judge for himself whether, if he cares to lend his aid in making this path into a high-road, it may not be possible to achieve before the end of the present century what many centuries have not been able to accomplish; namely, to secure for human reason complete satisfaction in regard to that with which it has all along so eagerly occupied itself, though hitherto in vain.[4]

This projection needs to be read together with Kant's prefatory statement of aim:

> In this inquiry I have made completeness my chief aim, and I venture to assert that there is not a single metaphysical problem which has not been solved, or for the solution of which the key at least has not been supplied.[5]

What Kant is projecting, what he is announcing as virtually accomplished, is the *completion* of metaphysics.

The same intention is expressed more vigorously and thought through more profoundly by Hegel—for example, in the Preface to the *Phenomenology of Spirit*:

> To help bring philosophy closer to the form of science, to the goal where it can lay aside the title '*love* of knowledge' and be actual knowledge—that is what I have set myself to do.[6]

What makes Hegel's grasp of the ending more profound is his awareness that the end cannot be extrinsic to the history that it completes, that it cannot be simply a matter of suddenly securing what throughout the history of metaphysics was sought in vain, that it cannot be an end which in this sense simply negates what has preceded. Rather, for Hegel—here the most schematic indication must suffice—it is a matter of bringing to a certain completion, of making actual, that knowing which has animated metaphysics throughout its history, that knowing which, more generally, consists in spirit's self-recognition, its self-appropriation, in every form of otherness. With Hegel, metaphysics would come to its end in the sense that its history would be gathered into the full actuality of spirit.

And yet, here too there can be a question of shadows, a question of reference back to the cave from which metaphysics would have emerged into the brilliant sunlight, a question of a return to the cave. The question is whether metaphysics in its completion simply persists or whether, on the contrary, it is as incapable of simply enduring as it is of simply terminating. Hence, in Schelling it is a question not only of the completion of metaphysics but then also of a certain shift, a displacement, of metaphysics thus completed. For instance, at the end of his *System of Transcendental Idealism,* having demonstrated the completeness of the system, Schelling continues as follows:

> There is one more conclusion yet to be drawn. Philosophy was born and nourished by poetry in the infancy of knowledge, and with it all those sciences it has guided toward perfection; we may thus expect them, on completion, to flow back like so many individual streams into the universal ocean of poetry from which they took their source.[7]

Such is, then, the second sense that I want to distinguish: the end of metaphysics as its completion—a completion which not only would gather what has preceded into the actuality of spirit but also would broach the question of a displacement, perhaps even of a displacement that would violate the sphere of completed metaphysics, that would transgress the limits of well-rounded truth.

It is Heidegger who gives the question of the end of metaphysics its contemporary form. Drawing upon Nietzsche and German Idealism, Heidegger rigorously redetermines the sense of the ending. This redetermination governs virtually all subsequent discourse on this question.

Heidegger's first move is to exclude simple termination: The end of metaphysics is not a matter of its stopping, its failing to continue, its decline into some kind of utter impotence. Rather, it is a matter of the completion of metaphysics. And yet, completion (*Vollendung*) is not to be taken in the sense of perfection (*Vollkommenheit*), hence not to be taken in the simpler of those senses given it in German Idealism. It is not a matter of metaphysics' coming to an end in which its highest perfection would be attained. Its end is not the locus, the place, of its perfection but rather the place of a radically different kind of gathering:

> The end of philosophy is the place, that place in which the whole of philosophy's history is gathered into its most extreme possibility. End as completion means this gathering.[8]

Such is, then, the third sense that I want to distinguish: the end of metaphysics as the place of such gathering, the place where the history of metaphysics is gathered into its most extreme possibility.

This sense needs to be determined more precisely and more specifically. Let me stress two points. The first is that end in the Heideggerian sense represents a kind of displacement of that classical sense of end as τέλος that was determined in the most profound way in German Idealism. According to this classical concept, something would come to its end in being gathered into its form of perfection, into the τέλος, as, for example, the preceding stages of development are gathered up, fulfilled, in the flowering of a plant. Such a gathering is thought by Hegel in the concept of *Aufhebung*. With this word—still not really translated, i.e., rethought, in English—Hegel designates a movement in which what is lower is surpassed and yet always essentially preserved by being elevated into what is higher, gathered up into it. In a different figure, *Aufhebung* is the process by which what is extrinsic and peripheral is gathered to the intrinsic, to the center. For Hegel such gathering constitutes the fundamental sense of actualization—that is, to be actual means to be gathered into the τέλος. With Heidegger, on the other hand, it is a matter of gathering into the most extreme possibility. The point is, then, that the displacement which determines the Heideggerian gathering is governed by the two oppositions center/extreme and actuality/possibility. It is a matter of gathering not to the center but to the most extreme and of gathering not into actuality but into possibility.

But there is a second point that is essential for grasping the radicalness of the Heideggerian sense of end. The point is that Heidegger uses the phrase "most extreme possibility" (*äusserste Möglichkeit*) not only in outlining the displaced sense of the end of metaphysics but also, much earlier, in *Being and Time,* in developing the existential analysis of death. In that earlier analysis Heidegger undertakes to determine the sense in which death is the end of Dasein. A number of senses he excludes as inappropriate: Death is not the end of Dasein in the sense of a mere stopping, as, for example, a road stops, terminates; nor is it the end in the sense of ripeness, in the sense that fruit, for example, reaches its end by ripening, for death is not the fulfillment of Dasein's life. Rather, death is the end in the sense that it is Dasein's *extreme possibility*. This means—if I may here merely allude to Heidegger's rich and complex analysis of death—that it is a matter of a possibility that cannot be outstripped, that is unsurpassable, of a possibility that withdraws all possibilities, of a possibility that closes off decisively the opening to a future.[9] The point is that the same holds for the "death" of metaphysics, determining the Heideggerian sense of the end of metaphysics. For metaphysics, too, the end is one that cannot be outstripped, an end which metaphysics cannot circumvent, get beyond, while itself remaining intact. It is an end which withdraws all possibilities—that is, an end in which metaphysics' possibilities are exhausted. And it is an end which accordingly closes off all opening to a future. In short, it is an end which takes the form of *closure*.

Such is, then, the fourth sense that I want to distinguish: the end of metaphysics as its closure.

And yet, closure is not something that suddenly supervenes at the end, constituting that end. Closure does not figure in metaphysics only in our time; on the contrary, the operation of the figure of closure can be discerned, at least retrospectively, throughout the history of metaphysics. Let me here merely refer in the very briefest way to a decisive moment that Heidegger and Derrida have identified in the basic constitution of metaphysics. That constitutive moment consists in the determination of knowledge as essentially *intuition*. This does not, of course, mean that metaphysics regards all knowledge as intuition—not all knowing is intuiting. The point is, rather, that intuition is regarded as knowledge in the most genuine sense, as the ideal at which all knowledge aims. In turn, that knowledge is essentially intuition means that ideally it is a pure seeing, a sheer beholding, of what is simply there, *present* to one's gaze, of what ideally would be totally open to one's gaze, something fully present. Thus, in granting a privilege to intuition, metaphysics would also grant a privilege to the correlate of intuition, namely, presence—or, rather, the granting of such privilege to the correlates intuition/presence belongs to the very constitution of metaphysics.

This privilege is what generates the figure of closure and inscribes it within metaphysics from the beginning. Ideally, intuition would be full presence to what is present. Completely self-sufficient, it would require no means, no mediation, no other resource of subjectivity such as might otherwise come to supplement intuition. Likewise, what would be present to such intuition would be fully and self-sufficiently present; it would present itself without reserve, and there would be no need for any detour of the sort that would pass beyond what is present in order to recover its presence indirectly. One could, for example, refer here to that original intuition which Kant contrasts, though precisely as the ideal, with the derivative intuition to which man is bound; original intuition would be so complete and self-sufficient that it would require no supplement on either side, neither the aid of another faculty such as reason nor the workings of other things to produce what would be intuited.[10] It would be a matter of sheer intuition of full presence, utterly closed off from everything else, utterly self-enclosed, a perfect figure of closure.

The point is, then, that this figure of closure, intrinsic to metaphysics and operative throughout, is completed, comes fully into force, in and as the end of metaphysics. One could trace it almost endlessly, but perhaps it is most obtrusive in German Idealism's proclamation of absolute self-presence, in Nietzsche's theory of will to power, and in the phenomenological reduction of being to a pure noematic correlate of a transcendental consciousness.

And yet, the force of such an analysis of metaphysics lies in its insistence that the completion of the figure of closure is at the same time a gathering of the history of metaphysics into its most extreme possibility, that it represents for metaphysics the exhaustion of all possibilities, the closing off to a future. The closure of metaphysics is a completion of its history and at the same time a termination of that history, its termination in the sense that its essential possibilities are exhausted and that history thus gathered into its most extreme possibility. Yet, still, closure is, most decidedly, not simple termination. Indeed, quite the contrary. In its closure metaphysics remains intact and in certain respects may assert itself still more forcefully. Let me cite from Heidegger's lectures on Nietzsche:

> The end of metaphysics that is to be thought here is but the beginning of metaphysics' "resurrection" in altered forms; these forms leave to the proper, exhausted history of fundamental metaphysical positions the purely economic role of providing raw materials with which—once they are correspondingly transformed—the world of "knowledge" is built "anew."[11]

In its closure metaphysics remains intact precisely in its essential exhaustion, a well-rounded sphere turning perpetually on its axis, on the same axis, an eternal recurrence of the same.

(B) TRANSGRESSION

Any opening to the future must intervene in the recurrence, must disrupt the operation of closure, transgressing its limits. Inasmuch as the figure of closure belongs intrinsically to metaphysics, such a move will also disrupt, dislodge, displace metaphysics itself. Such transgression, deconstructing metaphysics itself, will constitute, in Heidegger's phrase, the task reserved for thinking at the end of metaphysics.

Let me outline as briefly as possible some of the strategies by which such transgression is attempted in contemporary thought. Specifically, let me sketch, ever so briefly, three strategies of transgression.

The first strategy is that adopted by Derrida in his critique of Husserl, i.e., his critique of closure in its phenomenological form. What the Derridean critique undertakes to show is that every such form of allegedly pure enclosure, pure interiority—whether it be that of pure expression, of transcendental consciousness, or of the living present—always of necessity is invaded by exteriority, that the very constitution of the "inside" always already involves an outside.

Consider the most elementary case of self-enclosed presence, that of the living present. By bringing fully into play Husserl's own analyses of retention and protention, Derrida shows that there can be no simple self-identical present or "now," because the present is essentially connected to the immediate past and future. For example, in listening to a musical melody, the hearing of one note of the melody involves an essential reference back to the earlier notes just heard and, perhaps more indeterminately, to the notes still to be sounded. Were this not the case, were it simply a matter of a sequence of hearings, a sequence of unrelated "nows," one could never hear a melody *as* a melody.

Derrida stresses that the connection of the present to the immediate past and future is an essential, i.e., constitutive, connection. It is not as though there is a present "now" which somehow comes to be connected to past and future; rather, these connections belong to its very constitution as a present "now." Derrida elaborates this peculiar complexity of the "now" by bringing into play the concept of repetition. The "now" essentially involves repetition not only in the sense of retention of the previous "now" (as in the example of the melody) but also in the sense that the "now" as the form of presence, as ideal, is infinitely repeatable.

This operation, this figure, of repetition Derrida calls the *trace*. It is, as it were, the figure into which Derrida deconstructs that figure of closure which for phenomenology would be primordial. It is a figure which one could call more "primordial," were it not that the deconstruction calls into question the very determination of primordiality, indeed calls into question primordiality as a determination of the matter for thought. This figure, the operation of the trace, has another name: *différance*.[12]

Such is, then, the first of the transgressive strategies, a strategy of exposing the operation of the trace, the movement of *différance*, of exposing in the very citadel of self-enclosed presence an operation, not itself a matter of presence, which conditions and limits all presence. The Derridean strategy is to transgress the limits of presence in the direction of *différance*.

The second strategy is that adopted by Heidegger in his critique of the metaphysical question of Being. It is a strategy which, precisely in transgressing Being, would transgress also the limit of metaphysics, its closure. It is a strategy by which metaphysics would thus be displaced, its closure disrupted; or, in the Heideggerian phrase, it is a strategy by which to accomplish a *Verwindung der Metaphysik*—that is, an overcoming of metaphysics not in the sense of simply getting rid of something and leaving it behind but rather in the sense in which, for example, one overcomes profound grief over the death of a loved one, overcomes it by taking it on and yet still opening oneself to the future.

Consider, first, the metaphysical question of Being at which Heidegger's transgressive critique is directed. The question is not just one question alongside other metaphysical questions but is, rather, the question by which, according to Heidegger's analysis, metaphysics is constituted. Let us look briefly at that analysis as Heidegger presents it in his text "The End of Philosophy and the Task of Thinking."[13]

In this text Heidegger offers three interconnected determinations of metaphysics. The first is framed as the fundamental question, the metaphysical question of Being: "Metaphysics thinks beings as a whole—the world, man, God—with respect to Being." The second adds the determination of Being as ground and thus determines the fundamental question as a question of fundament, of ground: "Metaphysics thinks beings as beings by way of a representing which supplies the ground." But, in turn, ground shows itself as presence in the sense of that which brings beings into their presencing, that which lets them come to presence. In this connection one should think especially of the Platonic determination: Being is determined as εἶδος or ἰδέα, as the pure look of whatever would be offered up to vision, the sheer aspect of whatever would present itself to intuition. The force of the Platonic determination lies in the connection which it establishes between the presencing of beings and the shining of their εἶδος, their look: Something can come to presence only if there shines in and through it an εἶδος, a pure look. In other words, the shining of the εἶδος is what lets the thing come to presence; it is what lets there be a presencing and what in this sense may be called presentness or presence. Thus, according to Heidegger's third determination, metaphysics represents presencing beings in their presence, in the Platonic instance referring them to the εἴδη that shine through them and empower their coming to presence.

Thus, to bring together the three determinations, metaphysics represents beings with respect to Being, i.e., ground, i.e., presence; metaphysics refers beings back to their Being, i.e., their ground, i.e., their presence; and this representing, this movement of referral, is precisely that fundamental questioning in which metaphysics is constituted, the metaphysical question of Being. It should be noted how in this connection the privileged role of presence is maintained, that privileged role that was found to generate the figure of closure. Indeed, one could say that the privilege enjoyed by presence becomes even greater in the present context: Now it is a matter not only of beings getting understood as present but also of their Being as such getting understood as presence.

Again the figure of closure begins to take shape, comes to be the shape of metaphysics: As the movement of referring beings to their Being, i.e., ground, i.e., presence, metaphysics is closed off within this circuit, enclosed within the space of the difference between Being and beings. This is to say that metaphysics does *not question beyond Being*. It is imperative, then, to distinguish between the metaphysical question of Being and another question of Being to which metaphysics is necessarily closed. This other question of Being, the questioning beyond Being, ἐπέκεινα τῆς οὐσίας, is what defines the Heideggerian transgression.

For Heidegger, then, it is a matter of transgressing beyond Being. Beyond to what? In Heidegger's first formulation of his project, the "beyond" of Being is called the *meaning* of Being, and the Heideggerian question of Being is the question of the meaning of Being. The aim of his project is to identify the meaning of Being as temporality, that is, to show that time is the horizon for all understanding of Being. The transgression would thus occur precisely in the movement beyond Being to time as the meaning of Being. But transgression is also at work in the specific analyses that constitute most of *Being and Time* as published. In these analyses one finds conspicuously at work a kind of transgressive opening, an opening beyond the closure generated by the privilege of presence. Precisely such opening is at work, for example, in Heidegger's refusal to regard things as compactly present objects of intuition, i.e., as present-at-hand, in his insistence, instead, on extending them beyond themselves into an open contexture of world; or, again, it is at work in his refusal to apply to the subject the measure of self-presence, in his transformation of the concept of subject into that of Dasein as Being-in-the-world, as having "in its ownmost Being the character of not being closed off."[14]

The transgression is more explicit in Heidegger's later texts, especially its character as a transgression of the limits of metaphysics. It is perhaps in "The End of Philosophy and the Task of Thinking" that he introduces the movement of transgression most directly. He begins with the classical demand that philosophy be rigorous, the demand vigorously renewed in Husserl's appeal "to the things themselves" but indeed operative since the Greeks, expressed, for example, in the Platonic insistence in the *Seventh Letter* that thought bind itself to τὸ πρᾶγμα αὐτό. Heidegger's question concerns this turning of thought to things themselves, this turning by which thought would let the things show themselves, would let them shine forth in such a way as to show themselves, thought being rigorous precisely by binding itself to such self-showing. Heidegger's question is: What remains unthought in this turn to the things themselves? In other words, the question is: What must already be in play in order for such self-showing to occur and in order that thought might turn to it?

First of all, Heidegger observes, such shining requires light; something can shine in such a way as to show itself only in a certain brightness, an illumination. But this movement—from the shining of Being and hence of beings *to* the light required for such shining—is only the first step and does not decisively transgress the limit. What is decisive is the further step, the other condition to which the first points back:

> But brightness in its turn rests on something open, something free.... Brightness plays in the open and wars there with darkness.[15]

This openness, this open space in which brightness and hence showing can occur, Heidegger calls clearing (*Lichtung*).

> Light can stream into the clearing, into its openness, and let brightness play with darkness in it. But light never first creates the clearing. Rather, light presupposes the clearing.[16]

Beyond the enclosure of subjectivity, beyond the enclosed, allegedly self-enclosing round of shining and showing, of presence to intuition, beyond Being thus rounded out, there is the open space, the clearing, in which can play the light that the shining of Being reflects.

Such is, then, the second of the transgressive strategies, the Heideggerian strategy of questioning beyond Being to the open, the clearing.

One might also broach such transgression in still another way. This third strategy of transgression—I refer to it here only in the very briefest way—would be elaborated by exploiting the peculiar openness of *imagination*. In this regard what is decisive is the freedom of imagination from the metaphysical privileging of presence and intuition, the threat, as it were, that imagination poses to the operation of metaphysics' governing ideal. The point is that imagination is simply not governed by the ideal of presence; rather, to take as typical the Kantian definition, imagination makes present something decisively absent, hence always mixing presence and absence—for example, presenting in a phantasy-image a castle thousands of miles away, presenting in his self-portrait of 1500 the man Dürer, who is also absent, indeed in the most absolutely decisive way. Hovering between presence and absence, resistant by its very nature to being governed by the ideal of presence, imagination does not accord with the figure of closure that this ideal generates. Over against metaphysical closure, imagination is discordant, disruptive, transgressive. Even when repressed, even when limited by metaphysical closure—when reduced, for example, to simple phantasy—imagination retains its impetus toward opening, expanding, into the beyond. In the words of Rousseau:

It is imagination which extends for us the bounds of the possible, whether for good or ill, and therefore stimulates and feeds desires by the hope of satisfying them.[17]

Opening up, extending, the bounds of the possible, imagination awakens desire within us, sets astir that eros capable in the most profound sense of opening us beyond ourselves and beyond what can ever be, even ideally, present.

The third of the transgressive strategies would involve radicalizing this opening power of imagination. It would involve applying it to an opening beyond Being. And this would amount to installing imagination at the very heart of the task of thinking at the end of metaphysics.

THREE

The Gathering of Reason

There can be no question of responding to the issues and criticisms raised in reference to *The Gathering of Reason* unless I attempt to draw them into a retracing of that project, into the orbit, if you will, of a new preface to it. Otherwise one could expect little more than a *Hin- und Herreden* between very different readings of Kant and, only thinly disguised behind those different readings, very different philosophical projects. And though I am hardly inclined to expect much from such arguing back and forth, here the question can be left open whether this could be in general an appropriate form of philosophical discourse. However this may be, it is not the discourse called for in the present event, which, on the contrary, is defined by a single reading and a single project, by a single text bearing my signature.

Before I begin, something needs to be said about the signature—at least by way of suggesting a certain caution. For it would be easy to allow the event being staged here and now to be understood and played out in accordance with a structural schema which one ought no longer to take for granted. The structure most determinative for this event is that by which is defined an author's relation to what is usually called—quite carelessly, no doubt—that author's text. What one ought to forego taking for granted is that simple schema by which a text would be merely the expression of certain intentions or thoughts had by the author, who might then subsequently be called upon, as in the present event, to reawaken those intentions so as to explain that text in which they are— perhaps too imperfectly—expressed. This schema would assign the author indisputable authority over the text, requiring only that he exercise that authority by reproducing the moment of inception of the text, by reawakening in its noetic purity what has been externalized, expressed, in the text.

Contribution to a discussion of *The Gathering of Reason* (Athens: Ohio University Press, 1980) held at the meeting of the Society for Phenomenology and Existential Philosophy at Pennsylvania State University on 28 October 1982. The other participants were Reiner Schürmann and Charles Sherover.

Even without beginning to expose the vast system of metaphysical oppositions that had to be taken for granted in order for this schema to assume that aura of self-evidence that it has, until recently, enjoyed, it can be shown that the relation of author to text involves a degree of complexity not accountable by this simple schema. Rather, a certain dispersion, a scattering, of the relation can always be discerned, whatever the text.

But let me speak of the particular text which is at issue here and which bears my name, my signature.

The most obtrusive splitting of the I who speaks in the text is marked by the difference between the text proper and the preface. Without pretending to rehearse the problem of the preface as it has been developed since Hegel, let me simply note that the I who speaks in the preface does not have the same relation to the text proper as does the I speaking in that text. Among other things, the prefatorial I tells of aims, circumstances, alliances, which guide or condition the discourse of the text proper; whereas the other I, which one might want to call the proper I, speaks that discourse itself. The additional signature attached to the preface marks the difference most appropriately, provided it is not simply conflated with the other signature, the one shown on the title page.

Even within *The Gathering of Reason,* within the text proper, there is no uniform relation of author to text but rather a dispersion of the relation, a splitting and scattering of the textual I. The text is, of course, grafted onto the Kantian text, and throughout an extensive portion of it I write, so to speak, in Kant's name, that is, in such a way that no incoherence would arise were Kant's signature to be attached to this portion of text. Or, rather, I write *almost* in Kant's name, for clearly there are divergencies; and in terms of a very old opposition, it is already an interpretation, distanced from what is usually called—quite carelessly, no doubt—the original text. In *The Gathering of Reason* the contours of this discourse are clearly marked as being determined by what I call the strategy of duplex interpetation. My relation to the text, the identity of the textual I, varies in those other portions of text that are marked as determined by other strategies. In part, the scattering is determined by the series of distances from the Kantian text characteristic of the other strategies—that is, moving from each strategy to the next, I speak more in my own name and less in the name of Kant.

There is also another kind of distancing brought into play. One thing that is demonstrated about the Kantian text, that I, speaking at a distance from that text, undertake to demonstrate, is that that text works against itself, against certain explicit intentions of its author. In this sense, the Kantian text gets withdrawn from being merely the fulfillment of those intentions, detached from the author. Were the relation of author to text, his ownership of his text, still to be understood in accordance with the simple schema of expression, then within such a copyright system I could legitimately be charged with having stolen Kant's text from him— or at least with having attempted, at least in part, such a theft.

By the very fact of its possibility, this mercurial theft points to another order of complexity in the relation of author to text, a complexity which in principle an author could never mark in composing the text. This complexity lies in the capacity of language to outstrip the intentions of the author, so that what is said diverges from, perhaps exceeds, what the author intends to say. An author has always already begun to be dispossessed of his text.

Even if the conditions and necessity of such dispossession have been elaborated only recently, it can nonetheless be affirmed in Kant's name. It is, in fact, affirmed in his name in a passage from the *Critique of Pure Reason* which I have already cited in *The Gathering of Reason*:

> I need only remark that it is by no means unusual, upon comparing the thoughts which an author has expressed in regard to his subject, whether in ordinary conversation or in writing, to find that we understand him better than he has understood himself; as he has not sufficiently determined his concept, he has sometimes spoken, or even thought, in opposition to his own intention (A 314/B 370).

Certain events can serve to scatter my signature still more broadly. Suppose I acquire a copy of *The Gathering of Reason,* read it, and write in its margins a series of comments. Suppose also I sign my name in the book in order not only to indicate ownership but also to identify myself as author of the marginal comments. Need it be said that this signature marks a very different relation to the text, that it functions quite differently from that signature printed on the title page? The scattering is still broader, the signature still more complex structurally, the intertextuality explicit, if certain other texts related to *The Gathering of Reason* and bearing the signatures of the other participants in the present discussion have in my marginal writing also been in play (in a way which I shall not undertake to analyze here). Suppose, finally, that I extract the marginal comments, fitting them together and filling them out so as to make a new text, which also I sign—the text which I am now going to read to you and which, bearing its signature differently, I want to mark off from this preface which I have just been providing for it.

The Gathering of Reason undertakes a certain subversion of metaphysics. More precisely, it undertakes to confirm and develop positively a subversion that has long since been in play, a subversion that was rigorously renewed in the Kantian critique of metaphysics. And yet, critique, too, sought in the end to restore metaphysics beyond the threat of further crisis. Attempting to respond to that deeper crisis that ought not to have broken out, *The Gathering of Reason* undertakes, then, a certain subversion of Kantian critique, a certain displacement of it into a sphere in which it might communicate with the crisis that besets contemporary humanity. I would insist that the subversion is developed from within rather than being imposed from without—insofar as the strategies adopted and the subversion undertaken leave intact the relevant opposition between inner and outer. The very means for subversion are borrowed from critique, drawn from it by a series of interpretive strategies.

Let me distinguish between two cases of subversion exercised by *The Gathering of Reason* with respect to the *Critique of Pure Reason.* In each case it is a matter of showing that a peculiar shift is in play in Kant's text, a peculiar slippage which throws the text off balance, out of joint. Let me identify the two cases of subversion by now naming the respective shifts: encroachment and transgression. And let me organize the present discourse around this distinction.

(A) ENCROACHMENT

The two cases of subversion, which are prepared by the strategies of inversive and projective interpretation respectively, are, in fact, clearly distinguished in *The Gathering of Reason*, at the beginning of the final chapter: There they are characterized as "two severe shocks" that have been absorbed by the structure constitutive of metaphysics at considerable cost to its security. One of these shocks, the more violent one, has resulted from the installing of imagination at the origin of the gathering of reason. Through this encroachment of imagination upon reason, the autonomy of reason is threatened, undermined. The reference is to the preceding, inversive interpretation of the Transcendental Dialectic, which undertakes to expose a complicity of imagination in dialectical illusion. In other words, within the horizon of that particular strategy, it is shown that imagination plays an essential role in bringing forth those transcendental ideas which would otherwise be regarded as simply posited by reason. That opening of the difference between sensible and intelligible in its broadest (if constitutively empty) extent is a task to which reason unmixed with imagination is unequal. The problem is that to mix imagination with reason is precisely to subvert reason, to corrupt it, to pervert it.

The subversive power of this encroachment can best be gauged by thematizing the relevant terms with respect to the opposition between presence and absence. Taken in a broad, traditional sense, intuition and reason may both be said to be directed to the thing itself; both aim to make it itself present. But reason supervenes only insofar as the sensibly immediate proves recalcitrant to intuition; it is then that recourse is had to reason in order by this indirect way to recover the sensibly immediate thing in its original or essential presence. One would, to cite the founding example, recur to the εἶδος which shines in and through the sensibly immediate and which constitutes its presence. Such recourse, opening the distinction between sensible and intelligible, is taken by *The Gathering of Reason* as the definitive gesture of metaphysics. Both intuition and reason are, then, to be contrasted with imagination, which, to speak in Kant's name, is "the faculty of representing in intuition an object that is not itself present" (B 151). The point is that imagination irreducibly mixes presence and absence. It makes present something essentially absent, something which is not (as with intuition) recoverable by recourse to a more originary making-present. What imagination brings forth, the image, is such as both to present something, the original (as it is usually called), and at the same time to let it remain absent. Here it must suffice merely to mark this global contrast without even broaching those complex phenomenological analyses that would eventually be required.

What the inversive interpretation of the Transcendental Dialectic shows is that that gathering which would be the gathering of reason has instead the structure of a gathering of imagination. The dominance of such a structure, though it can be rigorously established only by a careful reading of the entire Transcendental Dialectic, can be at least indicated by reference to that decisive failure which the Dialectic demonstrates in the gathering. Whatever its mechanism, that failure lies in the peculiarly mixed character that the ideas prove to have: What in them would be presented in its essential presence (most notably the soul and God) proves to be essentially absent, withheld from every actual gathering into presence. To this extent—an extent which would eventually have to be measured much more precisely—the ideas prove to have the structure of images, that peculiar mixing of presence and absence.

Let me merely mark in passing the further result implied by the Dialectic: Even as imaginal, the presentation accomplished in bringing forth the ideas is still illegitimate. An idea is not a legitimate offspring even of imagination, much less of reason, but rather—and I take the phrase from Kant—"a bastard of imagination." Yet even if the idea is not actually akin to that which it would feign resemble, even if it is a deceptive image, it is nonetheless imaginal.

The encroachment of imagination upon reason produces a shock to the entire system, to the entire Kantian system insofar as it renews and is governed by the definitive gesture of metaphysics. Specifically, the encroachment serves to *inhibit* that drive to *presence* which governs that gesture, that having recourse to reason; for in place of that original presence in which the metaphysical gesture would come finally to rest, there proves to be an irreducible mixing of presence and absence, the space of a play of imagination. This perversion of presence is at the same time a perversion of whatever allegedly pure intelligible would be put forth as *ground*; the encroachment thus serves equally to inhibit the metaphysical drive to ground.

(B) TRANSGRESSION

The other shock is brought by the projective interpretation, which undertakes to recover λόγος in the Kantian determination of reason—that is, to show how in its systematic functioning in the Kantian text, if not explicitly in its determination, reason retains subliminally, as it were, the sense of λέγειν, which I venture to render in English as "gathering." It is a matter of opening up within the Kantian text the space of a retranslation of reason into λόγος, of attempting to subvert the Kantian concept of reason by confronting it with its forgotten origin.

The way in which gathering is outlined initially—that is, in the first chapter of *The Gathering of Reason*—is easily resumed. Its locus is traced out between the concept of an absolutely unlimited knowledge and the configuration of limits, the conditions of fragmentation, which define the beginning of actual human knowledge. Gathering occurs, then, within this difference, specifically as a gathering into the unity of presence by which the fragmentation would be repaired and human knowledge constituted in an affinity with that absolutely unlimited knowledge that could be attributed only to the divine. What the *Critique of Pure Reason* undertakes is to test the various phases of this gathering. What the Transcendental Dialectic, in particular, demonstrates is the failure of the final phase of gathering, of that phase which coincides with metaphysics. It shows how human knowledge falls short of that ideal toward which it is carried by the power of gathering.

This sketch of gathering is, of course, only a point of departure, the point of departure for that subversive movement which I now want to mark by the word *transgression*. For it is not just a matter of repeating the classical gesture of ascent so as to mark anew, perhaps more legibly, the limits which were marked classically by such schemata as that of ὕβρις and νέμεσις; it is not just a matter of exposing the trace of this classical gesture in the Kantian text. Rather, it is a matter also of letting the Kantian text efface that trace, of letting this classical structure be radically displaced. It is a matter of letting the failure of metaphysical gathering serve to displace the very sense of gathering, displace it in the direction of its preclassical origin. It is precisely because I want especially to mark this displacement that I insist on the word *gathering*—that is, λόγος in that preclassical, Heraclitean sense that has been recovered by Heidegger.

This displacement is, then, a broaching of the Heideggerian question, and the very title *The Gathering of Reason* an explicit recognition of the question of Being in the *Critique*. But it is a broaching of that question in precisely such a way as to transgress metaphysics and the manner of raising the question proper to metaphysics. The question is *not* to be raised *merely* as a matter of distinguishing between Being and beings, *as* metaphysics distinguishes between the intelligible and the sensible. What is rather to be raised is what Heidegger calls the question of the truth or the clearing of Being. It is a matter of displacing the sense of gathering in such a way as to raise the question of that opening, that space, that field, in which the metaphysical gesture, the turn from the sensible to the intelligible, the classical ascent, first becomes possible.

Even in the initial sketch it is clear that *gathering* does not name either an act of knowledge or a faculty of the knower but rather the dynamics which runs throughout the field of knowledge, empowering even the constitution of the objects of knowledge. *Gathering* names the dynamics by which the entire field of human knowledge is opened up and structured.

But the *Critique of Pure Reason* contributes still more decisively to the displacement, to diverting gathering from reason even in its most expanded sense, to diverting gathering to the limit of metaphysics. It does so by the way in which it installs at the heart of gathering an irreducible absence, an essential withdrawal, a self-withholding of that which would be gathered into presence. This moment of negativity, to which I have already referred as it occurs in the transcendental ideas, may at the level of understanding be located in the problem of the noumenon. It is, however, much more in accord with the transgressive strategy to thematize this withdrawal structurally—for example, in terms of what in *The Gathering of Reason* is called an arc of absence (cf. 166)—than to regard it as a mere precritical residue in the critical system.

I would propose such an approach to the problem of thinking the root or ground from which the fourfold fragmentation of gathering arises. I would propose it as a more appropriately critical, transgressive, or, if you will, postmetaphysical way to think this ground than the way which installs in the critical system a precritical concept of existence. I would propose it, were not the subversion demanded such as to inhibit the very demand for the radical, were it not such as to inhibit, as I have tried to show, the very drive to ground.

(C) ABYSS

Let me try, finally, to outline somewhat more explicitly that transgression put into play in *The Gathering of Reason*. It is put quite directly into play in the first paragraph of the Introduction, in the broaching there of the schema of crisis.

According to this schema, crisis is constituted by the lack of sense capable of fulfilling certain essential intentions. The schema is compounded in the case of a crisis of reason, for that very means, reason itself, by which in every other case a fulfilling sense would be sought out and opened up, becomes itself questionable in the highest degree. Even to thematize crisis of reason by way of this schema, this schematic account of reason as that to which recourse is had in the face of crisis, is to lay claim to a certain resolution of the crisis of reason; it is to claim to have opened up a fulfilling sense that would to some degree resolve that crisis. Thus, a crisis of reason is intrinsically self-effacing; it is such as to withdraw the very means by which it could be thematized as crisis.

The very project of a critique of reason is exposed to such a breach. This project is linked to crisis, to a crisis of reason which inhibits the turn, the typically metaphysical recourse, from sense to reason, requiring instead that reason turn upon itself. This turning is the event of critique, the event in which reason is summoned before a tribunal which, however, can be none other than itself. But if reason has entered into self-effacing crisis, how is the judgment pronounced by reason serving as its own tribunal to be capable of resolving the crisis? To cite *The Gathering of Reason*:

> Could reason ever be so detached from itself as to be capable of constituting its own tribunal? Can such distance ever be opened up within reason? (2f.).

The difficulty lies in the hinge on which reason would turn upon itself—or, rather, in the breach, the space, by which reason would in the turn come to be separated from itself. The question is: What would be required in order that this space be such as to isolate the tribunal from that crisis which its judgment is intended to resolve? How can such a space be granted? How can such distance be assured?

Kant is undoubtedly assured of such distancing of reason from itself. One might well suppose that this assurance—or, rather, a strategy for producing it—is what underlies the otherwise outrageous semantics of the word *reason* in the *Critique of Pure Reason*, its open but unmarked ambiguity. More thematically, the assurance rests for Kant on his assurance of reason's essentially total self-presence, his assurance that whatever self-concealment has plagued reason in the history of metaphysics, turning it unsuspectingly against itself (as in the antinomies)—that such self-concealment is ultimately nonessential. Kant is assured (to speak now in his name) that it is only a matter of "trial, practice, and instruction"—in a word, that *discipline* will suffice to open the requisite distance and to bring effectively into play reason's essential self-presence.

What is astounding is how little Kant's assurance is borne out by what is actually carried through in the *Critique of Pure Reason,* how little assurance it provides of the essential integrity of self-presence, for example, in the theories of inner sense, of apperception, of freedom. What is astounding is how much these developments seem instead to withdraw that self-presence that reason would require in order, even retrospectively, to be assured of its critical distance.

It is little wonder, then, that the encroachment of imagination upon reason, that encroachment which *The Gathering of Reason* seeks to release, broaches a transgression of the entire metaphysical schema. For this encroachment serves to install within the very upsurge of reason an irreducible nonpresence, what one could call an essential absence, an essential withdrawal, were its effect not in the end to undermine or at least to displace the very sense of essence. The space of reason's critical self-presence proves to be the opening of an abyss and points transgressively beyond reason's turning upon itself, beyond to the opening of the space of the turning, beyond to that which, itself withdrawn, self-effacing, closed, first opens up the space of metaphysics and of critique.

I conclude with a single pointed comment—pointed to an exposure of the textual I on which one critic insists. The exposure, introduced by a reference to the question which *The Gathering of Reason* raises regarding the dismantling of subjectivity, alleges that this book itself is evidence of a certain subjectivity thinking its way through certain issues, that this activity as well as the present discussion presupposes an individual subject. Remarkably, it is as though to dismantle subjectivity were some species of self-forgetfulness in which an author would deny the very existence of those beings who for the past several centuries have been understood by way of the concept of subjectivity. It is as though to dismantle subjectivity were not to disrobe it, to uncover subjectivity so as to reveal the constitutive lines connecting this concept to those of ground and presence—revealing it, thus, as a concept which could be resumed only at the cost of also taking for granted, probably unawares, those drives to ground and presence about which surely we ought finally to question. It is also as though to dismantle subjectivity were not to take it apart, to scatter it, to disperse the I—or, rather, more precisely, to understand that being which one would otherwise call subject in a way capable of granting certain kinds of dispersion that would not be matters of ground and presence—for instance, the kind of dispersion which I have been constantly mimicking, if not enacting, to which I referred at the beginning, and to which now again I direct your attention.

II.
OPENINGS—TO THE
THINGS THEMSELVES

FOUR

Hegel's Concept of Presentation

Its Determination in the
Preface to the *Phenomenology of Spirit*

For the first issue of the *Critical Journal of Philosophy*, which appeared in January 1802, Hegel wrote a long introduction entitled "On the Nature of Philosophical Criticism in General and Its Relation to the Present Condition of Philosophy in Particular." One of the issues taken up in this Introduction is the peculiarly esoteric character of philosophy. Hegel writes that "philosophy is by its nature something esoteric." He explains: "It is philosophy only by being opposed to the understanding and therefore still more to common sense [*gesunder Menschenverstand*]. . . . In relation to the latter the world of philosophy is in and for itself an inverted world."[1]

Philosophy is esoteric—and yet not in the sense that would entitle it to an indifferent aloofness. It is not such as can remain merely the esoteric possession of a few specially gifted individuals. Hegel is emphatic on this point in the Preface to the *Phenomenology of Spirit*: The elaboration, the form, demanded of philosophy is precisely such as to render it universally intelligible, "capable of being learned and of thus becoming the property of all"—that is, such as to render it "exoteric."[2] Philosophy is esoteric in its way of comporting itself to its *Sache*, its world an inverted world, but it is exoteric in that it offers to all who would undertake it the possibility of undergoing the inversion into philosophy. The formulation in the Introduction of 1802 is succinct: "Philosophy must indeed recognize the possibility of the people elevating themselves to it, but it must not lower itself to the people."[3]

The peculiar esoteric character of philosophy prescribes the rigor demanded of the beginner who would elevate himself to philosophy: The displacement into philosophy requires a radical inversion. And this inversion has as an essential moment a disorientation so radical that only

---

Originally published in *Hegel-Studien*, Band 12 (1977).

the name "skepticism" is appropriate to it. Yet being in another regard exoteric, philosophy is obliged to hold out to the beginner the possibility of entering into this disorienting inversion, of offering (in the strictest sense) an *introduction* to philosophy. The radically disorienting, inverting movement into philosophy must be *presented*. An initiatory presentation (*Darstellung*) is demanded. The *Phenomenology of Spirit* is intended to satisfy this demand.

Just as philosophy in the form of science cannot begin straightaway as though "shot from a pistol," just as it requires the prior presentation of the movement up to philosophy, so likewise the initiatory presentation has its "prerequisite." The presentation requires a prior determination (appropriately preliminary) of the concept of presentation. Such determining—the introduction to the introduction to philosophy—proves actually to be an anticipatory leap, and as such its necessity for the presentation itself can, at best, be clarified only in and through the determination, not at the outset. My task is to thematize this determination of the concept of initiatory presentation—or, more specifically, to exhibit it up to the point where its necessity for the presentation begins to show itself from out of the determination. I accordingly restrict my attention to the Preface to the *Phenomenology of Spirit*—in fact, to its earlier sections. Rather than proceeding to that second phase, that more specific determination of the concept of presentation which Hegel carries out in the Introduction, in which the considerations, becoming more "procedural," are narrowed down to that point at which the presentation itself can commence—rather than proceeding thus, I shall remain with the Preface and attempt to think through to its end the connection between presentation and presented, as this connection is manifest within that larger sphere opened up by the more dangerous anticipatory leap which Hegel dares in the Preface.

(A) THE FAILURE OF THE PREFACE

Of the nineteen sections into which the Preface is divided,[4] the first is the most starkly reflexive. The theme with which the Preface here begins is *itself*—that is, the idea of a preface as such. More specifically, it begins with a consideration of the questionableness that necessarily infests any preface to a philosophical work, a questionableness rooted in a basic conflict between the character of a preface as such and the demand under which philosophy stands.

Hegel begins: Such explanation as customarily is offered in a preface—an explanation of the aim of the work and of its relation to other treatments of the same subject—"seems in the case of a philosophical writing not only superfluous but in regard to the nature of the thing [*um der Natur der Sache willen*] even unsuitable and inappropriate" (*Phän.* 9).

The thing (*Sache*) to which philosophical writing pertains is of such a nature as to render all such prefatory explanations inappropriate. More precisely, such explanations stand in opposition to the way in which philosophy must comport itself to its *Sache,* to its way of having regard for the thing, its way of being for the sake of the thing itself, its letting the thing itself be: "For instead of occupying itself with the thing, such talk is always outside it; instead of abiding in the thing and forgetting itself in it, such knowing always reaches out for something else and really remains involved with itself rather than being involved with the thing and devoting itself to it" (*Phän.* 11).[5] The way of comportment characteristic of prefatory explanations, hence, what is said in such explanations and the manner in which it is said—such "can not hold as the way in which philosophical truth is to be presented" (*Phän.* 9).[6] The Preface determines preliminarily the nature of presentation, but such determining is not itself a presentation. The Preface falls short of those very "standards" which it determines.

From the outset the Preface is thus destined to fail; from its beginning it is already a failure. This character must be directive for the interpretation of the Preface if such interpretation is to avoid duplicating in itself the violence which the Preface does to the *Sache* of philosophical thought. The interpretation is called upon to let the violence ultimately recoil upon and be absorbed by the Preface, to let the things themselves simply stand. There is required, on the side of the interpretation, a certain suspension of judgment regarding those things, a certain "parenthesizing," which is also in a sense a complicity in the violence, or, to the extent that it understands itself, more properly a restraint. This restraint is required most of all in those connections in which the Preface is addressed to such things as the true, knowing, the absolute, God. In *our* time the restraint is more difficult and the demand for it of an entirely different order to the extent that our time is determined by the "death of God"—that is, by the positive lack of a true that could stand correlative to knowing and converge with it in absolute self-consciousness—that is, by the negation of precisely those things which Hegel's presentation would allow to show themselves as the *Sache* of philosophy.

But the Preface cannot allow them genuinely to show themselves. Measured by the demands of the things themselves, it is a failure. This failure of the Preface and its way of determining the further character of the Preface are variously elaborated in the first section. Hegel draws a curious analogy between philosophy and anatomy: Just as no one would suppose that he could learn anatomy merely by acquiring the general idea without mastering the particulars, so in philosophy mere consideration of aims and of other such generalities is inadequate to the thing itself. In fact, the inadequacy is much greater in the case of philosophy, it is even of an entirely different order; for, in the end, anatomy has no right at all to the name of science, and thus the very distinction between the actual elaboration and mere prefatory considerations breaks down, both being equally unscientific. The collapse of this distinction in the case of anatomy and the correlative breakdown of the analogy with philosophy serve, however, to render the distinction still more prominent in the case of philosophy. There is a fundamental opposition between a philosophical work and such general considerations as customarily go to make up a preface. This disparity generates, in turn, a disparity within the Preface itself: "In the case of philosophy, on the other hand, there would arise the disparity that use would be made of such a way [i.e., an unscientific procedure, as an anatomy] and yet, by means of this way itself, it would be exhibited as incapable of grasping the truth" (*Phän.* 10). Such a disparity characterizes the Preface to the *Phenomenology of Spirit*: Its procedure, its way of showing something, is such that the procedure itself gets shown up as inadequate. The Preface is such as to revoke itself. Its exhibition of what is required in order to be equal to the task of grasping the truth recoils upon the Preface itself, which manifestly does not meet the requirement thus exhibited. Nevertheless, in this self-revocation a certain content is preserved, namely, the determination of the nature of presentation; it is preserved inasmuch as it is carried over into *enactment*. The Preface sublates itself; its fundamental movement is an *Aufheben*.[7]

(B) SUBSTANCE AND SUBJECT

The basis for the determination of the concept of initiatory presentation is prepared in sections 5–6 of the Preface. Sections 7–8 explicitly carry through the determinations thus prepared. The subsequent sections of the Preface are then devoted largely to elaborating the determination in various regards and to applying it to certain polemical contexts.

The preparatory sections will require most careful attention and most deliberate restraint. As a guide for thematizing that basis which they prepare for the determination, focus on three principal statements from these sections.

The first of these statements occurs at the beginning of section 5:

> According to my view, which must justify itself [only] through the presentation of the system itself, everything depends on comprehending and expressing the true not as substance but just as much as subject.[8]

Two general observations need to be made before focusing on the principal content of the statement. First, note how the cast of the statement accords with the preliminary, prescientific character which both the determination and the provision of its basis have. The statement incorporates a self-characterization: Hegel is expressing his view (*Einsicht*) to which other views could be opposed, views whose claims to truth could not be effectively countered. Such expression does not belong to the presentation in the proper sense that is to be determined, and consequently what is expressed will eventually need to be genuinely established within the presentation. Second, note Hegel's reference to "comprehending and expressing." This reference poses on the horizon two relevant dualities: the duality of presentation (the comprehending and expressing) and presented (that which is comprehended and expressed); and, within the presentation itself, the duality of comprehension and expression, of thought and language.

The true is to be comprehended and expressed "not as substance"— i.e., not merely as substance, not as though it were substance and nothing more—"but just as much as subject." The true is to be taken as *both* substance and subject, yet in such fashion that the taking of it as subject involves a *negation* of the taking of it as mere substance.

In this context substance is to be understood primarily in the sense determined for it in Spinoza's *Ethics*: "By substance I understand that which is in itself and is conceived through itself."9 Substance is that which is in itself in the sense of suffering no dependence on anything external to itself, which is absolved from all such dependence and in this sense absolute. Thus, Spinoza poses substance (i.e., the one substance, God) as encompassing both thought and extension as its attributes— hence, as encompassing both subject and object. But, in the end, substance as determined in Spinoza's work proves not to be so encompassing; as Fichte explicitly recognized,10 substance as so determined remains bound on the side of things. Indeed, as Hegel notes in the present context, Spinoza's own age was outraged by his concept of God as the one substance because of "the instinctive recognition that self-consciousness was only drowned in it and not preserved." To take the true as mere substance is to remain on the side of the object, that is, to establish the identify of subject and object only on the side of the object. In the language of Hegel's *Differenz-Schrift*,11 Spinoza's substance is, at best, merely an objective subject-object.

What is thus required is that the true be "just as much" subject, that it be not merely substance but *also* subject. In this connection "subject" has, as the primary sense from which Hegel in reforming and further developing its sense will proceed, that sense determined for it in Fichte's *Wissenschaftslehre*: the subject "has no being proper, no subsistence" [*kein eigentliches Seyn, kein Bestehen*] but rather is sheer "act" [*Handeln*] and nothing but act, specifically, the act of positing itself.12 The subject is a movement of self-positing, hence, as both positing and posited, is "a necessary identity of subject and object: subject-object."13 However, it is an identity of subject and object on the side of the subject, a subjective subject-object.[14] What is thus required is that it unite "with itself the being of the substance" (*Phän.* 19), that is, that the true be both subject and substance. What is required is a synthesis which will yield the identity of subject and substance, that is, the identity of subjective subject-object and objective subject-object, that is, the identity of identity and nonidentity.[15]

But everything depends on how this uniting of subject and substance is carried through, on whether it falls back into "inert simplicity" so as to end up presenting "actuality in a non-actual manner" (*Phän.* 19f.)—that is, on whether this uniting results in an indifference with respect to subject and object in which the negation and opposition between them would be finally eliminated, so that the movement and struggle corresponding to such negation and opposition would be revoked in the end rather than being taken up into the end in that manner which Hegel expresses by restoring to the word "actuality" the fundamental sense which the ancient philosophical tradition gave it. It is not sufficient that the true merely be *also* subject; rather, its way of being subject must be such as to sublate its way of being substance, its being-subject must constitute a sublation of its being-substance. This means that its being-subject must both negate and preserve its being-substance.[16]

Hegel's expression of the relevant negation consists mostly of a recapitulation of the general Fichtean determination of the nature of the subject. He begins: "The living substance is, further, that being which is in truth *subject* or, in other words, which is in truth actual only insofar as it is the movement of self-positing" (*Phän.* 20). It is to be noted how Hegel refers here to *living* substance, which (to say the least) is meant to indicate substance in a sense which, in contrast to that determined in Spinoza's thought, does not remain merely on the side of things. Substance (as living) is in truth subject; that is, substance in respect of its being in the truth, in its character as constituting the truth, *is* subject. Substance, in that sense that would allow one to say "The true is substance," is such as to require that in the end one say instead "The true is subject." Furthermore, "end" is here to be understood as τέλος,[17] thus, in correlation with actuality in the sense of ἐνέργεια. Substance, as being gathered up into its τέλος, as actual, is movement—specifically, the movement of self-positing, the movement which, in the Fichtean determination, does not just belong to the subject but rather *is* the subject.

Hegel continues: "As subject, it is pure, *simple negativity* and thus the bifurcation [*Entzweiung*] of the simple. . . ." This means: As the positing of itself, the subject is both the subject (which posits) *and* the object (which is posited); the subject as posited is object, is what it is not, is pure, simple negativity. As subject, as positing of itself, it is a positing of bifurcation; it posits within itself the bifurcation into subject and object.

Hegel continues, describing the subject, which is the bifurcation of the simple: ". . . or the doubling which opposes [*die entgegensetzende Verdopp-lung*], which again is the negation of this indifferent diversity and of its opposite." The bifurcation is an opposition *within* the subject; the opposition between subject and object is an opposition within the subject. Thus, it belongs to the movement of the subject (the movement which the subject *is*) to overcome the opposition, to negate the sheer diversity and reestablish its own unity. This overcoming, this reestablishing of its own unity, is not merely something added on, as it were, to the subject's self-positing, to that movement of self-positing which the subject *is*. On the contrary, the movement of self-positing *is* such a reestablishing of unity from out of diversity; it is a self-gathering—neither unity nor diversity but the gathering of diversity into unity. In Hegel's words, "Only this sameness which reconstitutes itself or the reflection into itself in being other—not an *original* unity as such or immediate unity as such—is the true."

The true is subject, that is, the movement of self-gathering into its end: "It is the becoming of itself, the circle which presupposes its end as its aim and has it for its beginning and which is actual only through its execution and end." The true is *not* substance: There can be "alongside" the subject no substance which, as object, would together with the subject constitute the true. There can be no such object, for the very distinction between subject and object is itself posited within the subject. The only being which, in the end, measures up to the Spinozistic criterion of substance is subject, not substance; only subject is "in itself" and "conceived through itself," whereas substance (as object) falls decisively within the sphere of that self-positing which is the subject.

Yet in the issue of subject and substance there is not only the moment of negation but also that of preservation; the opposition between subject and substance is not simply abolished at the level of the true in its actuality but also preserved in a new form. This requirement, that a moment of opposition to the subject be preserved, suddenly bursts forth at the very center of the issue—bursts forth in a language of such sheer strength that it holds together as its content the utmost abstractness and the most stark concreteness. Hegel writes of how matters would stand if such a moment were lacking, if there were merely the moment of negation, if subject were just the negation of substance in the sense of excluding the latter from the true in its actuality: "Thus the life of God and divine knowing may indeed be spoken of as a playing of love with itself; this idea sinks to the level of edification and even insipidity when seriousness, pain, the patience and work of the negative are lacking in it." This playing of love with itself, this play of unification, of self-gathering into unity—what is that seriousness which, if lacking in the idea of such play, reduces what would be the idea of absolute knowing to the level of mere edification?

Hegel continues: "In itself that life is indeed untroubled sameness and unity with itself, which is not serious about otherness and estrangement, nor with the overcoming of this estrangement." Thus, that seriousness which is so crucial is a seriousness regarding otherness; and the insipid idea which fails to include this seriousness is an idea of the divine life merely as *in itself.* What is the character of this seriousness regarding otherness such that it shatters the untroubled unity with self of the divine life in itself? Seriousness about otherness can be thus effective only if it corresponds to an otherness which is in truth serious, a serious otherness. What, then, is other than life, knowing, subject? And how is it *seriously* other than these? The relevant otherness is simply that of object to subject. It is that otherness constituted by the subject-object bifurcation. What, then, is required in order that this otherness be a *serious* otherness? It is required that the bifurcation be no mere correlate of self-positing, that the otherness of object to subject not be such as to be immediately and totally dissolved into the subject's identity with itself. The bifurcation, the eruption of otherness, must be a rending, a tearing apart, to which belongs the *pain* of dismemberment, a rending which no sheer self-assertion can heal but which requires "the patience and work of the negative." Serious otherness is no mere moment within the identity of the subject; and the overcoming of serious otherness is not to be accomplished by a mere positing of unity correlative to such identity, by a mere positing of a unity that would immediately abolish the diversity of dismemberment. What is required is rather the toilsome gathering of diversity into unity, a gathering which, in overcoming diversity, otherness, lets it nevertheless be preserved in a new form.

Referring still to the divine life regarded in itself, as lacking seriousness about otherness, Hegel continues: "But this in-itself is abstract generality in which is disregarded both the nature of this life *to be for itself* and thus the self-movement of the form." To surpass the level of mere edification, it is thus required that the divine life be regarded in its nature as being-for-itself. For it to be for itself means: to establish the unity of its self-identity (to posit itself) from out of an opposition of such seriousness as to require toil, an opposition of such seriousness that mere negation of it cannot stand, an opposition which, in being overcome, must also be preserved by being granted a new form, an opposition which must be *sublated.* The true is not merely the untroubled self-positing of the divine life, not merely "the pure self-contemplation of the divine"; it is such only *in itself,* not in its *actuality.* The true becomes actual only by troubling itself with the gathering of serious otherness into itself; the true in its actuality is the gathering which *forms* diversity into unity, the gathering movement of informing, "the self-movement of the form."[18]

Hegel concludes: "The true is the whole." He explains: "It should be said of the absolute that it is essentially *result,* that it is only in the end what it is in truth; and precisely in this consists its nature: to be actual, subject, or that which becomes itself." The absolute is the whole of that movement in which self-identity is reconstituted from out of a bifurcation involving serious otherness; it is the whole of the movement in which the otherness of what is seriously other is sublated and that other thus established in its proper identity with the subject; it is the whole of the movement of gathering diversity into unity. And yet, the absolute is *in truth* "only in the end," only as "result." In its way of being the true as such, the absolute is the whole of the movement of gathering *as itself gathered up* into its fulfillment in the end; for what gathers and what is gathered are established in their identity precisely through the gathering, and so the absolute is the self-gatheredness into the τέλος, that is, the absolute is ἐνέργεια.

The true cannot be merely substance in that Spinozistic sense that remains on the side of objects; the true must *also* be subject. Yet, the true cannot be merely both substance and subject; its being-subject must also sublate its being-substance. This means, first, that its being-subject negates its being-substance, i.e., that there can be no mere substance (as object) alongside the subject, since the very distinction between subject and object is posited within the subject; and it means, second, that in its being-subject its being-substance is also preserved, namely, as serious otherness. Yet, now it can be seen, further, that the being-substance which is sublated by being-subject falls as much on the side of the subject as on that of the object: the true in-itself, the divine life as lacking serious otherness, is substance—Hegel calls it "immediate substance"—which the subject, the true in its actuality, negates and preserves in that movement of self-gathering which it is.

(C) KNOWING AS SYSTEM

The present concern is to thematize the basis which Hegel lays in sections 5–6 as preparation for the determination of the concept of presentation. To this end, I have proposed to focus on three principal statements from these sections. The second of these statements occurs at the beginning of the next-to-last paragraph of section 6:

> Among several conclusions which follow from what has been said, one may be singled out: it is only as science or as *system* that knowing is actual and can be presented.[19]

It needs to be asked: From which of the previous considerations does this conclusion follow? And how?

It can be related, first of all, to the consideration of language, specifically, of the proposition, that occurs in the middle of section 6 (*Phän.* 21–23). This consideration falls into two parts, which are separated in the text by a paragraph in which Hegel develops his concept of actuality by bringing it into explicit connection with Aristotle's concept of purposiveness.

The first part of the consideration of language occurs as a response to those who would object to understanding the absolute as result, who would object to doing so on the ground that it introduces mediation into the absolute. Hegel answers this objection by showing how it is based simply on a misunderstanding of the nature of mediation and of the bond between mediation and determination. If the absolute is spoken of *immediately,* if one utters such words as "God," "absolute," "eternal," then the absolute *as* so expressed is merely something general, and such expression is hardly an adequate expression of the absolute. Such single words "do not express what they contain" (*Phän.* 21)—just as the phrase "all animals" does not constitute a zoology. But if to such words anything else is added, if the transition is made to a proposition, then mediation is involved. If, for example, instead of saying merely "God," one says "God is the eternal," then there occurs within the expression the transition from God to something other, the eternal, and then the taking of this other back into God—that is, mediation, which Hegel defines as "nothing else but self-moving self-identity" (*Phän.* 21). Without mediation there could be nothing beyond the mere uttering of names.

The second part of the consideration of language in section 6 is, in effect, an elaboration of Hegel's definition of mediation. In order to express the absolute more adequately than in the previously mentioned single words, one might employ the proposition "God is the eternal." Here one begins with the word "God," which, however, taken by itself, is "a senseless sound, a mere name"; only the predicate gives the name content (*Phän.* 22). And so, one might well ask: Why not just speak of "the eternal"? Why add the senseless sound in the first place? Hegel answers: "But this word signifies that what is posited is not a being or essence or mere generality but rather something reflected into itself, a subject" (*Phän.* 23). The point is that the structure of the proposition anticipates the structure of the absolute as subject: It involves a transition into otherness (bifurcation) and the leading of this other back into the unity of the subject. Nevertheless, the structure of the proposition does *not* duplicate that of the absolute, does not mirror it perfectly; it *only* anticipates it: "The subject is accepted as a fixed point to which the predicates are affixed as to their support, by a movement which belongs to those who know about it and which is not supposed to belong to the fixed point; but only through this [i.e., the recognition that the movement belongs to the subject itself] could the content be presented as subject." The limitation thus lies in the fact that the movement between subject and predicate is taken to belong to the one who knows or asserts the proposition, *not* to the subject itself, which is, rather, posited as a fixed point.

How is this consideration of language linked to that conclusion which Hegel draws: "It is only as science or as *system* that knowing is actual and can be presented"? It is linked, specifically, to that side of the conclusion which pertains to presentation in general; this is indicated at the end of the consideration of language by Hegel's reference to what would be required in order for the structure of the proposition to be more than a mere anticipation of the structure of the absolute, in order that its content be, as Hegel says, "presented as subject." Such presentation would require that the subject (of the proposition) into which the predicate is taken back not be treated as fixed, as unaffected, unchanged, by the synthesis, that the movement not be regarded as belonging on the side of a detached knower who would have the proposition as object of his knowing. Rather, the subject must be treated as moved, as having become a different, more determinate subject by virtue of its taking of the predicate into itself. Yet, this is precisely what a proposition is prevented from accomplishing by its static subject-predicate structure; a proposition can *only anticipate* that movement which the absolute is. The structure of the proposition is such that this movement of becoming determinate cannot be *presented* in a single proposition. This means that the conception of the nature of philosophy in terms of basic propositions (*Grundsätze*) or principles (*Prinzipien*), that conception which dominates almost all modern philosophy up to German Idealism, is decisively transformed in Hegel's development of the issue of presentation. Any such proposition, "if it is true, is also false insofar as it is merely a basic proposition or principle" (*Phän.* 23). How, then, can the movement be presented? Its presentation will (at least) require a *system* of propositions, that is, a chain of propositions systematically connected in such a way that each proposition leads over to another which has as its subject that more determinate subject that results from the determination accomplished through the first proposition.[20] For the sake of presentation, the advance must be made not only from word to proposition but also from proposition to system of propositions. The absolute can be presented "only as science or as system."

Here it is appropriate to recall that peculiar disparity within the Preface of which Hegel spoke at the outset, that disparity which gives to the Preface its self-revoking character: It is to show that the way of showing characteristic of a preface does not measure up to what is required for a *presentation* of philosophical truth. Already this self-revocation is under way: The Preface is not itself such a *system* of propositions as it has shown to be required for the presentation of the truth.[21]

In the statement to which concern is now directed there is a peculiar duality, Hegel referring not only to presentation but also to what is to be presented in the presentation. On the one hand, he says that knowing can be *presented* only as science or as system, the reference being primarily to the requirement that the presentation take the form of a system of propositions, in contrast, for example, to an attempt at presentation through an alleged basic principle. On the other hand, Hegel says also that knowing is itself actual only as science or system. Not only must knowing be presented as science or as system, but also it *is* science or system; and only because it is such does its presentation stand under the requirement that it assume the form of science or system. Knowing, as actual, *is* system, and this is why it must be presented as system. A more fundamental sense of "system" thus begins to emerge: According to this sense, a system is not merely a system of propositions but rather a system of knowing, the system which knowing *is*. But what is this knowing which is actual only as system? It is the knowing *of* the absolute (in the double sense of the genitive). It is the self-knowing of the absolute, in which the absolute reconstitutes its self-identity from out of a serious otherness. Yet, this movement of self-knowing is just the absolute itself; and so in its fundamental sense the system *is* the absolute.

In the first statement that was considered, Hegel calls the absolute "the true"; and, explicitly expressed "not as substance but just as much as subject," it is called "the true in its actuality," "the true as actual." In the second statement, on the other hand, he calls the absolute "knowing," or, more fully, "knowing as actual." The absolute in its actuality is called both "knowing" and "the true." But in so calling it, Hegel has let it become manifest why it may be called by both names: In its actuality, in that self-gatheredness into the τέλος, the absolute finds itself in the other so as to reestablish its own self-identity; such reestablishing, as sublation of the otherness of the object, and, hence, of the otherness of the known, *the true*—such reestablishing is thereby an establishing of the identity of knowing with the true. In its actuality the absolute is both knowing and the true, for in this actuality knowing and the true are identical; the absolute is, most properly, the movement of establishing this identity, the movement in which knowing and the true are gathered into their identity.

(D) SPIRIT

According to the first principal statement, the absolute (the true as actual) is to be comprehended "not as substance but just as much as subject." If the terms are taken in the senses to which the development of this statement leads, that is, if substance is taken as the true in itself, as the "essence" (*Phän.* 20), and subject as the true for itself, as the true in its actuality, then the result of this development may be expressed by saying: Substance is essentially subject. The second statement—that "it is only as science or as *system* that knowing is actual and can be presented"—may be similarly abbreviated if the subordination of presentation to what is presented is taken as granted. It then says: Knowing, i.e., the absolute, i.e., the true as actual, is system; that is, the true is actual only as system. The third of the statements, which stands at the beginning of the final, most crucial paragraph of section 6, brings the results of the other two statements together in the concept of spirit:

> That the true is actual only as system or that substance is essentially subject is expressed in the representation which speaks of the absolute as *spirit*.[22]

It is in the paragraph which this statement introduces that the basis is decisively laid for the determination of the nature of presentation.

The crucial connection is that of spirit to actuality: "The spiritual alone is the actual" (*Phän.* 24). The determinations of spirit are thus to be worked out in terms of the concept of actuality, as the latter has been unfolded throughout sections 5–6. Hegel gives four determinations. First, spirit is "the essence or being-in-itself"—that is, it is immediate substance, the divine life as pure self-contemplation, as involving no serious otherness, as not having undergone the pain of that bifurcation which brings with it radical opposition. In this determination spirit still lacks form and actuality, that is, it is not yet that concrete movement which forms diversity into the unity of the τέλος, into actuality; it is no more than the abstract, still indeterminate assertion of unity, the possibility of self-positing. Second, spirit is "that which relates itself and is determinate" [*das sich Verhaltende und Bestimmte*]—that is, spirit is that which can become determinate, which can concretely posit itself, *only* insofar as it relates itself to an other, only insofar as it undergoes that bifurcation by which radical opposition is brought forth. The third determination is stated together with the second, as though they were one: Spirit is "that which is other and for itself" [*das Anderssein und Fürsichsein*]—that is, the other, which according to the second determination must be brought forth, is brought forth in a rending of spirit itself. It is an other which, however serious its otherness, is ultimately nothing other than spirit itself, an other in which spirit is object for itself. Fourth, spirit is that which "in this determination or being outside itself remains in itself—or it is in and for itself" [*in dieser Bestimmtheit oder seinem Außersichsein in sich selbst Bleibende;—oder es ist an und für sich*]—that is, spirit is the sublation of that bifurcation from which both otherness (being outside itself) and determinateness emerge; it is the gathering of otherness into itself, the positing of the identity of the other with what was subject in itself but is now, through this movement of determination, a reconstituted self-identity. In this fourth determination the others are gathered up: Spirit is being-in-and-for-itself.

Hegel proceeds to develop a curious "doubling" of these determinations:

> This being-in-and-for-itself, however, it is first for us or *in itself*; it is the spiritual *substance*. It must also be this *for itself*, must be the knowing of the spiritual and the knowing of itself as the spirit (*Phän.* 24).

This doubling indicates a movement. It is a movement of spirit (as being-in-and-for-itself). But, it is characterized in two somewhat different ways. This difference is decisive.

According to the first characterization, the initial term of the movement, i.e., that *from* which there is movement, is: being-in-and-for-itself (only) in-itself. This term Hegel describes as "spiritual substance." At the first level it has, in a sense, no lack: as spirit, as being-in-and-for-itself, it has undergone the pain of bifurcation and the reconstitution of unity out of the diversity. But, at the level of the "doubling" it is only substance, not yet subject; it lacks actuality. Yet, the levels must be brought together, and that requires that this term be regarded as spirit in that condition in which that reunification, without which it would not be spirit, is indeed accomplished *but remains merely implicit*. It is the movement of gathering in that condition in which the moment of being itself gathered up, i.e., the identity of what gathers with what is gathered, is still implicit. In this condition spirit is reunited with itself in the object; it knows itself in the object without, however, knowing that it is itself that it knows. The relevant movement is, then, from spirit in this condition *to* being-in-and-for-itself (also) for-itself—i.e., *to* spirit in that condition in which it knows itself explicitly in its other. Thus, the movement is a movement from spirit in-itself to spirit for-itself, to spirit which is actual in the highest sense. Yet, spirit is itself movement; and so the movement being described is not something which spirit passively undergoes (in the sense, for instance, of a substratum that would remain unchanged through the movement), but rather the movement must belong to that very movement which spirit *is*.

But there is a second, quite distinct characterization given of this movement. According to this second characterization, the relevant movement is a movement from being-in-and-for-itself *for us* to being-in-and-for-itself *for itself*. Taken superficially, this characterization suggests that "we" know something about the absolute which it does not know about itself (namely, that it knows itself in its object). It suggests, in other words, that we know more about the absolute than it knows about itself, so that what would be required is that the absolute raise itself to that level of knowledge which *we* already have. The relevant movement would, then, be a movement by which spirit would come to know as much about its own self-knowing as we knew already before the movement. But clearly this suggested sense of the movement is a *comic sense*; and it collapses as soon as one asks seriously about such knowledge of the absolute as we would presume to have from outside the absolute. What must be the character of a knowing of the absolute in which we—or, more precisely, I—would be the subject of the knowing and the absolute its object? In order for it to be a genuine knowing, it must be true, that is, it must be a knowing of the true. But, the development of the second of the three principal statements has shown that a knowing of the true in its actuality is precisely a movement in which is established the identity of knowing with the true. For genuine knowing there is thus required in the present case a movement through which the mutual externality of the I and the absolute would be retroactively revoked. In other words, the knowing must be such that what the subject knows in knowing the object is just itself and such that the subject comes to recognize this knowing *as* a knowing of itself. Thus, in knowing the absolute, the I would know itself *in* the absolute and would recognize its unity with the absolute. Hence, in the course of knowing the absolute, the I would cease to be a subject situated outside the absolute; its knowing would be, as it were, appropriated to the self-knowing of the absolute.

What, then, is the character of the movement and of its terms? It is a movement *from* a knowing of the absolute which presumes to be outside the absolute and for which spirit would be merely in itself (i.e., its object) *to* a knowing of the absolute which knows itself as not being external but rather as belonging to the absolute's self-knowing. It is a movement of the knowing I *into* the absolute—that is, it is a movement by which the I's knowing is appropriated to the absolute's self-knowing. Considered with respect to its final term, it is a movement in which spirit becomes for-itself by appropriating the self-conscious I, the immediate *cogito*. Contrary to the comic sense at first suggested, the movement is not a movement of the absolute up to the I but of the I up to the absolute; yet, even this conception grants too much externality and so requires qualification, for the I can move up to the absolute only because the absolute is already with it,[23] or, still more strictly, the movement is not something which the I accomplishes alone but is rather a movement of the absolute, i.e., belongs to that movement which the absolute *is*. These qualifications point to a more fundamental perspective on the movement. If the absolute is absolute, then the I cannot have been initially outside it, so as then to undergo movement into the absolute. Rather, the I must already be in the absolute from the beginning, and the movement thus a movement within the absolute. It must be a movement by which the I, which takes itself to be outside the absolute, comes to the awareness that it is always already within the absolute.

Hegel's conclusion to section 6 poses the connection between spirit and science:

> The spirit which, so developed, knows itself as spirit is *science*. Science is the actuality of spirit and the realm that the spirit builds for itself in its own element.

Thus, science is not a theory about spirit, not an account of spirit—just as system is not merely a system of propositions. Rather, science *is* spirit in its actuality. Science *is* the absolute.

The posing of the identity between spirit and science brings to completion the preparation of the basis for the determination of presentation. With this completion two further issues are opened up which point ahead into the complexity of the problem of presentation.

The first concerns the title "System of Science," which Hegel places at the beginning of his work. The title now says: system of spirit in its actuality. Yet, system in its fundamental sense is identical with spirit as actual, the gathering of diversity into the unity of the τέλος. Hence, the title, in this formulation as well as the first, just says the same thing twice—or, it says: system (science) which is spirit in its actuality. "System," "science," "spirit in its actuality"—in their fundamental senses all three say the same thing. And, as long as one adheres solely to this fundamental sense, it makes no sense to speak of *Hegel's system*—or, at best, to speak in this way is only to allude to the problem of withholding from the primary sense of "system" (and "science") a secondary yet in some measure distinct sense; it is to allude to the problem of presentation.

The second issue concerns the becoming of science—specifically, the way in which the sense of such becoming is determined by the posing of the identity of science with spirit in its actuality. Such becoming must belong (in a still to be determined way) to that movement of gathering which is spirit itself. The becoming of science must thus belong to science itself, just as the gathering movement of spirit is itself gathered up into the end. To the extent that the structure of presentation accords with that of what is presented, the presentation of the becoming of science, which Hegel is about to identify as the phenomenology of spirit, constitutes a part of science (as presentation). The presentation of the inverting movement into philosophy falls within philosophy and separates itself decisively from the (self-revoking) prefatory determination of the nature of presentation.

(E) PRESENTATION

In sections 5–6, Hegel has laid the basis for that determination of the concept of presentation that is to be carried out and elaborated in the

subsequent sections of the Preface. This basis consists primarily of the
determinations of spirit and the peculiar "doubling" then built on these
determinations, a "doubling" through which is distinguished, within that
whole movement which is spirit as such, the particular movement from
spirit in-itself (or for us) to spirit for itself (i.e., spirit in its full actuality).
With this basis laid, Hegel proceeds in section 7 to introduce the issue of
initiatory presentation and to relate it to that particular movement that
has been distinguished.

Hegel introduces into the considerations the peculiar esoteric and
exoteric characters of philosophy. These characters in their tension
generate the problem of presentation, at least in its most immediate form
as that of presenting the inverting movement into philosophy. The
esoteric character is expressed first: "Science on its part demands of self-
consciousness that it should have elevated itself into this ether to be able
to live—and to live—with it and in it" (*Phän.* 25). Science—i.e., in its
fundamental sense, spirit as actual and, in its derivative sense, philosophy—brings a demand. It places this demand upon self-consciousness,
that is, upon the individual I, the immediate *cogito*, which as such lays
claim to knowing. The demand is that the I elevate itself "into this ether,"
i.e., into the sphere of "pure self-recognition in absolute otherness"
(*Phän.* 24)—i.e., up to the level of being-in-and-for-itself for itself, of
spirit in its full actuality. That to which elevation is demanded is identical
with that which places the demand. And what is demanded, the elevation
of self-consciousness into the "ether," is precisely that movement which
Hegel distinguished at the end of section 6: the movement of the I into
the absolute.

Hegel proceeds to consider the exoteric character of philosophy:
"Conversely, the individual has the right to demand that science should
at least offer him the ladder to this standpoint and show him this
standpoint within himself" (*Phän.* 25). The ladder would lead from the I
into the absolute—that is, it would make available to the I the way of that
movement into the absolute—that is, it would *present* it. The ladder
which the individual can rightly demand is simply the presentation of the
movement into the absolute, of the movement up to philosophy. Yet,
how does the ladder, the presentation, lead the I to the standpoint of
science? It does so, not in the manner of a mere connecting of two
otherwise unrelated points, but rather, as Hegel says, by showing the
individual "this standpoint within himself." The presentation is to let the
standpoint of the I develop itself into what it already implicitly is, the
standpoint of science.

However, the movement to be thus presented is not a mere uninter-
rupted, untroubled unfolding; it is not a movement lacking serious
opposition, resistance, tension. In fact, the relevant tension has already
come into view in previous considerations as the tension between the I's

taking itself to be outside the absolute (such that the absolute would be its *object*) and the I's always already belonging to the absolute. Hegel now extends this into a fundamental tension between science and natural consciousness:

> If the standpoint of consciousness, to know of objective things in opposition to itself and to know of itself in opposition to them, is considered by science as the *other*—that in which it knows itself to be at home with itself, is considered rather as the loss of the spirit—so, on the other hand, the element of science is to it a distant beyond in which it no longer has possession of itself. Each of these two appears to the other to be the inversion of the truth. That the natural consciousness immediately entrusts itself to science is an attempt it makes, attracted by it knows not what, to walk for once also on its head (*Phän.* 25).

The opposition is fundamental. Science stands at the point of explicit unification of subject and object, of being-in-and-for-itself *for itself*, of "pure self-recognition in absolute otherness"; and at this point the I cannot remain outside as a subject having science (spirit) as its object; the I cannot have "possession of itself" in the sense on which natural consciousness insists. Natural consciousness stands at the point of *merely* implicit unification, and what it asserts is precisely the bifurcation into subject and object; at this point the movement of the I into the absolute is opposed, and the I posited as subject over against object. Therefore, each "standpoint" appears to the other as a perversion, as inverted. The movement into philosophy is a radically disorienting, *inverting* movement.

At the end of section 7, the consideration of the movement into philosophy is explicitly connected with the previous characterizations of this movement (at the end of section 6). Hegel speaks of the demand that the I, "which seems to itself to stand outside science," be appropriated to science, that the belongingness of the I to the absolute be made explicit, that science "show that and how" the I "belongs to it" (*Phän.* 26). At the same time, this movement is precisely the becoming of science, that is, spirit's coming to be for itself:

> As lacking such actuality, it [science] is merely the content as the *in-itself*, the *purpose* which is still only something inward—not yet spirit, only spiritual substance. This *in-itself* has to express itself and to become *for itself*; this means: it has to posit self-consciousness as one with itself (*Phän.* 26).

It is now possible to formulate the issue of initiatory presentation, that is, to lay out the principal distinctions and questions. The most fundamental distinction is that between the presentation itself and that which is to be presented in the presentation. With respect to the presentation, one can distinguish between two kinds of questions. First, there is the question of the *standpoint* of the presentation, i.e., the question of its stand with respect to what it presents. Second, there is the question of the *form* of the presentation—a question for which Hegel has made preparations in his consideration of the way in which the demand for system is placed upon the presentation by the presented and in his consideration of the structure of the proposition, especially that of the way in which its structure anticipates the movement of the absolute itself.

On the other hand, that which is to be presented in the presentation is that particular movement which Hegel distinguished in his considerations at the end of section 6. It is a movement from being-in-and-for-itself in itself to being-in-and-for-itself for itself; and as such it is identical with the movement from being-in-and-for-itself for us to being-in-and-for-itself for itself. It is the movement of the I into the absolute—that is, the appropriation of immediate self-consciousness to the absolute.

What is especially important at this stage, as the most fundamental development of the issue of presentation is approached, is that the principal items, presentation and presented, be kept sufficiently distinct to allow their intertwining to unfold.

(F) PRESENTATION AND PRESENTED

In sections 5–6 of the Preface, the basis is prepared for the determination of the concept of initiatory presentation. This preparation consists in the distinguishing of the movement that is to be presented in the presentation. In section 7 the demand for initiatory presentation is then introduced, and the movement previously distinguished is identified as that which such presentation is to present. With the presentation and the presented thus identified and distinguished, the task is to determine the precise manner in which they belong together.

Hegel expresses this determination in section 8. I shall attempt to work out the relevant determining methodically, in order then to be able to take up Hegel's expression at its proper level.

At the level of the mere distinction, there is the movement (from being-in-and-for-itself in itself to being-in-and-for-itself for itself), and there is the presentation of this movement. The movement is a movement of spirit, of the absolute. The presentation of the movement would be accomplished by an I, an individual self-consciousness, outside the absolute. Clearly, however, this formulation cannot stand, and the items distinguished cannot remain so totally distinct. For, in this formulation what is manifestly operative is the standpoint of natural consciousness: the formulation is, in effect, an affirmation of sheer bifurcation, of bifurcation between the moving absolute (as object of the presentation) and the presenting I (as subject of the presentation). Such an affirmation

cannot stand, because the very movement being presented (the becoming of spirit, of science) is an overcoming of such bifurcation, an inverting of natural consciousness. The character of that which is to be presented must be allowed to recoil upon the determination of its relation to
the presentation; the recoil destroys the mere externality that natural
consciousness would assert.

Even in the preparatory distinguishing of the movement to be presented, Hegel already points beyond such natural representation by
giving a second characterization of the movement, a characterization by
which the presenting I is drawn into the movement rather than being
simply posed over against it. The movement is a movement from being-
in-and-for-itself for us *to* being-in-and-for-itself for itself, and the movement so characterized amounts to a movement of the I into the absolute.
Thus, there is the movement of the absolute and the movement of the
presenting I into the absolute; that is, the movement of presentation is a
movement into the very movement (i.e., the absolute) which it presents.

The connection between these two movements must be determined
more precisely. So, the question is: In what way can the presentation be a
movement into the very movement presented? What must be the character of this *way* of movement into movement?

The general character of this way is already prescribed by the terms in
which the way has become an issue. At a general level it may be said:
There can be movement into movement only insofar as the first movement blends into the second. Thus, the presentation can be a movement
into the movement presented only if it is of such a character that it comes
to coincide with the movement of the presented. The problem is to
determine the character of this "coming into coincidence," to exhibit it in
terms of the specific character of the two movements involved.

The issue is no simple coincidence, no mere static coinciding, but
rather a *coming* to coincidence. That which thus comes to coincidence
brings something along to that with which it comes to coincidence, at
least a doubling of self. Regarded from the end, the movement of
presentation, moving into the movement presented, brings the latter to a
completion. The presentation constitutes, in a still to be determined
sense, the *completion* of the movement presented; it brings it into its final
phase.[24]

Yet, on the other hand, the two movements are the same and not
merely coincident in the end. Movement from spirit in itself to spirit for
itself and movement of the I into the absolute—these were offered by
Hegel as two characterizations of one and the same movement. But, how
can the presentation remain in any sense a presentation if it is simply the
same as that which it presents? Clearly it cannot remain a presentation if
it is *simply* the same as what it presents—that is, the relevant sense of
sameness must be other than that of such simple sameness as would

exclude all difference. There must be an element of difference which grants to the presentation its distance from the presented, even if the presentation should prove such as to abolish that distance in the end. Such distance is, of course, something utterly different from that distance of subject from object on which natural consciousness would insist.

How, then, can the presentation be the final phase of the movement, that which brings it to completion, and yet be in some determinate sense the same as the movement? Especially if one attends to the peculiar gathering character that belongs to the "ending" of the movement, which would constitute its "final phase," then it can be seen that there is only one way in which this is possible: The presentation must be a retracing of a movement which otherwise is already completed before the inception of the presentation. The presentation as a re-*tracing* is thus identical in content with the presented, but as a *re*-tracing it differs in form and has, thus, its proper distance. The presentation is to retrace the presented in such a way as to gather it into its τέλος. The presentation is a *gathering reenactment.*

In section 8, Hegel characterizes the presentation as such a gathering reenactment—that is, as recollection, which is further described as the movement proper to education. It is, more specifically, the recollecting of the past stages of spirit. It is a passage through the contents of the educational stages through which spirit has passed in coming to its present stage, a passage which reenacts, "relives" those stages, not in their original form, but "as shapes already cast off by the spirit": "The content is already actuality reduced to possibility, vanquished immediacy, and the shapes have been reduced to abbreviations, to simple determinations of thought" (*Phän.* 27, 28). What are recollected are the past stages of spirit reduced to simple determinations of thought.

Hegel says that the content thus reduced is something possessed by spirit in its present stage; the reduced content is its property. In other words, the past shapes of spirit are gathered up into spirit in its present condition. Rather than simply leaving its past stages behind in moving to new shapes, spirit reduces these stages in such a way that they can be gathered up into the new stage; with respect to its shape, spirit is a movement of gathering into the τέλος. As so gathered, the content of the past shapes of spirit is "property that has already been acquired by the general spirit which constitutes the substance of the individual" (*Phän.* 27). They belong to spirit as substance, as still in itself to the extent of leaving the gathering of shapes implicit. The gathering has itself still to be gathered into the determination of spirit.

The recollection which the presentation is to accomplish is also a gathering. It is a passage which gathers up that through which it passes, which reenacts in such a way as to gather up that which it reenacts. That which it gathers up are just the stages through which spirit has passed; and it gathers these up in that form in which they now lie in spirit as its property, as thought determinations which are already gathered up. The gathering recollection is a regathering of what is already gathered; it is a regathering which reenacts the self-gathering of the shapes, which lets them show themselves as self-gathering, which thus lets the gathering be itself gathered into the determination of spirit. The presentation brings the gathering which spirit is to its completion by bringing to it the moment of its ending, the gathering of the gathering itself into the end; the presentation, leaving everything on the side of the presented, brings to it the doubling of explicit self-consciousness.

Hegel describes the movement of education, the enactment of initiatory presentation, from the point of view of the individual and from that of the general spirit. With respect to the former, it consists fundamentally in his gaining what is already given over to him, in his appropriating his spiritual substance to himself as self-consciousness. From the point of view of the general spirit as substance, "it is nothing else than that this acquire its self-consciousness [*sich ihr Selbstbewußtsein gibt*], bring forth its becoming and its reflection" (*Phän.* 27). Initiatory presentation has its distance, but only in order that it might properly "rejoin" the movement which is spirit itself and bring the latter to its completion, draw it into the end.[25]

The initiatory presentation, now explicitly identified by Hegel as a "*phenomenology* of spirit," presents the "becoming of science as such" (*Phän.* 26). That is, it presents the movement from spirit in itself (i.e., spiritual substance) to spirit for itself—or, more specifically, the movement from "immediate spirit," which Hegel now identifies as "sensible consciousness," to genuine knowing, i.e., spirit's knowing of itself. Yet, what is distinctive about such presentation is the fact that it is no mere copy set over against an original already complete in itself. It is no mere copy, for it presents the relevant movement, the movement of spirit through its shapes, not in its "original" form, but rather as reduced to thought determinations, to property—that is, *as* already gathered up. Yet, even so regarded, that which is presented is not an "original" already complete in itself, of which the presentation would provide merely a pale reflection easily dispensed with. On the contrary, the presentation brings the reflection by which the presented first comes to its completion, by which spirit becomes for itself, by which the gathering (which spirit is) is itself gathered into the end.

Such is the "standpoint" of the initiatory presentation, that is, its *stand* with respect to what it presents. It is a stand which leaves everything on the side of the *Sache* itself, which lets the *Sache* be, not by turning away and ignoring it but by turning toward it and tending it. The presentation is to free the *Sache* to itself, to let that self-gatheredness (which the matter is) come to fulfillment. The presentation is devoted to that midwifery which assists in the birth of the true; and to that extent it is Socratic.

But what is required in order that thought be able to tend the *Sache* for thought, in order that it be able to free that matter to itself? Must not such thought already have presupposed something in order to occupy the standpoint demanded? Are its presuppositions not then foisted, in turn, upon the *Sache* itself, in such a way that the presentation would end up binding the *Sache* in alien forms rather than freeing it to itself?

Indeed, such thought must already presuppose something in order to attain the required stand with respect to its *Sache*. However, what is of fundamental importance is that its presupposing is not such as to impose upon the *Sache* something alien to that *Sache,* as when, for example, an empirical concept is imposed upon a thing without regard for the nature shown by that thing. The thought which would present the *Sache* has its proper directedness, and without such directedness it could never, for instance, present the transition from one shape of spirit to another, the transition which is unknown to the consciousness within those shapes. But the directedness, rather than imposing the transition onto the *Sache,* only frees the transition that is already in the *Sache* itself, only regathers what is already itself implicitly gathered, or, more precisely, lets it show itself as self-gathering. The presenting thought has undeniably a directedness to unity; more precisely, it has a directedness to gatheredness as such, to unity in the sense of gathering unity. But it does not *impose* this unity upon the diversity that reigns among and within the shapes of spirit. Rather, it *holds out* this unity to the shapes, *lets* them develop into it, that is, lets them show themselves as already self-gathered into such unity.

Indeed, something is required of the thinking that would present the *Sache*. Such thinking does not just observe—as Hegel himself finally grants when he comes to the end of the determination of the concept of initiatory presentation (*Phän.* 74). Yet, all that is required of such thinking is in service to that reticence capable of freeing the *Sache* to itself.

It is to this stand of reticence that the determination of the concept of presentation would provoke one willing to undergo the inverting movement into philosophy. Indeed, the Preface does violence to the *Sache des Denkens*—but precisely in order to contribute to drawing thought to that stand from which it can let the *Sache* be.

FIVE

Image and Phenomenon

Phenomenological thinking is the practice of self-effacement in the face of the things themselves. The rigor thus required of such thinking must be such as to allow it to stand under the demand to attend solely to the things as they present themselves. Phenomenological thinking is directed toward evidence, that is, toward experiences in which the things at issue "are present to me as 'they themselves,'" and it places itself under the demand that what it presents as scientific judgment be grounded in evidence so understood.[1] This demand for evidence constitutes what Husserl calls the principle of all principles: "that whatever presents itself originarily to us in 'intuition' (as it were, in its bodily actuality) is simply to be accepted as that as which it gives itself but only within the limits in which it there gives itself."[2] Phenomenology means: λέγειν τὰ φαινό-μενα: phenomenology lets "that which shows itself be seen from itself as it shows itself from itself."[3] Phenomenological thinking would "leave the last word to the things themselves."[4]

However, such an exclusive attending to the things themselves is radically different from the passivity and indolence of a thinking that would purport to be merely descriptive. For it is precisely in that pose in which thinking would simply leave itself out and straightforwardly go about describing the things themselves—it is precisely then that its preconceptions remain most stubbornly (because concealedly) in force so as to render it least attendant to things as they present themselves. Thus it is that allegedly descriptive accounts of the same thing are notoriously various, lacking even that provisional accord which is made possible in modern empirical science by the interplay of conceptualization and intuition. Every attempt at immediate recourse to mere description fails, because it refuses to consider what such recourse requires of it. Its pose is thus self-forgetful, that is, comic, and it is at best only a comic prelude to genuinely phenomenological thinking.

Mere decision does not suffice to bring one into a position from which to attend to the things themselves; nor is it sufficient merely to enforce

Originally published in *Research in Phenomenology*, vol. 5 (1975).

such decision with resolution. Such a position—hence, the initiation of an attendance to the things themselves—is not something immediately attained. On the contrary, its attainment demands of thought an effort which is immeasurably more strenuous than any mere "methodological" decision. It is thus that there is a *problem* of methodology in phenomenological thinking—because there is need to raise questions regarding what is required of a thinking that would genuinely attend to the things themselves. There is need of a methodological reflection occupied with determining what is required of thinking in order that it be capable of attending to the things themselves, in order that it be capable of freeing these things to themselves in letting them show themselves. In general, such reflection is two-sided. On the one side, it seeks to determine the character of that *reticence* by which thinking holds itself aloof from the things themselves in such fashion as to grant them the free space in which to show themselves. On the other side, such reflection seeks to determine the character of that *engagement* of thought with the things themselves by which it entices them into the open, draws them out, invokes their self-presentation, aids in the birth of their truth. In practice, phenomenological thinking, bound by its commitment to attend to the things themselves, is a peculiar midwifery; the methodological reflection is charged with bringing into that practice the reflexive determinations which first grant it its proper bearing.

This study takes up such methodological reflection and carries it through within a certain domain of problems. Specifically, it will be shown that, in the domain of perceptual apprehension, images belong so fundamentally to the structure of the phenomenon that to attend to the phenomena (as the things themselves) requires a correlative attending to the relevant imaging. The image-structure thus intrinsic to the phenomenon will hence be exhibited in its way of prescribing the reticence and the engagement required of genuinely phenomenological thinking.

(A) IMAGE AND INTENTIONALITY

In the breakthrough into phenomenology which Husserl accomplished in the *Logical Investigations,* the issue of images played a significant role. This role was, however, largely negative. The understanding of consciousness as intentional experience marked for Husserl the decisive overcoming of a certain misunderstanding of presentation in terms of images, a misunderstanding that had dragged on through the centuries and had especially plagued much of modern philosophy. In view of this connection, Husserl added to chapter 2 of the Fifth Investigation—the chapter in which the concept of intentionality is thematically introduced—an appendix devoted explicitly to criticism of the so-called "image-theory." In order that our present efforts be posed from the outset at

that level achieved by Husserl in that breakthrough, the sense of image needs to be brought under this criticism and purged of the remnants of nonphenomenological thinking that still accrue to it—that is, the sense of image needs to be redetermined in consonance with the demands of phenomenological thinking.

Husserl's critique of the so-called image-theory is explicitly designated as a development of his considerations of intentionality. More specifically, the critique refers back primarily to those considerations[5] in which Husserl seeks to ward off a certain misunderstanding of the sense "intentional object." The relevant misunderstanding lies in the supposition that in the concept of intentional relation "it is a matter of a relation between two things, both in the same way really [*reell*] present in consciousness, an act and an intentional object." Over against this misconception, Husserl insists that an intentional experience directs itself to the object in a specifically *intentional* sense: the object is "meant" or "aimed at." Thus:

> There are . . . not two things experientially present; we do not experience the object and beside it the intentional experience directed upon it . . . : only one thing is present, the intentional experience. . . . If this experience is present, then, *eo ipso* and through its own essence (we must insist) the intentional "relation to an object" is achieved and *eo ipso* an object is "intentionally present."

Thus, the intentional object is not a component of the experience. It is not of the same order as the intentional experience: The intentional object is not immanent or mental. On the other hand, those kinds of contents which are genuinely immanent, which do belong as components to intentional experience, are not intentional. What one sees are not color sensations but colored things; and colored things do not belong to the experience of seeing but are rather what that experience presents.

The force of this clarification lies in its expulsion of the intentional object from the intentional experience and, hence, from the sphere of immanence. This expulsion requires that the common distinction between merely immanent or intentional objects and transcendent or actual objects (which may correspond to them) be collapsed; for this expulsion is, on its other side, an affirmation that, as Husserl says, "the intentional object of a presentation is the same as its actual object."[6] But such a distinction is precisely what is presupposed by that "image-theory" which would explain presentation by supposing that there is an image in consciousness which serves as substitute for the thing itself which is outside consciousness. Husserl's stand against the image-theory is dictated by its basic conflict with the concept of intentionality.

Husserl elaborates the critique in such a way as to extend the contention beyond the basic conflict between the image-theory and the general

concept of intentionality; and, taking a stand in the contention, he then places the issue of images in the domain prescribed by that stand.[7]

(1) Husserl charges that the image-theory, posing the thing itself outside and an image representative of it in consciousness, completely overlooks "the most important point." This point is: "that in imaginal presentation [*im bildlichen Vorstellen*] we *mean* the imagined object (the original) on the basis of the appearing image." The image-theory, posing image inside and original outside, assumes as something self-evident that the former is capable of serving as representative for the latter. But the matter is not self-evident. It must be asked: How is it possible to *mean* the original on the basis of the image?

Nothing is gained by appeal to the resemblance between image and original. In order for such resemblance to be able to direct one beyond the image to the original, in order for it to allow one to mean the original on the basis of the image, the resemblance would need to be manifest. But, it could be manifest only if the original were itself already manifest—whereas it is precisely the function of the image to make the original manifest. Thus, lacking independent access to the original, one could mean it on the basis of the image only if the character of the image *as* image—even its character as image of just that original to be meant—were somehow manifest in the image itself. Only on the basis of such a manifest imaginality (*Bildlichkeit*) would one be able "to go beyond the 'image,' which alone is given in consciousness and to relate it *as* an image to a certain extraconscious object." Does the image manifest its imaginality?

This question poses the most crucial juncture in Husserl's consideration of the issue of images. It calls for a decision of the most profound bearing.

Husserl's decision is negative: The imaginality of the image is not manifest in the image itself. It follows that the image, essentially concealing its character as image, is utterly incapable of performing that representative role assigned it by the image-theory, which thus collapses. The consequence is momentous: The issue of images is decisively removed from the center of phenomenological concern. Of course, there remain problems regarding images, problems to which phenomenology would eventually need to turn; but they are problems which, ranged alongside other sets of problems, would be taken up by a phenomenological thinking confident of itself. Banished from the center, these problems do not bear upon the self-forming of the phenomenological pose as such— that is, the issue of images has no bearing on the determination of that reticence and engagement required of phenomenological thinking.

(2) Husserl can thus proceed to place the issue of images, to pose the problem of images as a peripheral problem to be taken up on the basis of the understanding of consciousness as intentional experience rather

than itself bearing on that understanding. As such the problem is that of the instituting of the image-original relation. In order that one object be an image of another, more is required than mere resemblance between them: The image-original relation must be instituted, one object must be constituted by consciousness as image-representative of the other. Husserl is explicit: "The constitution of the image as such takes place in a peculiar intentional consciousness." Thus:

> A painting is an image only for an image-constituting consciousness, which through its imaginative apperception (here founded in a perception) first gives to a primary, perceptually appearing object the "status" and "meaning" of an image.

Such constitution of the image is to be distinguished from those acts of fulfillment which, presupposing an already constituted image-original relation, achieve a concrete synthesis of image with original.

(3) The very posing of the problem of images, the setting of the issue in its proper domain, thus presupposes a certain settling of the issues belonging to the domain in which phenomenological thinking is still a problem for itself. Clearly the settling of these issues cannot proceed through the issue of images. More specifically, the intentional givenness of an object to consciousness, an issue belonging to the domain of fundamental problems, cannot be clarified in terms of images:

> Since the interpretation of anything as an image presupposes an object intentionally given to consciousness, it clearly would lead to an infinite regress were we again to let this object be itself constituted through an image or to speak seriously of a "perceptual image" immanent in the simple percept *by way of which* it relates to the "thing itself."

(4) Husserl refers, finally, back to the domain of fundamental problems, to what is preeminently at issue in that domain, namely, intentionality: It is imperative to realize that an object is present to consciousness, not because a content similar to the object is somehow present in consciousness, but rather because it is constituted as object in and through the intentional experience.

(B) IMAGE AND IMAGINALITY

The basic clarification which Husserl achieves in introducing the concept of intentionality is a principal moment of that breakthrough into phenomenology accomplished in the *Logical Investigations*. The insistence on the distinction between presentation and presented, i.e., between intentional experience and intentional object, and the correlative expulsion of the presented from the sphere of immanence serve decisively to eliminate the mental object—the "idea" in one of those several, inadequately distinguished senses which the word had for Locke.[8] In turn, the elimination of the mental object serves to clear the way for the return to the things themselves, for an attending, not to mental contents that stand for, and thus stand in the way of, the things themselves as they show themselves. The basic clarification, which prescribes the expulsion of the object from the sphere of immanence, stands directly under that demand which defines phenomenological thinking.

However, the question is whether, granting what is demanded in this demand, it is, then, necessary that the issue of images be banished from the domain of fundamental problems. It is not a question of that "image-theory" which Husserl criticizes. Clearly the basic thrust of Husserl's criticism is decisive: To retain that view according to which an image within consciousness substitutes for the actual object outside consciousness is to fail to make that demanded clarification which Husserl achieves through the concept of intentionality. The question is, rather, whether the expulsion of such images from the sphere of immanence *also* requires that the issue of images be banished from the domain of fundamental problems. Once all images are placed on the side of the object, is it possible to redetermine the sense of image in such a way that the issue of images remains at the center of the problematic of phenomenological thinking? This question prescribes two tasks: On the negative side, it is to be shown that the criticism by which Husserl would banish the issue of images from the domain of fundamental problems is *limited,* that the recognition of its limit prompts a redetermination of the sense of image, and that, granted this redetermination, it is not necessary for the issue to be banished to the periphery of phenomenological thinking—that is, it is possible for this issue to be retained at the center without violating the sense of Husserl's breakthrough into phenomenology. The second task is, then, to show, positively and concretely, how the issue of images belongs to the domain of fundamental problems—that is, how the very demand for attending to the things themselves brings with it a demand for attending to images.

On what does the removal of the issue of images from the domain of fundamental problems depend? It does not follow from the general demand that the intentional object be expelled from the sphere of immanence—that is, it is not a direct consequence of the introduction of the concept of intentionality into the domain of fundamental problems. The general concept of intentionality prescribes only that images be expelled from the sphere of immanence—that is, that the sense of image be redetermined in such a way that images are regarded as located on the side of the object. Granted such redetermination, there is nothing in the general concept of intentionality to prevent the issue of images from remaining in the domain of fundamental problems.

What drives the issue of images out of this domain is Husserl's way of developing that "most important point" that is overlooked by the image-theory: that one *means* the original on the basis of the image—that, consequently, the possibility of such a meaning must be accounted for. Granted the lack of independent access to the original, that is, granted that the original "needs" the image in order to become manifest, the question becomes: Does an image in any way announce its character as an image? Does an image manifest its imaginality? Husserl's negative answer to this question entails that no image is capable of performing its representative function, or, more generally, its function of revealing the original. To the extent that the capacity of images to perform this function is what places the issue of images within the domain of funda-mental problems, the denial of this capacity entails the removal of this issue to the periphery.

(1) But Husserl's answer and, hence, his decision regarding the place of the issue of images are limited—that is, they hold only within the limits of the ontological analytic that is brought to bear on the issue. This ontological analytic is at work in Husserl's specific formulation of his denial that images manifest imaginality:

> The imaginality of the object which functions as image is, however, ob-
> viously no intrinsic character (no "real predicate"); as though an object were
> imaginal as, for example, it is red and spherical.[9]

Imaginality is no real predicate; it is not given with the image-object in the way that the redness and the spherical shape, for example, are given. The point is indisputable: Imaginality is not a qualitative or quantitative property adherent to the image-object. But from this Husserl concludes, in effect, that imaginality is *nothing* manifest in the image-object.

This conclusion is dependent upon a decisively limited ontological analytic; the latter is expressed in Husserl's appeal to "real predicates" as the standard to which imaginality would need to measure up in order to be admitted as something genuinely manifested by the image-object. Is this an appropriate standard for measuring something such as imag-inality? Hardly.

If considered in categorial-ontological terms, specifically, if measured itself by reference to the categorial reflections of the *Critique of Pure Reason,* it proves to be a narrow standard: It does not cover all of the categorial determinations of objects. In the strictest sense, a real predi-cate is one which expresses a specific, positive determination in the category of quality. An extension of this sense is critically quite impor-tant: The sense of real predicate is extended so as to include all "deter-mining predicates," that is, all predicates "which could be added to the concept of a thing."[10] Such inclusion marks, however, the limit of the extension; further extension beyond this limit would inevitably lead back to that confusing of "idea" and object (as in the ontological proof for the existence of God) which Husserl, no less than Kant, is intent on eliminating.[11] Thus, there are categorial determinations which are not also real predicates. Among these are the determinations of the category of modality (possibility, existence, necessity).

Thus, it can be granted with Husserl that imaginality is no real predicate *without*, however, also drawing the further conclusion that imaginality is nothing whatever manifested in the image-object; that is, it is possible for imaginality to be a specific determination of a category not covered by the concept of real predicate. Let me, then—in an effort to preserve manifest imaginality and, hence, the revelatory power of the image—regard imaginality as the specific determination of existence (actuality) that pertains to whatever presents itself as image. That is, imaginality is to be regarded, not as a property belonging to the image, but rather as the way in which the image *is* (actual), as its mode of actuality. That is, the actuality of the image is to be regarded as identical with its image-character, and thus it can be said of the image that *it is as an imaging*. But in that case the mode of actuality (the "is") of an image is different from that of an object, and there is need, accordingly, to call into question the seemingly obvious assumption that whatever is an image must also (and even more fundamentally) be an object—that is, there is need to call into question every account of images which takes it for granted that the image-character of the image is founded on its object-character, which assumes that an image is, first of all, an object which then has acquired, as it were, some further character that makes it an image. Shadows and reflections are not objects in the sense in which the things shadowed and reflected are. And they are apprehended, not as objects which then have the further character of being images, but rather *as* shadows and reflections of things, that is, *as* images. To grasp a shadow or reflection as an object requires both an artificial perceptual pose and a considerable extension of the concept of object beyond its usual range.

Like shadows and reflections, imaginality is too delicate for a measure that takes its directives solely from objects, and the attempt to apply this measure to it only succeeds in completely dispelling it. The delicacy of the image is to be granted—that is, phenomenological thinking is bound to attend to the image in such a way as to let it show itself in its peculiar delicacy.

Nietzsche offers a glimpse of this delicacy. Reflecting on the character of dream-images in order to trace in our apprehension of them that forming power which he names "Apollonian," he attends especially to the peculiar *shining* of the image-form: In the dream, however lively, we always have "*die durchschimmernde Empfindung ihres Scheins.*"[12] The image shines in such a way as to betray in a "fleeting sensation" that it is just appearance; its shining is a shimmering, a tremulous gleaming, which fleetingly and delicately betrays that it is mere image, not original. Its shimmering lights up its imaginality, lets it be (delicately) manifest, not as a property of an object, but as a moment of that very shining in which it is betrayed.

(2) If imaginality is thus freed from objectivity, then the basis for the banishment of the issue of images to the periphery collapses: It can no longer be supposed that the constitution of images presupposes the constitution of objects and that, consequently, the problems concerning the latter are simply prior to those having to do with images. For a regard that is attentively phenomenological, it is not as though a painting were, first of all, an object, on which an image-character would subsequently be superimposed; when such a stratification is supposed, one has simply transferred to perceptual apprehension, i.e., to that which is perceptually apprehended, something which one "knows" about the painting on quite different grounds. On the contrary, a painting is, from the outset, apprehended *as an image*—as revealing an original which it itself is not. When one looks at Dürer's self-portrait of 1500, one looks through the image at Dürer himself. In such a case one does not see an object to which one then gives the status of an image by imaginatively referring it beyond itself; it requires a very artificial perceptual pose in order to see a painting as merely a canvas covered with splotches of color. One does not even see just the image itself, for only in an abstract sense can there be an image by itself; one sees an image *of* Dürer, that is to say, one looks at Dürer himself through the image. One apprehends the image *as* already linked up with the original of which it is an image, as opening onto the original, as letting the original show itself. And thus, paintings have a revelatory power which surpasses what one could grant them through a constitutive extension back toward an imaginatively projected original. Their revelatory power flows, as it were, in the other direction.

(3) If imaginality is freed from objectivity, if it is not presupposed that an image must always already be an object, then there is no formal argument to vitiate from the outset the attempt to understand the constitution of objects in terms of images. Nor does such an attempt conflict with the general demand of phenomenological thinking so long as all images are regarded as situated beyond the sphere of immanence. The question is granted: How (if at all) do images belong to the constitution of objects? And, though subordinate, there is also the question: How can one and the same thing sometimes be constituted as both object and image?—i.e., how do these senses, as constituted, fit together?

(4) To allow the issue of images to remain in the domain of fundamental problems is not to deny that what is preeminently at issue in that domain is intentionality—as long as images are regarded as situated

beyond the sphere of immanence. Yet, it does serve to provoke questions as to how intentionality is to be put at issue in this domain. Granted that the supposition of a mere content in consciousness (i.e., a mental image) does not suffice to account for experience of objects, nevertheless, the phenomenological redetermination of the sense of image and the correlative expulsion of images from the sphere of immanence open up the possibility of regarding images as providing the peculiar way in which content is offered up to consciousness (understood as intentional experience). In this regard the task would be to show how the *form* of the linking-up of images with original corresponds to the *form* which belongs to intentional consciousness with its capacity "to pass over through synthesis from ever new and very disparate forms of consciousness to a consciousness of unity."[13] The task is to exhibit the structural correspondence between the imaginal *offering* up of content and the intentional *taking* up of content by consciousness in the constitution of the object.

(C) IMAGE AND OBJECT

But as yet I have not even begun to show *concretely* how the issue of images belongs to the domain of fundamental problems. One way of beginning such is by showing that the issue of images pertains to certain specific moments in the constitution of objects as such—that is, by exhibiting some respects in which imaging belongs to that kind of showing in which an object comes to show itself to perceptual apprehension. In the beginning such concrete attending should bind itself to the phenomena, even at the cost of being fragmentary—yet realizing that its indifference to questions of completeness and totality exposes it to the risk of eventually being compelled to reform its matters.

In coming to show itself, a visible object belongs to a visual field, which contributes in several significant ways to the structure of the showing and, hence, to the determination of the content that gets shown. One such way is through the *lighting* of the field, that is, its peculiar configuration of shadows, of intensity of illumination, of gloss and reflection. For the most part, the lighting is not itself really seen; it remains, as it were, in the background—or, rather, it is that foreground which directs one's gaze to the thing, which already prepares an articulation of the visual field, an articulation which vision resumes so as to embrace the contours of the perceptual object.[14] In the lighting of the field, there is imaging already in play, not only the imaging between the lighting articulation as a whole and the visual sweep which resumes it, but also at a more rudimentary level—at the level of mere shadows. These "poorest" of images are integral to the lighting of the visual field, and their shadowing is what, perhaps most of all, gives the lighting its power of articulation. Through these images one sees the contours of the field; their imaging is a shadowing forth of the contours. It is an imaging which, in laying out contours, prepares the showing of the object.

In the actual showing, the object presents itself perspectively. One sees it always from somewhere, and, correlatively, it presents itself one-sidedly, offers to vision only one of its faces. It shows itself by way of profiles, yields up to perceptual apprehension some profile or other. Normally, one can, of course, change one's perspective on the object by moving around it, for instance; then the object offers a new profile, though in doing so it ceases to present the previously offered profile. Never, in fact, does one get all the profiles of the object simultaneously in one's perceptual grasp. One cannot see the object from everywhere simultaneously. Except under very artificial conditions, one cannot even see it from two perspectives simultaneously; each profile withdraws all others from one's gaze, conceals them.

A profile of an object is not itself an object; it lacks that peculiar structure of unity within multiplicity which is required of objects and which belongs to them especially through their way of being linked up with profiles. Furthermore, a profile is not an independent part, from the totality of which the object would somehow be composed; it is not in this sense that profiles are "partial." A profile is always a profile of the object as a whole. Of course, there is a certain correlation of profiles with the front, the back, and the various sides of the object: In the profile which one gets from one perspective, the front of the object is dominant and the back probably not immediately visible at all; if the object is looked at from the side, both front and back will, if immediately visible, be seen obliquely, and that particular side of the object which faces one's vantage point will dominate the profile offered. Yet, however much one or another independent part may dominate a particular profile, that profile remains, nevertheless, a profile of the object *as a whole*. Faced with a profile one intends in perceptual apprehension, not just the parts immediately presented in the profile, not just the sides seen from the present perspective, but rather the object as a whole; nor is the object apprehended *as* it presents itself in a profile, but rather *as* it shows itself as a whole through the profile. A plate seen obliquely is not seen as an ellipse but rather as a circular plate seen obliquely. The perceptual apprehension surpasses in the direction of the object itself what is immediately offered up to vision.

Thus, a profile opens onto the object of which it is a profile. A profile serves as that through which something else, something which the profile is not, shows itself; and, correlatively, one looks through the profile to the thing, to such an extent that, in a quite definite sense, one does not really even see the profile. Hence, the structure of the linking-up of profile with object is identical with that by which image is linked up with original; that is, profiling is a specific form of imaging, a profile a specific kind of image, in that redetermined sense by which imaginality is freed from objectivity. And, like every image, a profile not only lets the object show itself but also, in its irreducible difference from what shows itself, compels that object to hold itself back—that is, guarantees concealment and sets the object at a distance from perceptual apprehension, a distance which serves precisely to free the object from one's grasp of it, to grant it its aloofness from the perceptual apprehension of it.

There is still another character of profiles that needs to be noted: Although it is possible to determine in a certain disengagement from the object a series of discrete profiles corresponding to various fixed positions from which one might gaze upon the object, such determination covers up the continuity that is primary in perceptual apprehension. This continuity is such that, concretely regarded, profiles are never really discrete but rather shade into one another so thoroughly that any establishing of limits by which particular profiles would be distinguished within this course of continual variation would betray its character as an imposition coming from the side of a seer enacting a series of viewings of the object from discontinuous positions. Profiles blend into one another, and what is primary is the profiling of the object, not the profiles—just as with images, once freed of the weight of objectivity, what is primary is the imaging, not the images, which, as long as they are regarded apart from the imaging, inevitably get considered as quasi-objects rather than being freed to their proper delicacy.

(D) IMAGE AND PHENOMENOLOGY

It has been shown that the issue of images belongs to the domain of fundamental problems, that image-structures are integral to that total structuration in which the constitution of the object comes to pass. (The extent and the depth of the involvement of image-structures in the constitution of the object are matters here left undetermined.)

Yet, the principal issue in the freeing of imaginality from objectivity is the granting of the delicacy of the image, that is, the dissolving of the image as a quasi-thing into the effervescent shining, that is, the release of image into imaging. Through this issue, what has been shown is itself released into a new domain, the domain of showing as such, in distinction from that of objects shown. Granted that the attending has been fragmentary, what has been shown—within the limits imposed by that fragmentariness—is that *imaging belongs to showing*: That showing in which an object comes to show itself to one's perceptual apprehension *comes to pass as imaging*. Still granted these limits, it has been shown that showing is a shining in which something shines through so as to become manifest, a shining which, however, is also a shimmering betrayal of its own lightness, a shining suffused with a glimmer which lightly veils that which shines through. *A showing of showing as imaging*—it is thus that the present efforts are gathered up.

Because imaging belongs to showing, the issue of images is an originary issue for phenomenological thinking, that is, an issue which bears upon the self-forming of the phenomenological pose as such. For phenomenological thinking is bound to attend to the things themselves in such a way as to let them show themselves from themselves—that is, in the case of the objects offered to perceptual apprehension, in such a way as to let the *showing as imaging* come to pass *from* the objects themselves. What is required of such an attending? In the first place, reticence is required of it—a holding itself aloof from the imaging in order that it might come to pass from the things themselves, the reticence of a thinking which holds open the space of imaging, of a thinking which grants place to the play of indeterminate duality. But also, engagement is required of such an attending—an engagement, not specifically in those objects of perceptual apprehension that it would let show themselves, but rather in that showing proper to them, an engagement in showing-imaging as such. Granted the showing of showing as imaging, phenomenological thinking comes under the demand that it form itself into an attending which, in engagingly holding out as provocation the form of showing as imaging, reticently gives way to the play of imaging in the things themselves.

SIX

Research and Deconstruction

At the beginning of his Marburg lectures of 1927, *The Basic Problems of Phenomenology*, Heidegger explicitly identified phenomenology as "the method of scientific philosophy as such."[1] This identification echoed the classic formulation that had been given by Husserl in his *Logos* article of 1911: It is only as phenomenological research that philosophy can become a rigorous science. It is a matter of placing philosophy under the demand that the last word be left to the things themselves.[2] To cite that text of 1911, *Philosophie als strenge Wissenschaft*: "The impulse to research must proceed not from philosophies but from things and problems."[3] Husserl adds that philosophy is, however, a science of beginnings, that it must be not only rigorous but also radical science. It must, for example, avoid simply identifying the things themselves with empirical facts, must avoid thereby understanding itself as simple empiricism. More generally, it must be radical even as regards the identity of the things themselves, hence ultimately as regards its own identity, its own self-understanding.

This addition, this supplement to the demand for rigor, is of utmost significance. Through it phenomenology becomes two-sided. On the one side, phenomenology has the character of *research*, of actual theoretical work on the things themselves, work by which the things themselves would be explicated as they show themselves. This side would be essentially determined by the demand for rigor: It is a matter of attending carefully and exclusively to the things themselves. And yet, if it would be radical, phenomenology must, on the other side, expose itself to the question of the identity of the things themselves, must let it repeatedly be asked "Which things are things themselves?" and "How must one attend in order genuinely to attend to the things themselves?" In other words, a radical phenomenology must be prepared to have its field of research disrupted by a questioning more negative, more skeptical than any explicative research. It must be prepared for a questioning which inverts

Presented under the title "Forschung und Dekonstruktion" to the Deutsche Gesellschaft für phänomenologische Forschung in Trier on 12 April 1980; published (in German) in *Phänomenologische Forschungen*, ed. E. W. Orth, vol. 11 (1981).

and displaces the fundamental oppositions by which the field of research is determined, a questioning which thus throws out of joint the structure within which research would otherwise securely proceed. It must be prepared for, must invite, must invoke against itself, the *deconstruction* of the field of research.

My concern here will be to trace the interplay between these two sides, between research and deconstruction, though only in a very limited and fragmentary way. In more precise terms, I shall focus on a series of structural shifts produced by this interplay within phenomenological thought—that is, on a certain discontinuous movement generated by the recurrent tension between research and deconstruction, the movement of phenomenology's self-constitution and self-dissolution. In more comprehensive terms, I shall venture a few very tentative steps toward what might eventually warrant the title "presentation" ("*Darstellung*") of phenomenological thought—or, to recall, cautiously, Merleau-Ponty's phrase, "a phenomenology of phenomenology."[4]

I shall trace in merest outline three stages of this movement. At each stage it will be a matter of thinking through the phenomenological injunction "to the things themselves" both as principle of rigor and as itself subject to the demand for radical questioning.

(A)

Phenomenology attends to the things themselves as they present themselves. Setting aside all prior interpretations, setting all presuppositions out of action, it attends to things as they show themselves in their immediate intuitive presence, regardless of whether the relevant intuition be sensible or categorial. Attending to the things themselves as thus present requires of the phenomenologist a reflective adherence to the intuitively presented. The task is to explicate the moments of that intuition.

And yet, precisely such explication serves to bring to light certain structures of experience that repel such merely adherent attending to the intuitively present. The most important examples are horizonal structures. A sensibly presented thing presents itself within a horizon of other things, an outer horizon; and it presents itself as capable of being perceived from an indefinite number of other perspectives to which it would offer itself in different profiles—that is, it presents itself as having an inner horizon of other possible profiles which are somehow cointended. What is distinctive about horizonal structures is their inconspicuousness, their submersion in the texture of experience. A horizon does not simply show itself but rather holds itself back in order that something else might show itself within that horizon. This holding back, this not showing itself, is essential to its very character as a horizon; and one could succeed in thematizing it, in making it simply present, only at the cost of robbing it of its character as horizon. It is therefore incumbent upon the phenomenologist to pay heed to such horizonal reserve. It is a matter of bringing somehow to show itself something which, submerged in the texture of experience, ordinarily does not show itself as such but rather holds itself back as the condition under which things can show themselves. Bringing it to show itself cannot be a matter of transforming it into something nonhorizonally present to which one could merely adherently attend. On the contrary, the phenomenological attending must exercise enough reticence to allow the horizon its reserve, must discern it in the texture of experience without detaching it from that texture and transforming it into something simply present.

Thus, through actual work on the things themselves, a decisive shift is introduced, a broadening of the scope of the things themselves so as to include not only the directly present but also another component, the horizonal structures. This shift broaches a correlative shift on the side of the phenomenological attending, which now comes to include not only a reflective adherence to what immediately shows itself but also another component, a reticent discerning of something which for the most part does not directly show itself. It is a matter of bringing something to show itself without violating its reserved, withdrawn, submerged character. If an interpretive character is ascribed to such reticent discerning of submerged structures, then it may be said that with this shift phenomenology has become hermeneutical, has undergone a *hermeneutical shift*.

This hermeneutical shift is also deconstructive with respect to the opposition between interpretation and reflective adherence to the immediately present. This opposition was initially posited as a simple opposition and as thus posited provided the basis for the initial exclusion of interpretation from phenomenological attending: Leaving all interpretation aside, phenomenology would attend solely to the things themselves as they show themselves. And yet, precisely in its rigorous attending to the things themselves, precisely through phenomenological research, phenomenology comes to require what is previously excluded, comes to include an interpretive component, though of a kind that is no longer simply the opposite of adherence to the directly present. In other words, the opposition by which phenomenological attending was initially defined has been deconstructed in such a way that its terms are no longer simply opposed.

(B)

Yet, if these terms are no longer simply opposed, this does not mean that they are now securely composed moments, merely coordinate components of phenomenological attending; it does not mean, correlatively, that the things themselves are simply, conclusively determined as the sum of the directly presented and the horizonal structures within which it is presented. On the contrary, the hermeneutical shift already prepares another shift, a shift in which the opposition is reconstituted in another dimension and its deconstruction thus resumed and extended. Again it is a shift linked to certain necessities uncovered in actual phenomenological research.

One can find this second shift traced in Merleau-Ponty's *Phenomenology of Perception,* perhaps most succinctly in that remarkable chapter entitled "The Thing and the Natural World." In that chapter a certain reductive movement is enacted, this movement serving as the organizing structure for the entire discourse. Beginning with the full, concrete perceptual object, there is movement through a series of reductions aimed at isolating what is immediately sensibly presented. Beginning, for example, with the full perception of a die, yet breaking with the natural attitude and ceasing merely to live in that perception, one introduces a series of reductions which gradually decompose the initial perceptual object. One notices that the die is really perceived only through sight and that as a result all that is really immediately presented is the outer surface; the die loses its density, its materiality, and becomes merely a visual spectacle. All that one actually perceives are certain properties such as size, shape, and color. But even these are given only fragmentarily. One does not see the die from all sides simultaneously; one does not see its cubical shape but only certain distorted faces of the cube, meager profiles which, if their detachment from the thing were enforced, would eventually be decomposed into sheer sensible content. If one then sought, beginning with such sheer content, to reconstitute the full perceptual object, if, in other words, one sought to trace the movement in the opposite direction, one would presumably need to invoke a certain synthetic activity capable of composing that object from the manifold of fragmentary material actually given.

It is in the determination of the character of this synthesis that the distinctively phenomenological orientation of Merleau-Ponty's analysis becomes evident. Instead of an intellectual synthesis, which would "substitute for the thing itself in its primordial being an imperfect reconstruction,"[5] Merleau-Ponty's analysis uncovers a synthesis that is always already under way within the material itself. It is a matter of synthesis by a subject that is bodily, that is saturated with its objects and consequently never detached from the material to be synthesized, that could never simply bring that material under its synthesizing gaze. When, for example, one runs one's hand over a rough surface, there is not first a series of tactile sensations which the movement of one's hand would then link together into the perception of the rough surface; rather, one's hand is from the outset paired off with the surface, and its movement is what allows there even to be anything like tactile sensations. In Merleau-Ponty's words:

> Tactile experience adheres to the surface of our body; we cannot unfold it before us, and it never quite becomes an object. Correlatively, as the subject of touch, I cannot flatter myself that I am everywhere and nowhere. . . . It is not I who touch, it is my body; when I touch I do not think a manifold, but my hands rediscover a certain style. . . .[6]

So then, it is never a matter of sheer sensible content devoid of synthetic connection and over against it an activity of synthesis that would compose the full perceptual object from that content. Rather, the effect of Merleau-Ponty's analysis is to deconstruct the very distinction between synthetic form and sensible content. Instead of an external correlation of form and content, his analysis uncovers at every level a sensible content that is already informed—or, more precisely, a sensible fragment that is already installed within a horizonal structure and through that structure already engaged in synthesis. What his analysis uncovers are properties that are always already linked up with other properties and with the thing, e.g., the woolly red of a carpet; or profiles that always already merge into other profiles so as to let, for example, a plate seen obliquely be seen not as an ellipse but rather as a circular plate viewed obliquely.

What is, then, the character of the shift introduced by Merleau-Ponty's analyses? It is a shift away from the simple duality that was introduced by the previous, hermeneutical shift, away from the duality of merely presented content coordinated with horizonal structures. It is a shift of the horizonal structures into the very core of the content in such a way that there virtually ceases to be any merely presented content. Through this disruptive shift such content is reduced to being, at most, only a vanishing moment in the perceptual hold on the thing.

This same shift is traced in *Being and Time*—traced perhaps most conspicuously in Heidegger's analysis of the environing world in its relation to projective understanding, the analysis by which the derivative character of the present-at-hand is demonstrated. In effect, that demonstration carries through, though at a quite different level, the same kind of disruption of pure intuitive content as does Merleau-Ponty's analysis. It displaces the merely intuited present-at-hand, exhibits it as derivative from the ready-to-hand; and the latter it exhibits as thoroughly installed within those structures which in the environing world of equipment correspond to the horizons that structure the perceptual world. The sight which is operative in one's dealings with the ready-to-hand is a sight by which is held in view the referential totality correlative to projective understanding; it is a sight which to that extent is grounded in understanding and correspondingly is remote from immediate intuition.

What is especially significant in the Heideggerian development of the shift is the way in which that shift is shown to be related to the Western metaphysical tradition as a whole and to have profound consequences with regard to that tradition. This connection is perhaps most explicit in Heidegger's lecture course *Logik* (1925–26).[7] Here he undertakes to show that within this tradition knowledge has continuously been regarded as intuition—that is, that a paradigmatic status has been accorded to intuition such that all knowledge, to the extent that it is not simply intuition, is charged with compensating for what it lacks in intuition. For the entire tradition knowledge is ideally the sheer beholding of what is present, sheer intuition adherent to the simply present. Therefore, the shift away from such priority of intuition is in effect a shift away from the entire metaphysical tradition; it is a *counter-metaphysical shift*. It is a break with what Derrida, in a thoroughly Heideggerian move, calls the metaphysics of presence. And according to both Heidegger and Derrida, it is a break also with phenomenology itself to the extent that phenomenology simply retains its initial injunction to attend to the things themselves as they show themselves *in intuition*—that is, to the extent that phenomenology retains what now has appeared as its solidarity with the metaphysical tradition.

Thus, this second shift, deconstructing the distinction between horizonal structures and the intuitively presented, proves so radical as to turn phenomenology against itself, against its founding injunction. And it is equally a turning against metaphysics, a shift away from the center of metaphysics, a shift by which phenomenology is driven to the very edge of metaphysics. The question is whether phenomenology, turned thus against itself by this counter-metaphysical shift, can somehow be reconstituted at the edge of metaphysics.

(C)

Perhaps the most decisive consequence of the disruption of the merely intuited lies in the fact that it is also a disruption of the identity of the thing, a deconstruction of the principle of identity. Once horizonal structure has been installed at the very core of all allegedly pure content, once the thing has been inserted into the horizonally structured world, it is no longer possible to regard the identity of the thing as a matter of persistent self-sameness, as enduring presence to intuition, as the permanent possibility of presenting itself intuitively throughout all structural variations. This is why Merleau-Ponty, having traced out this shift, goes on to observe:

> A thing is, therefore, not actually *given* in perception, it is internally taken up by us, reconstituted and experienced by us insofar as it is bound up with a world, the basic structures of which we carry with us and of which it is merely one of many possible concrete forms.[8]

And yet, if this shift disrupts the identity of the thing as permanent presence, it also broaches still another shift, a third shift, by which that identity would be reestablished in a new way. The thing is reconstituted, constituted in a new identity, "insofar as it is bound up with a world"— that is, its identity, dislodged from intuitive presence, differentiated from simple self-sameness, is reestablished as mediation with itself, as mediation through the world of horizonal structures in which it is insert- ed. Through and from the world, the thing is given back to itself, constituted in its identity. The relevant shift is, then, a *mediational shift*.

The problem of identity is of crucial importance for the reconstitution of phenomenology. For the phenomenological injunction "to the things themselves," if taken at its highest level of generality, prescribes a certain reflexive operation of the principle of identity; the phenomenologist is enjoined to let the thing itself show itself from itself, in contrast to a procedure in which something different from the thing itself would obtrude into the showing. But such an injunction can be coherently heeded only if there is a thing *itself*, only if the thing is constituted in its identity. Only in this case does phenomenological research become pos- sible—that is, only through the shift by which identity is reestablished as mediation with self through world does it become possible to reconstitute phenomenology at the edge of metaphysics.

But how would phenomenology be actually reconstituted at this ex- treme to which it is driven by the deconstruction of the principle of identity? How could phenomenological research again commence at this extreme? How could it again bind itself to the injunction that it attend to the things themselves? How could it attend to the things themselves if, in the immediate sense, there are no things themselves? Its only possibility would lie in an orientation to another sense, a nonimmediate sense, in which there are things themselves. More precisely, phenomenological research could be reconstituted only as an attendant traversing of that circuit of mediation by which the thing would at the edge of metaphysics be established in its identity. Phenomenology at this extreme would become a reflective recovering of the thing itself, returning it through the world to itself. Phenomenology would become in this sense an attentive letting-be.

Yet here least of all would the driving tension between research and deconstruction be resolved and phenomenology securely established in its domain of research. On the contrary, here at the edge of metaphysics the questions become still more radically deconstructive, the shifts which they broach still more unsettling and ambiguous. Even the security of the position of phenomenology at the edge of metaphysics comes into question, perhaps in the most radically deconstructive way. The question is whether, by the shift to mediated identity, phenomenology really succeeds in securing itself at the edge of metaphysics; whether even in mediated identity the τέλος of presence, hence of metaphysics of presence, does not remain decisively operative; whether, consequently, a phenomenology as recovery of the thing itself would not be doomed almost immediately to fall back from the edge, back into metaphysics merely rendered dialectical. The question is whether phenomenology must not be ready to relinquish the identity of the thing, to relinquish it beyond the possibility of mediation and of dialectical recovery, to let the thing be withheld by the self-withholding world, withheld not only from immediate intuition but even from itself. The question is that of a *differential* shift, of a shift which would decisively install difference within what one would previously have called, but could no longer simply call, the thing itself. But what then of the injunction "to the things themselves"?

III.
CLEARING(S)

SEVEN

The Origins of Heidegger's Thought

Delphi schlummert und wo tönet das
grosse Geschik?
—Friedrich Hölderlin,
"Brod und Wein"

Heidegger was among those for whom the untimely death of Max Scheler in 1928 brought an experience of utter and profound loss. In a memorial address, delivered two days after Scheler's death, Heidegger paid tribute to Scheler as having been the strongest philosophical force in all of Europe and expressed deep sorrow over the fact that Scheler had died tragically in the very midst of his work, or, rather, at a time of new beginnings from which a genuine fulfillment of his work could have come. Heidegger concluded the address with these words:

> Max Scheler has died. Before his destiny we bow our heads; again a path of philosophy fades away, back into darkness.[1]

Heidegger's death, however, seems different. It came not in the midst of his career but only after that career had of itself come to its conclusion. His last years were devoted to planning the complete edition of his writings, and he lived to see the first two volumes of this edition appear. The reception of his work seems likewise to have run its course, from violent criticism and misunderstanding to an appreciative assimilation of his work. Today Heidegger's thought is acknowledged as having been a major intellectual force throughout most of this century—a force which has drastically altered the philosophical shape of things and given radically new impetus and direction to fields as diverse as psychology, theology, and literary criticism. But now, it seems, that impact is played out.

Memorial lecture presented at the University of Toronto on 21 October 1976 and at Grinnell College on 12 November 1977. Published in *Research in Phenomenology*, vol. 7 (1977).

Heidegger's thought, now assimilated, is being enshrined in the history of philosophy. It is as though a well-ripened fruit had finally dropped gently to the ground.

Perhaps, however, the death of a great thinker is never totally lacking in tragedy. For even if his life is lived out to its conclusion, as was Heidegger's, his work is never finally rounded out. The case of Socrates is paradigmatic: the philosopher engaged in questioning even through-out his final hours, exposing himself to the weight of the questions asked by his friends, and, most significantly, letting his positive thought, his "position," be decisively fragmented by a great myth just as it is about to be sealed forever. The work of a genuine thinker never escapes the fragmentation, the negativity, to which radical questioning exposes him; and death, when it comes, seals the fragmentation of his work. Death fixes forever the lack, the negativity, and testifies thus to the inevitable loss by casting that loss utterly beyond hope. Death brings philosophy to an end without being its end, its τέλος, its fulfilling completion. Death stands as a tragic symbol.

Even in its external appearance, Heidegger's work is fragmentary. His book *Being and Time,* first published in 1927, remains unfinished, even though he always considered it his magnum opus. Moreover, its un-finished state is precisely such as to leave the entire project in suspension, for that part which remains unpublished is just the one in which Heideg-ger would actually have carried through the task for which the entire published part is only preparatory. Heidegger did not succeed in deter-mining the meaning of Being as time, and by ordinary standards *Being and Time,* falling short of its expressed goal, is a failure—or, at best, a torso. That failure is not redeemed by the later writings. To the extent that they take up and deepen the questioning of *Being and Time,* they do so only at the expense of still greater fragmentation. With Heidegger's death, too, a path of philosophy fades away, back into darkness. Though in a different way, Heidegger's work remains as tragically fragmentary as Scheler's.

The response to Heidegger's death can be thoughtful—rather than merely biographical—only if one reenacts, as it were, a strand of this tragedy. This requires that one release Heidegger's work from that seal of fragmentation brought by his death; that is, one needs to let that fragmentation assume the positive aspect which it has in living thought. What is this positive aspect? It is that aspect which Heidegger designated by referring to his thought as *under way.*

If one would reenact such thought, it is imperative to understand what set it on its way—that in response one might set out correspondingly. It is imperative also to understand what sustained it on that way, what shaped the way itself—in order also to keep to that way. One needs, in other words, to understand the origins of Heidegger's thought.

This, then, is my primary question: What are the origins of Heidegger's thought? I shall deal with this question at three progressively more fundamental levels. These three levels correspond to three distinct concepts of origin. Initially, I shall take origin to mean historical origin and thus shall pursue the question of origins by asking about those earlier thinkers whose work was decisive for Heidegger's development. Secondly, I shall consider origin in the sense of original or basic issue, and accordingly shall attempt to delimit this issue and to indicate how it serves as origin. Finally, I shall understand origin in its most radical sense as that which grants philosophical thought its content. At the level of this most radical sense of origin, it is perhaps possible for death to regain a signifying power for philosophy which, despite all differences, could match that which it had among the Greeks.

(A) THE HISTORICAL ORIGINS OF HEIDEGGER'S THOUGHT

Taking origin, first, in the sense of historical origin, consider: Who are those thinkers whose work served to set Heidegger's thought on its way? If, in posing this question, one lets the concept of origins expand into that of mere influences, then the question proves right away to be unmanageable. With the exception of Hegel, no other major philosopher has so persistently exposed himself to dialogue with the tradition. And if one began to count up influences, even excluding all lesser ones, one would have to name Dilthey, Nietzsche, Kierkegaard, German Idealism, Kant, Leibniz, Descartes, Medieval Scholasticism, and Greek philosophy, that is, virtually the entire philosophical tradition—to say nothing of Heidegger's contemporaries or of such poets as Pindar, Sophocles, Hölderlin, and Trakl, all of whom were profound influences on Heidegger. Clearly such reckoning up of influences comes to nothing unless one first grasps the basic engagement of Heidegger's thought—that engagement on the basis of which he is then led to engage in his extended dialogue with nearly every segment of the tradition. Let me, then, pose the question in a more precise and restricted way: What are the historical origins of the basic engagement of Heidegger's thought? But the question is still inadequate. Engagement of philosophical thought involves two moments: It is an engagement *with some issue,* and it is an engagement with it *in some definite way.* In other words, engagement involves both issue and method, and it is of these that one needs to consider the historical origins. The question is: What are the historical origins from which Heidegger took over the issue and the method of his thought?

The method is that of phenomenology, which Heidegger took over from his teacher Edmund Husserl. It was for this reason that Heidegger dedicated *Being and Time* to Husserl and therein expressed publicly his gratitude for the "incisive personal guidance" that Husserl had given him. In various later autobiographical statements, Heidegger speaks of the fascination which Husserl's *Logical Investigations* had for him during his formative years and of the importance which his personal contact with Husserl had for his early development. In *Being and Time* phenomenology is explicitly identified as the method of the investigation; and in the recently published Marburg lectures of 1927, Heidegger works through almost the entire problematic of *Being and Time* under the title "Basic Problems of Phenomenology."

But what exactly did Heidegger take over from Husserl? What in this regard is to be understood by phenomenology? It is, in the first instance, the methodological demand that one attend constantly and solely to the things themselves. It is the demand that philosophical thought proceed by attending to things as they themselves show themselves rather than being determined by presupposed opinions, theories, and conceptual formulations. And so, in *Being and Time* one finds analyses such as that which Heidegger gives of tools. A tool, for instance, a hammer, normally shows itself within a certain context, namely, as belonging with other tools all suited to certain kinds of work to be done; only through a severe narrowing of perspective can one come to regard the hammer as a mere thing. Or, take the case of hearing; and consider: What sort of things does one usually hear? One hears an automobile passing, a bird singing, a fire crackling—whereas, as Heidegger says, "it requires a very artificial and complicated frame of mind to 'hear' a pure noise."[2] Yet, as a method, phenomenology extends beyond the sphere of things even in this enriched sense: Whatever the matter (*Sache*) to be investigated, the phenomenological method prescribes that it be investigated through an attending to it as it shows itself. Thus, *Being and Time*, dedicated primarily to the investigation of that being which we ourselves are, proceeds by attending to the way in which that being, Dasein, shows itself. What complicates the methodological structure of Heidegger's work is the fact that Dasein is also the investigator so that it becomes a matter of Dasein's showing itself to itself. Nevertheless, this complexity does not render the investigation any less phenomenological.

On the contrary, in that project to which his investigation of Dasein belongs, Heidegger seeks to be more phenomenological even than Husserl himself. He seeks to radicalize phenomenology by adhering even more radically than Husserl to the phenomenological demand to attend to the things themselves. As he expresses it in a later self-interpretation, he sought "to ask what remains unthought in the appeal 'to the things themselves.'"[3] This dimension, tacitly presupposed in the phenomenological appeal to the things themselves, this dimension to which Heidegger's radical phenomenology would penetrate, constitutes the basic issue of Heidegger's thought.

What is this issue? What is fundamentally at issue in Heidegger's thought? One name for this issue—perhaps not the best—is Being. This name betrays immediately the historical origin from which Heidegger took the issue, namely, Greek philosophy, especially Plato and Aristotle. For it was in Greek philosophy that Being was most explicitly and most profoundly put at issue, in works such as Plato's *Sophist* and Aristotle's *Metaphysics*. Heidegger considers all subsequent reflections on Being, all later ontology, as a decline from the level attained by the great Greek philosophers: Gradually Being ceased to be held genuinely at issue, and what Plato and Aristotle had accomplished, what they had wrested from the phenomena, was uprooted from the questioning to which it belonged, became rigid and progressively emptier. *Being and Time* is thus cast explicitly as an attempt to raise again the question about Being. It is cast as a renewal, a recapturing, of the questioning stance of Greek philosophy. This is why it begins as it does: The very first sentence of *Being and Time* is a statement not by Heidegger but rather by the Eleatic Stranger of Plato's *Sophist,* a statement of his perplexity regarding Being. *Being and Time* literally begins in the middle of a Platonic dialogue.

Yet, on the other hand, *Being and Time* is no mere repeating of Greek philosophy. Heidegger does not seek to reinstate the work of Plato and Aristotle, as though historicity could just be set out of action in this exceptional case; nor does he propose merely to revive the questioning in which their work was sustained. In his lectures of 1935, later published as *Introduction to Metaphysics,* his intent is clear:

> To ask "How does it stand with Being?" means nothing less than *to recapture* [*wieder-holen*] the beginning of our historical-spiritual Dasein, in order to transform it into a new beginning. . . . But we do not recapture a beginning by reducing it to something past and now known, which need merely be imitated; rather, the beginning must be begun again, more originally, with all the strangeness, darkness, insecurity that attend a true beginning.[4]

Heidegger would take up more originally the beginning offered by Greek philosophy, take it up by taking it back to its sustaining origin, make of that beginning a new beginning.

The historical origins of Heidegger's thought, in the restricted sense specified, are thus constituted by Husserlian phenomenology and Greek ontology. From the former Heidegger's method is taken; from the latter it receives its fundamental issue. However, method and issue are not simply unrelated. Rather, as already noted, Heidegger's penetration to what becomes the fundamental issue for his thought is, by his own testimony, an attempt to radicalize phenomenology, "to ask what remains unthought in the appeal 'to the things themselves.'" How is it that Being is what remains unthought in the appeal to the things themselves? How is it that a radical phenomenology must become ontology?

Consider again the approach prescribed by the injunction of phenomenology, "to the things themselves." What remains unthought here? What does the approach fail to take into account? The injunction prescribes that things are to be regarded as they show themselves. In thus attending to their showing of themselves, one easily passes over that which makes such showing possible, which makes it possible in the sense of being necessarily always already in play in the commencement of every such showing. Consider again the example of a tool. What is required in order for a hammer to show itself in its specific character as a hammer? It is required that it be linked up with a certain context of other tools, all oriented toward certain kinds of work to be done—especially if, as Heidegger insists, the hammer most genuinely shows itself as a hammer, not when one merely observes it disinterestedly, but rather at the moment when one takes it up and uses it for such work as it is suited to. In order for the hammer to show itself as a hammer (when one takes it up and uses it), there must be already constituted a context from out of which it shows itself—that is, a system of involvements or references by which various tools and related items belong together in their orientation, their assignment, to certain kinds of work to be done. Such a system of concrete references is an example of what Heidegger means by *world*.

So, what exactly is required in order that it be possible for the hammer to show itself as such? It is required that there be something like a world from out of which the tool can show itself and, more significantly, that that world be *disclosed* in advance to the one to whom the tool would show itself. The hammer can show itself in that action in which one takes it up and uses it *only if* the system of involvements by which tools and tasks are held together is itself already in view, only if one is already in touch with it, only if it is already disclosed. The possibility of things' showing themselves requires a prior disclosure of a world, of an open domain or space, for that showing. Radical phenomenology, as Heidegger pursues it, would penetrate to the level of such disclosure.

Still, however, it is not clear why radical phenomenology must become ontology. How is it that the investigation of such fundamental disclosure comes to coincide with a renewal of questioning about Being? This connection can be seen only if one considers with more precision just how Being is put at issue in *Being and Time*. What is asked about in the questioning of *Being and Time*? It is the *meaning* of Being that is asked about. But what is asked about in asking about meaning? What is meaning? According to the analyses in *Being and Time* in which the concept of meaning is worked out, meaning is that from which (on the basis of which) something becomes understandable. To ask about the meaning of Being is thus to ask about how Being becomes understandable; it is to ask about Dasein's understanding of Being. Yet, understanding of Being is, in general, that which makes possible the apprehension of beings as such. Hence, to question about the meaning of Being, about Dasein's understanding of Being, is to ask about that understanding which makes it possible for Dasein to apprehend beings. It is to ask about that understanding which makes it possible for beings to show themselves to Dasein—that is, about that understanding which constitutes the ground of the possibility of things showing themselves. It is to ask about the opening up of the open space for such showing, about the disclosure of world, about *disclosedness*. To ask about the meaning of Being is to ask about Dasein's disclosedness.

It is clear, therefore, how ontological questioning and radical phenomenology converge in the basic problem of disclosedness. This matter of disclosedness is the fundamental issue. In it the issue and method which Heidegger takes over from his historical origins are brought together and radicalized. It is this issue, disclosedness, that can thus more properly be called the origin of Heidegger's thought.

(B) THE ORIGINAL ISSUE OF HEIDEGGER'S THOUGHT

As a result of thinking through the way in which Heidegger takes over his historical origins, there has emerged a second, more fundamental sense of origin, namely, origin in the sense of original issue, the issue from which originate Heidegger's approach to other issues and his extended dialogue with the tradition. This issue is disclosedness.

In the various existential analyses in *Being and Time,* it is readily evident that disclosedness is the original issue. For example, Heidegger's analysis of moods aims at exhibiting moods as belonging to Dasein in a way utterly different from the way in which properties belong to objects, different even from the way in which so-called inner states such as feelings have usually been taken to belong to man. He seeks to exhibit moods in their disclosive power, to exhibit them as belonging to Dasein's fundamental disclosedness. His analysis seeks to show that, among other functions, moods serve to attune one to the world, to open one to it in such a way that things encountered within that world can matter in some definite way or other—in such fashion that, for instance, they can be encountered as threatening.

Heidegger's analysis of understanding is similarly oriented. Understanding is regarded not as some purely immanent capacity or activity within a subject but rather as a moment belonging to Dasein's disclosedness. Understanding is a way in which Dasein is disclosive. In understanding, Dasein projects upon certain possibilities, comports itself toward them, seizes upon them as possibilities; and from such possibilities Dasein is, in turn, disclosed to itself, given back, mirrored back, to itself. Dasein is given to understand itself through and from these possibilities.

In addition, the possibilities on which it projects are disclosive in the direction of world, most evidently in the sense that they prescribe or light up certain contextual connections pertaining to the realization of the possibilities. When, for example, one projects upon the possibility of constructing a wooden cabinet, not only does one understand oneself as a craftsman, but also this possibility lights up and orients the context within the workshop.

Heidegger's analysis of death also remains within the compass of the issue of disclosedness, and indeed this is why it is so revolutionary. According to this analysis, death is Dasein's ownmost and unsurpassable possibility; it is that possibility which is most Dasein's own in the sense that each must die his own death, and it is unsurpassable in the sense that Dasein cannot get beyond its actualization to still other possibilities; it is the possibility in which what is at issue is the loss of all possibilities. Heidegger's analysis focuses specifically on Dasein's comportment to this possibility, its projection on it, its Being-toward-death. Such projection is an instance of understanding, that is, it is a mode of disclosedness. In Being-toward-death, Dasein is, in a unique way, disclosed to itself, given back to itself from this its ownmost possibility. Precisely because it is a mode of disclosedness, Dasein's Being-toward-its-end is utterly different, for instance, from that of a ripening fruit.

Thus, disclosedness is the original issue in Heidegger's analyses of Dasein. Through these analyses Heidegger seeks to display the basic ways in which Dasein is disclosive and to show how these various ways of being disclosive are interconnected. Indeed, not every basic moment displayed in the analyses of Dasein is simply a way of being disclosive. Yet even those structural moments that fall outside of disclosedness proper are still related to it in an essential way. More precisely, such moments are related to disclosedness in such a way that their basic character is determined by this relation.

Consider that moment which Heidegger calls "falling." This is the moment which he seeks to display through his well-known descriptions of the anonymous mass (*das Man*)—his descriptions of how it ensnares the individual by its standard ways of regarding things and speaking about them; how it entices the individual into a conformity in which everything genuinely original gets leveled down and passed off as something already familiar to everyone; how, more precisely, it holds Dasein from the outset in a condition of self-dispersal and opaqueness to itself. What does this moment, this falling toward the rule of the anonymous mass, have to do with disclosedness? It has everything to do with it, because it is nothing less than a kind of counter-movement to disclosedness. It is a propensity toward covering up, toward *concealment*. This counter-movement toward concealment is essentially connected with Dasein's disclosedness. The connection is best attested by the issue of authenticity: Dasein's own genuine self-disclosure, the opening up of a space for its self-understanding, takes the form of a recovery of self from that dispersal in which the self and its possibilities are concealed beneath that public self that is no one and those possibilities that are indifferently open to everyone. Dasein must wrest itself from concealment.

Thus, Dasein's disclosedness is no *mere unopposed* opening of a realm in which things can show themselves. On the contrary, there belongs to that disclosedness an intrinsic opposition; there belongs to it a contention, a strife, between opening up and closing off, between disclosing and concealing.

Disclosedness, thus understood, is the original issue not only in the Dasein-analytic of *Being and Time* but also in Heidegger's later work. In order to grasp this continuity, it is necessary to consider a basic development which Heidegger's work undergoes after *Being and Time*. Note, first, that already in the earlier work Heidegger brings the Dasein-analytic explicitly into relation with the problem of truth. He identifies the concept of disclosedness with that of truth in its most primordial sense; he presents disclosedness or original truth as constituting the ground of the possibility of truth in that ordinary sense related to propositions and the things referred to in propositions. Hence, the strife intrinsic to disclosedness may also be termed the strife of truth and untruth. For truth in this original sense, as that opening which provides the basis on which there can be true or false propositions regarding the things that show themselves in that opening, Heidegger appropriates the Greek word ἀλήθεια.

In his later work Heidegger speaks of the original issue primarily in these terms, in terms of original truth or ἀλήθεια instead of disclosedness. And, though the issue remains the same, there is, nevertheless, behind this shift in terminology a fundamental development. What is the development? It may be regarded as a progressive separation of two phenomena which in *Being and Time* tended to coalesce. Specifically, Heidegger comes in the later work to dissociate truth from Dasein's self-understanding—that is, he dissociates the contentious opening up of a realm in which things can show themselves (i.e., truth) from the movement of self-recovery by which Dasein is given to itself. The happening of truth is set at a distance from the reflexivity of human self-understanding. But original truth remains for Heidegger the original issue; and so, with its dissociation from self-understanding, Heidegger's thought is set more decisively at a distance not only from German Idealism and the tradition which led to it but also from that idealistic path which Husserl himself followed in his later work.

Granted this development, the original issue of Heidegger's thought remains in the later work what it was from the beginning, namely, the opening up of a domain in which things can show themselves—that is, the issue of original truth. Consider, for example, Heidegger's essay on the work of art. In this essay Heidegger opposes the modern tendency, stemming from Kant, to refer art to human capacities such as feeling that could be taken as having no connection with truth; contrary to such an approach, Heidegger seeks to show that original truth is precisely what is at issue in art. According to his analysis, a work of art makes manifest the strife of truth. It composes and thus gathers into view truth in its tension with untruth. A work of art presents the strife between world, i.e., the open realm in which things can show themselves, and earth, i.e., the dimension of closure and concealment.

Heidegger's analysis of technology in his later works is similarly oriented. This analysis, which is something quite different from a sociological, political, or ethical reflection on technology, is directed, strictly speaking, not at technology as such but rather at what Heidegger calls the essence of technology. What is the essence of technology? It is simply a mode of original truth, the opening of a realm in which things come to show themselves in a certain way. It is, specifically, that opening in the wake of which nature comes to appear as a store of energy subject to human domination. It is that opening in which natural things show themselves as merely things to be provoked to supply energy that can be accumulated, transformed, distributed, and in which human things show themselves as subject to planning and regulation. What is at issue in Heidegger's analysis of technology is that same original issue to which his thought is already addressed from the beginning. It is that issue in which converge his efforts to radicalize Husserlian phenomenology and to renew Greek ontology, the issue of disclosedness, of original truth.

(C) THE RADICAL ORIGIN OF PHILOSOPHICAL THOUGHT

There is still a third sense of origin which needs, finally, to be brought into play. This third sense is not such as to revoke what has been said regarding truth as the origin of Heidegger's thought. It is not a matter of discovering some origin other than truth but rather of deepening, indeed radicalizing, the concept of origin. It is a matter of grasping truth as radical origin.

In order to see how this final sense of origin emerges, it is necessary to grasp more thoroughly the methodological character of the analyses of Dasein in *Being and Time*. Contrary to what might seem prescribed by the phenomenological appeal to the things themselves, Heidegger's analyses are not simply straightforward descriptions of Dasein as it shows itself. Why not? Because ordinarily Dasein does not simply show itself. Rather, there belongs to Dasein a tendency toward self-concealment of the sort that Heidegger discusses, for example, in his analysis of falling. What does this entail as regards the method required of a philosophical investigation of Dasein? It entails that Dasein, rather than being merely, straightforwardly described, must be wrested from its self-concealment.

But how, then, one must ask, is the investigation to be freed of the charge of doing violence to the phenomena? How can such investigation claim to be phenomenological? How can it justify the claim of proceeding solely in accord with the manner in which the things themselves show themselves? There is only one way. The violence that is done must be a violence which Dasein does to itself rather than a violence perpetrated by the philosophical investigation. The wresting of ordinary Dasein from its concealment must be the work, not of a philosophical analysis which would inevitably distort it and impose on it something foreign, but of a latent disclosive power within Dasein itself. Heidegger is explicit about the matter: The philosophical analysis must, as it were, "listen in" on Dasein's self-disclosure; it must let Dasein disclose itself, as, for example, in anxiety. Attaching itself to such disclosure, the philosophical analysis must do no more than merely raise to a conceptual level the phenomenal content that is thereby disclosed.

This peculiar methodological structure is what determines the final sense of origin. How? By virtue of the fact that it simply traces out the connection of thought to its sustaining origin. More specifically, this structure prescribes that Dasein's self-disclosure is precisely what gives philosophical thought its content, what grants it, yields it up to thought. Dasein's self-disclosure, that self-disclosure on which philosophical thought "listens in," is thus the origin of that thought—not just in the sense of being the central theme for that thought, but rather in the sense of first granting to such thought that content which it is to think. Yet, Dasein's self-disclosure is simply a mode of Dasein's disclosedness as such—that is, a mode of original truth. Truth is what grants to thought that content which it is to think. The origin of thought is original truth.

The genuine radicalizing of the concept of origins comes, however, only in the wake of the development that takes place in Heidegger's later work. Within the framework of *Being and Time,* there is no exceptional difficulty involved in understanding how philosophical thought can attach itself to its origin, to original truth; for such truth, though perhaps merely latent, is not essentially removed from Dasein. Philosophical thought can attach itself to its origin, because that origin belongs latently to everyone, including whoever would philosophize. One is always already attached to original truth. The problem arises when, through the experience of the history of metaphysics, Heidegger comes in his later work to dissociate truth from self-understanding. For this amounts to placing original truth at a distance from Dasein—that is, at a distance from that thought whose origin that truth would be. Thus, Heidegger's later work has to contend with a separation between original truth and that thought to which it would grant what is to be thought. As a result, the granting becomes a problem. Truth, the origin of thought, essentially withdraws from thought, holds itself aloof. Truth is the *self-withdrawing origin of thought*. And thought, resolutely open to the radical concealment of its origin, lets itself be drawn along in the withdrawal. Here one arrives at the most radical sense of origin.

Heidegger's efforts to radicalize Husserlian phenomenology and to renew Greek ontology converge on truth, first, as the original issue or basic problem, and then, finally, as the origin which grants philosophical thought as such. What is most decisive in this most radical concept of original truth is that truth so conceived withdraws from that very thought which it grants and engages. It withholds itself from thought.

What is remarkable is that the same may be said of death. It too withholds itself from thought, withdraws from every attempt to make it something familiar. In distinction from all other possibilities, death alone offers nothing to actualize in imagination. It offers no basis for picturing to oneself the actuality that would correspond to it. It is sheer possibility, detached from everything actual, detached from Dasein, self-withdrawing—yet constantly, secretly engaging.

Death withdraws as does original truth—withdraws while yet engaging. And so, death has the power to signify original truth. Yet, the task of philosophy, the task to which Heidegger finally came, is to develop thought's engagement in such truth. And so, death, signifying original truth, signifies the end to which philosophy is directed. At this level death can become a positive symbol for philosophy.

Perhaps it is a more fitting memorial to Heidegger if, instead of merely dwelling on his death, one seeks to restore to death its power to signify the end and thus the task of philosophy.

EIGHT

Where Does *Being and Time* Begin?

Ich kann mir kein seligeres Wissen denken,
als dieses Eine:
daß man ein Beginner werden muß.
—Rainer Maria Rilke,
"Zur Melodie der Dinge"

From its very beginning a project of philosophical thinking must be directed toward the matter that is at issue for that thinking (*die Sache des Denkens*). It must be specifically directed so as to allow that thinking to set about its task of disclosing the matter at issue, so as to empower that thinking to entice the matter to show itself. Yet, in order for philosophical thinking to be capable of taking up such direction, that matter must already somehow be disclosed in such a way that thought, having the matter before it, can then direct itself accordingly. Indeed, even before any such self-directing, the matter must already have come into view in order even to become something *at issue* for thinking. But in that case, the beginning already takes the matter as granted—that is, negatively, it proves to be infested with presuppositions.

This reflexivity—starkly formal though it be, ever so close to that elusive limit that divides genuine thought from sophistry—suffices to prevent the question of beginning from degenerating into a mere ascertaining of a point from which thought would set out. It necessitates holding the question of beginning within the sphere of philosophical thought itself, letting the beginning *of* philosophy be itself a problem *for* philosophy.

The issue of beginning, then, has to do not with a point but with a circle. How does beginning have to do with a circle? Heidegger writes: "What is decisive is not to get out of the circle but to come into it in the right way."[1] What is the right way into the circle? How does the philosophical project initiated in *Being and Time* come into the circle? Where does *Being and Time* begin?

Preliminary version published in *Heidegger's Existential Analytic*, ed. Frederick Elliston (The Hague: Mouton, 1978).

THE UNTITLED FIRST PAGE OF *BEING AND TIME*: THE GREEK BEGINNING

In the most literal sense *Being and Time* begins with a passage from Plato's *Sophist*. The passage is cited on the untitled first page of *Being and Time*, first in Greek and then in Heidegger's translation, and it is literally the first statement in the work, the beginning of the work. This beginning is not to be passed over as though it were some innocuous preliminary, as though it were only an announcement, prior to the work itself, that the work to follow is to deal with some of the celebrated problems handed down since the beginning of philosophy among the Greeks. The passage from the *Sophist* is not merely preliminary but, on the contrary, bears importantly on the way in which *Being and Time* begins; it already belongs even to that beginning. With the passage from the *Sophist* the beginning of *Being and Time* is already both under way and at issue. One should, first of all, wonder at the fact that the first words of Heidegger's work are not his own but rather words spoken in a Platonic dialogue.

Where does *Being and Time* begin? It begins in the middle of a Platonic dialogue. Its first words are those of the Stranger from Elea. What is the context in which those words are spoken in the dialogue? Speaking with Theaetetus, the Stranger pretends to be addressing a group of men identified as those who seek to understand "how many [πόσα] and of what nature [ποῖα] the beings [τὰ ὄντα] are."[2] It is this identification which launches that section of the dialogue in which the passage occurs with which *Being and Time* begins. Along with it there is a second characterization of these same men, which indicates quite concisely what is principally at issue in this section. The Stranger says of these men that they always seem to tell us a story [μῦθόν τινα . . . διηγεῖσθαι]—that is, they tell of such things as the warfare and love in which beings come to be from other beings and pass away into them—that is they determine "beings as beings by tracing them back in their origin to some other beings, as if Being had the character of a possible being" (*SZ* 6). It is to these men and it is in view of their peculiar way of telling about beings that the Stranger speaks in that passage which stands at the beginning of *Being and Time*:

> For manifestly you have long been aware of what you mean when you use the expression "being" [ὄν—Heidegger translates: *seiend*]. We, however, who once thought we understood it, have now become perplexed.[3]

Yet, what the Stranger proceeds to show in the course of addressing these men is that they are not at all able to say what they mean by "being"—that, as long as they cling to their characteristic "story-telling," they can at best accomplish no more than to be led into just that perplexity with which their condition was ironically contrasted. In turn, this result brings about the transition to the next section of the dialogue in which the Stranger pretends to engage in questioning Parmenides. In other words, the Stranger carries through the transition from the level of the mere determining of beings through other beings, i.e., of a determining which is oblivious to being as such and which cannot say what being means, *to* the Parmenidean level at which a genuine discussion of what being means is possible, whatever difficulties may be encountered. Thus, in its original context that statement which Heidegger sets at the beginning of *Being and Time* occurs within the transition from the level of those who are oblivious to being *to* the level of those who, like Parmenides and the Stranger himself, are alive to questioning about being. What this transition and the ensuing questioning of Parmenides eventually provoke is the γιγαντομαχία περὶ τῆς οὐσίας.

Yet, *Being and Time* begins within the *Sophist* in order that, granting its distance from the ancients, it might then pose for itself, for thinking "today," that question which the Eleatic Stranger was engaged in posing to those of the ancients who told stories about beings. Heidegger asks: "Do we have today an answer to the question of what we really mean by the word 'being'?" (*SZ* 1). Attending to the original context from which the question is drawn, one hears behind it the issue of that fundamental transition within which the question was raised by the Stranger. And attending, furthermore, to the perplexity into which such questioning proved to lead and to the strenuousness of the battle that had then to be waged over this issue, the γιγαντομαχία περὶ τῆς οὐσίας, one is then prepared for the unqualified negative reply which Heidegger gives when the question is posed to us today. And so, since we "in no way" have an answer to the question of what we really mean by the word "being" ("*seiend*"), it is fitting that, following the Stranger, we "pose anew the question of the meaning of Being" [*die Frage nach dem Sinn von Sein*] (*SZ* 1). To what extent are we prepared to follow the Stranger into that transition which he enacts in the *Sophist*? What is required in order that we be able to pose this question anew? To what extent *can* the beginning of *Being and Time* correspond to that beginning which the Stranger enacts with respect to the question of the meaning of Being in the *Sophist*?

In the *Sophist* it is the Stranger himself who poses the question about the meaning of Being and who, having posed the question, is able to proceed into a genuine attempt to answer it. But in order to do so, it becomes necessary for him, in the pretended dialogue, to leave behind those who, telling stories about beings, remain unaware *that* they are unaware of what they mean when they use the expression "being." In his own perplexity regarding what Being means, the Stranger abandons those incapable of arriving at such perplexity and moves on to engage in a pretended dialogue with Parmenides. With respect to the attempt to raise the question anew, it is crucial to ask whether today we share, from the beginning, that perplexity by which the Stranger was driven on to genuine dialogue regarding the meaning of Being or whether, on the contrary, we belong on the side of those story-tellers who, remaining untouched by such perplexity, remain therefore closed off from pursuing the questioning about Being. Heidegger asks *where* we *are* today with regard to perplexity about Being. He asks whether we share, at the beginning, the perplexity which the Stranger had won; his answer is an emphatic "no":

> But are we today even perplexed at not understanding the expression "Being"? In no way. And so it is fitting first of all to awaken again an understanding of the meaning of this question (*SZ* 1).

We today belong on the side of those unperplexed ancients who told stories about beings—that is, we not only lack an answer to the question of what we mean when we use the expression "being" but also have still to come even to understand the question, have still to come into that state of perplexity out of which we could then genuinely unfold the sense of the question about Being. Where does *Being and Time* begin? It begins at that place where we of today already are in the beginning. Thus, the place of its beginning corresponds, not to that place which the Stranger has reached when he raises the question of the meaning of Being, but rather to the place occupied by those who are unperplexed about Being, who have no understanding for the question. But it is precisely the task of the beginning to bring us into that movement by which the Stranger leaves behind the unperplexed "story-tellers"—to set us on the way through perplexity into the unfolding of the sense of the question about the meaning of Being, into an engagement with the question.

Against the background of this projection of the place and task proper to the beginning of *Being and Time,* Heidegger poses the aim (*Absicht*) of the work as a whole: "Our aim in the following treatise is to work out concretely the question of the meaning of Being" (*SZ* 1). The statement is provocative. What does it mean to *work out* a question? To what end is such a working-out (*Ausarbeitung*) directed? Is its concern with *asking* the question—perhaps in the sense of unfolding and developing it as a question? Or, does it seek to *answer* the question? Or, is this question— and, hence, any questioning genuinely engaged in it—perhaps so radical that the very distinction between asking and answering gets called into question? Furthermore, what does it mean to work out this question *concretely*? Is it not, rather, the most abstract of all questions?

Heidegger adds, finally, a statement of the preliminary goal (*vorläufiges Ziel*) of *Being and Time*: "Our preliminary goal is the interpretation of *time* as the possible horizon for any understanding whatsoever of

Being" (*SZ* 1). The interpretation is to exhibit time as that horizon by reference to which Being becomes genuinely understandable. Yet, as Heidegger later indicates explicitly (section 6), time has, in fact, played an important role in the understanding of Being throughout the history of ontology, for example, in the demarcation of modes of Being. Even in the *Sophist* the γιγαντομαχία περὶ τῆς οὐσίας is an engagement in a questioning of Being largely in regard to its relation to γένεσις and κίνησις and to that extent Being is secretely held to time as its horizon. What has come to pass secretly is to be worked out openly.

(A) PERPLEXITY

The task of the beginning of *Being and Time* is to carry out that movement enacted by the Stranger: the movement into perplexity and then the movement from perplexity into an engagement with the question of Being. This task of beginning is accomplished in the first chapter of the Introduction. Here Heidegger determines the place of the work *Being and Time*—that is, he opens up the question for our perplexity, lets what is asked about in it become questionable, and *places* the question, lets it unfold into that place where it is to be worked out. The second chapter of the Introduction, taking the beginning for granted, then projects the stages of the work as a whole and, attendant to the placing of the question, lets the demand for method unfold toward that place. In accordance with my guiding question, I limit consideration to the first chapter.

Measured against the demands exhibited in the *Sophist*, we are today in *need of perplexity* regarding what we mean when we speak of Being. However, the form which this need assumes with us by no means coincides with the form in which it is exhibited by those ancient "story-tellers" of whom the Eleatic Stranger speaks. Because we are moderns, not ancients, the need takes a different form. What is the difference, and how does it bear on the way of moving into perplexity? What is required in order to begin where we today already are?

The relevant difference and the consequent requirement can be seen in the title of secton 1 and in the first sentence: "This question has today been forgotten"—and so there is, as the title says, "the necessity of an explicit repetition [*Wiederholung*] of the question of Being." The form which our need takes is different, because for us the question *has already been posed* (by Plato and Aristotle); and however much the question may today be forgotten, our way into a posing of it is, nonetheless, a way *back* into something once accomplished. Our need of perplexity is a need to regain a stance once attained, or, rather, to reenact that movement into perplexity and that posing of the question of Being which were accomplished by Plato and Aristotle; and, as once accomplished, the posing of the question is attested in such ancient texts as Plato's *Sophist,* which thus offers a place where we may begin. Even though this question—*the* question that occupied Plato and Aristotle—subsequently subsided as a thematic question, even though it lost that element of questionableness in which it belonged for the Greek thinkers, even though subsequent thinkers failed to hold themselves in that provocative perplexity about Being, nevertheless what the Greeks had accomplished, what they had "wrested from the phenomena," remained. It remained even though in the end it was trivialized by being torn loose from the perplexity and questioning out of which it arose and by which it was sustained. To us there are handed down *traces* of the question: both the ancient texts and the question itself in that trivial, almost empty form into which it has devolved. Thus, alongside the beginning granted us by an ancient text such as the *Sophist*—or rather, under the provocation of such a beginning—the question itself, in its virtual emptiness for us, is given as a place where we can begin. To this extent, less is demanded of us than was demanded of the ancients; our posing of the question about Being is a recollection, a "repetition" (*Wiederholung*).

On the other hand, such repetition must confront a difficulty which in this regard was unknown to the Greeks. As Heidegger projects the matter, not only has the question become empty in the sense of needing again to be set within its proper element of questionableness; but also, correlative to the removal of the question from contention, a dogma has been developed which sanctions the total neglect of the question, which claims to exempt us "from the exertions of a newly rekindled γιγαντομα-χία περὶ τῆς οὐσίας" (*SZ* 2)—that is, which positively conceals the need for posing again the question of the meaning of Being and thus holds us back from the perplexity which we need. This concealment, this covering over of the questionableness of the question, is all the more radical by virtue of its having its roots, according to Heidegger's preliminary projection of the matter, in ancient ontology itself. The very way in which the question was taken up by the ancients and brought to its highest point of development served at the same time to lay the ground for that concealment of the question, that forgottenness, into which later thought fell. The questionableness that belongs to the question about Being must be not merely renewed but wrested from concealment.

To restore such questionableness to the question about Being is tantamount to undergoing that perplexity in which the Eleatic Stranger found himself, the perplexity regarding the meaning of Being, the perplexity through which one can come into a genuine questioning about Being. What is required for the movement into perplexity and hence for the engagement in the question opened up by that movement—what such a beginning requires is a confrontation with those prejudices which serve to conceal the questionableness of the question.

More precisely, what Heidegger undertakes is *to invert* these prejudices
in such a way that, rather than covering over the questionableness and
directing us away from it, they may come to point into that very questionableness. He seeks to invert them in such a way that they draw us into
perplexity, provoke a repetition of the questioning.

Heidegger considers three such prejudices. The first has to do with the
generality of the concept of Being, a generality of unlimited extent:
Being is the most general concept. However, with Aristotle it was already
evident that the generality of the concept of Being is not the generality of
a genus but transcends all such generality. Being is a transcendental; and
its peculiar generality, distinct from "ordinary" generality, is something
unfamiliar and problematic. The generality of the concept of Being,
rather than rendering it the clearest of all and the one least in need of
becoming an issue for questioning, serves instead to exhibit it as the most
obscure, most questionable concept.

Heidegger gives a very brief yet suggestive sketch of the history of the
problem. He refers to Aristotle as having put the problem of Being on a
fundamentally new basis by grasping the unity of Being as a unity of
analogy. The reference is to Aristotle's consideration of "being" (ὄν) as a
πρὸς ἕν equivocal: "being" has an equivocity by reference; its unity lies
precisely in the reference which every being has to οὐσία.[4] Heidegger
refers also to the discussions of this problem in the Thomist and Scotist
schools. Finally, he insists that Hegel, in defining "Being" as the "indeterminate immediate," remains within the same perspective as ancient
ontology but no longer heeds Aristotle's problem of the unity of Being as
over against the multiplicity of "categories."[5] Even with respect to Aristotle, Heidegger stresses that clarity regarding the relevant categorical
interconnections was not achieved. It is appropriate to ask: Within what
limits can *Being and Time,* in taking up the question of Being by way of an
analysis of Dasein, be regarded specifically as a "repetition" of Aristotle's
thinking of the unity of Being as unity of analogy? Within what limits
does the thinking of Being as collected into unity by reference to Dasein
correspond (as a "repetition") to Aristotle's thinking of ὄν as collected
into unity by reference to οὐσία.[6]

The second prejudice has to do with the indefinableness of the concept
"Being." This indefinableness follows, Heidegger says, from the character of "Being" as most general. Indeed, it follows in two ways. First, if
definition is by means of genus and specific difference, then it will be
impossible to define the concept of "Being" since there is no higher (i.e.,
more general) genus in which it may be placed. The second way is
expressed in a passage which Heidegger cites from Pascal: "So in order
to define Being it would be necessary to say 'it *is*' and thus to employ in
the definition the word defined" (*SZ* 4n).

Heidegger concludes abruptly: " 'Being' cannot in fact be conceived as a being" (*SZ* 4). This is what the indefinableness of "Being" shows—rather than its showing that the meaning of Being is no problem. The sense of the conclusion is that Being cannot be determined as a definite being. It is not possible, by definition or, more generally, by collection and division, to determine Being as something more or less *definite*: "'Being' cannot be so determined as to be addressed as a being" (" *'Sein' kann nicht so zur Bestimmtheit kommen, daß ihm Seiendes zugesprochen wird"*— *SZ* 4). Being cannot be conceived as a being because it cannot be conceived as having that determinateness which must be had by a being. The indefinableness of "Being" simply testifies to this lack of determinateness and thus, rather than eliminating the question of the meaning of Being, lights up the very questionableness of this meaning.[7]

The third prejudice proclaims "Being" the most self-evident concept. Indeed, its self-evidence is incontestable: We make use of "Being" constantly and in every regard and understand what we mean by it. However, its understandableness is "an average understandableness" and serves only to demonstrate how nonunderstandable it remains. What is crucial is the tension: We live always already in an understanding of Being, and yet the meaning of Being remains obscure, so much so that we do not even raise the question regarding what Being means. Like the ancient "story-tellers" we constantly tell about beings and thus already understand what it means to be, yet are unable to say what we mean in using the expression "being." To experience this tension is to undergo the perplexity prerequisite to taking up the question about Being genuinely. It is to learn "not only that there is lacking an answer to the question of Being but even that the question itself is obscure and without direction" (*SZ* 4). From our distance we have rejoined the Eleatic Stranger: "We, however, who once thought we understood it, have now become perplexed."

(B) THE STRUCTURE OF THE QUESTION OF BEING

Perplexity lets the question of the meaning of Being obtrude in that almost empty form into which it has come to us today; it lets the question stand out so as to show what it *lacks,* namely, clarity and direction. At the same time, perplexity prepares us to take up the question in the almost empty form which it has for us—to take it *as a trace* of a genuine questioning about Being. We are able to *take up* the question only to the extent that we can *pose* it; to pose it appropriately (i.e., phenomenologically—cf. section 7) is to let the structure which belongs to the question unfold *from the question itself.* The task is, first, to exhibit the formal structure of the question, that is, the structure which belongs to it simply as a question; and, second, to show how the structuration unfolds once the formal structural moments are regarded as moments specifically of the question of the meaning of Being.

Heidegger proceeds to sketch the formal structure of questioning as such: "Every questioning is a seeking. Every seeking is guided in advance by what is sought" (*SZ* 5). Thus, the general structure of questioning is such as to involve two distinct items, the questioning-seeking and what is sought, between which there is a mutual relatedness, a "circularity." More specifically, the seeking is directed toward discovering certain determinations of what is sought; it can develop into an investigation (*Untersuchung*), in which case it becomes explicitly an exposing-determining of that which the question is about (*als dem freilegenden Bestimmen dessen, wonach die Frage steht*). Yet, on the other hand, the seeking is guided in advance by what is sought; only to the extent that the latter is held already in view from the beginning is it possible to set about determining it in the appropriate manner. Thus, questioning, though two-sided, involves on each side a certain relatedness to the other.

Heidegger proceeds, next, to articulate one of these items (what is sought) into its structural moments by distinguishing between (a) that which is asked about (*das Gefragte*), (b) that which is questioned (*das Befragte*), i.e., that which is made directly subject to interrogation, and (c) that which is to be found out by the questioning (*das Erfragte*); the latter is what is really *intended* in that which is asked about, and, thus, its disclosure constitutes the fulfillment of what is more or less emptily intended at the outset of the questioning; it is that with which the questioning reaches its goal.

This general structure has, then, to be specified with respect to the question about Being. Any questioning about Being, as a seeking, must be guided in advance by what is sought. Hence, the meaning of Being, as that which is sought in the questioning, must already in some way be available to us. Indeed, such "availability" was already indicated in the course of Heidegger's inverting of those prejudices that initially blocked the way into perplexity: We always already live within a vague, average understanding of Being. Yet, now Heidegger brings this already granted understanding of Being into more explicit connection with the posing of the question:

> We do not *know* what "Being" means. But if we ask, "What *is* 'Being'?" we already hold ourselves within an understanding of the "is," without being able to fix conceptually what the "is" signifies (*SZ* 5).

Hence, the very asking of the question about Being, even in that almost empty form in which it is handed down to us, is made to testify to that vague, average understanding of Being which is always already granted. *Being and Time* is able to begin with the question in that form which it has for us in the beginning: The almost empty question of the meaning of Being provides a place where *Being and Time* can begin—only because in that question the already granted "availability" of the meaning of Being is in play in the questioning. Where does *Being and Time* begin? It begins within the already granted understanding of Being. But it is not yet clear in what sense such understanding constitutes a *place.*

Heidegger proceeds to articulate "what is sought" into its three structural moments. The first moment, that which is asked about (*das Gefragte*), is Being. But what is being asked about when one asks about Being? How is Being "preunderstood" in this identification of Being as constituting what is asked about in the question of Being? It is preunderstood in the one and only way by which it is possible to avoid importing into the questioning something alien to it: It is preunderstood *from* the place where we who question *are* with regard to the meaning of Being, from the very place of the questioning—that is, it is preunderstood as it shows itself to us of "today," to us to whom the question of Being has become almost empty. Specifically, it is preunderstood in its utmost formality, merely in its character as Being *of beings.* It is preunderstood as "that which determines beings as beings" (*SZ* 6). Correlatively, it is also taken in its character of being always already granted—as "that in regard to which [*woraufhin*] beings, however they may be discussed, are always already understood" (*SZ* 6). This means that Being is the *a priori* in the broadest (not specifically modern) sense: It is that which must always already be "available," which must always be understood in advance, in order for beings to be accessible as such. The *a priori* character of Being is not, strictly regarded, an additional item in the preunderstanding operative in the formal articulation here under way: It is correlative to the formal preunderstanding of Being as "that which determines beings as beings." Insofar as Being determines beings in their character as being, beings can be grasped in such character only within the compass of a prior grasp of Being.

Abruptly Heidegger shifts to another correlative, a correlative in a different order: "The Being of beings 'is' not itself a being" (*SZ* 6). Being can be appropriately asked about in the questioning only if it is asked about in a way that accords with the preunderstanding of it as determining beings as beings; what such accord requires, first of all, is that Being be held in distinction from that which it would determine, i.e., that its peculiar indefinableness, its character as lacking all such determination as pertains to beings, be preserved in the questioning. It is at this point that Heidegger introduces a specific reference to those ancient "storytellers" who, determining beings by tracing them back to still other beings, failed to open up the decisive difference and so remained closed to questioning about the meaning of Being.

Just as Being, as that which is asked about, requires its own way of being exhibited, in distinction from the ways appropriate to beings, likewise it is necessary to take up in proper fashion that third structural moment in which what is intended in the first moment is fulfilled: That which is to be found out by the questioning, namely, the meaning of Being (*der Sinn von Sein*), requires its own conceptuality, in distinction from the concepts appropriate to the determination of beings. Already Heidegger has indicated by way of anticipation that this peculiar conceptuality has something to do with the way in which time can serve as a horizon for understanding.

The other structural moment, that which is questioned, is also determined by the formal preunderstanding of Being: "Insofar as Being constitutes what is asked about and Being means Being of beings, beings themselves turn out to be that which is questioned in the question of Being" (*SZ* 6). Beings are to be made directly subject to interrogation; the questioning is to occupy itself with them in such a way as to question them about Being. The question is: *Which* beings are to be questioned? From which beings are we able to learn the meaning of Being, to read it off (*ablesen*)? Which beings provide a place where *Being and Time*, dedicated to the question of the meaning of Being, can appropriately begin?

Finally, Heidegger focuses on still another structure, on a structural connection of a somewhat different sort. He begins by asking: How must the question of Being be worked out in order that it be *posed in its full transparency* (*in voller Durchsichtigkeit ihrer selbst*)? The sense of the question is focused in the phrase "posed in its full transparency." What does this mean? To pose a question in its full transparency is to pose it in such a way that what is in play in the questioning, what structures it and gives it its perspectives, gets made explicit, transparent, rather than simply remaining implicit, covertly operative. What, then, is in play, in this specific sense, in questioning about Being? Heidegger answers: In such questioning there must come into play a certain way of regarding Being, a certain conceptual means for understanding its meaning, a choice as to which being is to serve as exemplary, and a certain way of gaining access to that exemplary being. But all these elements that come into play are simply modes of comportment *of the questioner*, i.e., modes of Being of the questioner:

> Regarding, understanding and conceiving, choosing, access to are constitutive ways of comportment of the questioning and therefore are modes of Being of a particular being, of the being which we, the questioners, are ourselves (*SZ* 7).

What, then, is required in order that the question be posed in its full transparency? What is required in order that its deployment be transparent? Heidegger answers: It is necessary "to make transparent a being, the questioner, in its Being" (*SZ* 7). Thus, a transparent *Fragestellung* requires an explication of the Being of the questioner.

It is at precisely this point that Heidegger introduces the word *Dasein*:

> This being, which we ourselves are and which has questioning as one of its possibilities of Being, we denote as *Dasein* (*SZ* 7).

Dasein is thus posed as constituting the *place* where *Being and Time* can appropriately begin. The very deployment of the question is to commence with an explication of Dasein in its Being.

But what does Heidegger mean by *Dasein*? Precisely what he says, and nothing more. It is, first, the being which we ourselves are, the being which is our *own*, a being which has the character of being someone's own, the character of ownness; and it is, second, the being which has questioning as one of its possibilities of Being, which, more specifically, has questioning about Being as one of its possibilities of Being, that is, Dasein is a being whose Being is such that it can question about Being. It is significant that the word is introduced at precisely that point in the text at which there is broached a certain drawing of the questioner into the question, the point at which a certain belongingness of that being to the question of Being becomes consequential for the deployment of that question.

But why *Dasein* and not simply *man* (*Mensch*)? Certainly there could be no beings with the character of Dasein who would not also be men, nor conversely. The point is that the designation *Dasein* is open to a radically different way of thematizing the being so designated, in contrast to a designation such as *man*, in which a virtually uncontrollable complex of presuppositions is operative, most notably, those connected with the determination of *man* as "rational animal."[8] If, on the other hand, one takes this being as "subject," so narrowing one's sights as to regard this being as a bare I, then one has presupposed too little[9]—one has taken for granted something essentially less than that peculiar circularity in which *Being and Time* is to begin, the circularity which at this point in the text has just begun to unfold. To designate this being as *Dasein* is precisely to place it in that circularity, to place it from the outset in relation to Being; to designate it thus is to prepare an interrogation of it as the *Da* of *Sein*, as the place of questioning about Being.

What, precisely, is the structural connection on which Heidegger wants to focus in raising the question of transparency? He formulates it thus:

> The asking of this question, as a mode of Being of a being, is itself essentially determined by that about which it asks—by Being (*SZ* 7).

The asking is not simply distinct from that which is asked about, the questioning not simply over against what is questioned. Rather, the two sides of the question are intrinsically connected, so thoroughly interconnected that the very deployment of the question cannot but be engaged already in answering it, disrupting the simple opposition between asking and answering.

It might, as Heidegger notes, be charged that this connection amounts to a vicious circularity: In order to determine the meaning of Being, in order even to deploy the question transparently, one must explicate Dasein in its Being; and yet, a being could be explicated in its Being only if one already knew what Being means. Heidegger counters the charge by appealing to our always already granted understanding of the meaning of Being. Either the circle is such that "what is decisive is not to get out of the circle but to come into it in the right way" (SZ 153), that is, it is a circle prescribed by the very relatedness of the questioner to what is questioned; or else, if circularity is regarded more straightforwardly, it must be insisted that factically there is no such circle: We live constantly within an already granted understanding of the meaning of Being; we always have already an implicit understanding sufficient to direct the determining of a being in its Being. The decisive point is that one can determine a being in its Being without already having at one's disposal any explicit concept of Being, because that vague, average understanding of Being in which we always already move grants us the way into the circle; or, alternatively considered, it grants us the basis from which the "presuppositions" can be developed, from which the requisite preliminary understanding of Being can grow. What is required is that one leap into the circle, i.e., that one take up and set in motion in the proper way one's being already in the circle; or, alternatively considered, that one engage in that peculiar, radical relatedness that belongs to the question of Being, the relatedness back and forth between its two dimensions:

> In the question of the meaning of Being there is no "circular reasoning" but rather a remarkable "relatedness backward or forward" which what we are asking about (Being) bears to the questioning itself as a mode of Being of a being (SZ 8).

Thus, it has again become evident—now in a more originary way—that *Being and Time* begins within the already granted understanding of Being. Such understanding of Being, Heidegger now says explicitly, "belongs to the essential constitution of Dasein" (SZ 8). *Being and Time* can begin within the already granted understanding of Being by beginning with Dasein. And because of where *Being and Time* begins, there is no circle of the kind that could be brought forth as an objection.

Is it, then, to be concluded that Dasein has a certain priority that entitles it to serve as exemplary being in the working-out of the question of Being? Not yet. Though Heidegger grants that a certain priority has announced itself, he insists that Dasein's priority has not yet been demonstrated.

(C) FUNDAMENTAL ONTOLOGY

The task to which section 3 is devoted has to do with "the ontological priority of the question of Being." What kind of priority is at issue here? It is a priority in the order of grounding, the kind of priority which a ground has with respect to that which it grounds. To say that questioning about Being has such priority means that questioning about Being is the discipline which grounds other kinds of questioning. But why is this priority an *ontological* priority? Because what this discipline most directly grounds is all other ontological questioning, all other ontologies. To say that the question of Being has ontological priority amounts to saying that the discipline in which this question is worked out constitutes *fundamental ontology*.

It is the task of section 3 to exhibit this priority (though only in the degree and manner befitting an introduction). As such, section 3 may appropriately be regarded as a supplement or positive counterpart to section 1. Thus, whereas section 1 exhibits the questionableness of the meaning of Being by so inverting the traditional prejudices as to lead into perplexity, section 3 indicates that the question of the meaning of Being so underlies the entire edifice of knowledge that perplexity over the question about Being must eventually spread to all scientific knowledge.

Every science presupposes a demarcation of the region of beings to which it is directed as well as an establishing of the basic structure of that region by means of certain basic concepts. Initially this demarcating and establishing are done "roughly and naively" in terms of prescientific experience. But in the course of scientific research, the basic concepts of a science get brought into question by the results of that research, and it is precisely then that the most important kind of development takes place:

> The real "movement" of the sciences takes place when their basic concepts undergo a more or less radical revision which is transparent to itself. The level which a science has reached is determined by how far it is capable of a crisis in its basic concepts (*SZ* 9).

It is especially in the wake of such crises that the need for a genuine grounding of science is discerned. What such grounding requires is a rigorous, ontological determination of those beings to which the science is directed, that is, a determination of these beings with regard to their Being in such a way as to establish rigorously the basic concepts of the science, in contrast to the rough and naive way in which such concepts first arise. Heidegger describes such grounding:

> Laying the ground for the sciences in this way is different in principle from the kind of "logic" which limps along after, investigating the status of some science as it chances to find it, in order to discover its "method." Laying the ground, as we have described it, is rather a productive logic—in the sense that it leaps ahead, as it were, into some area of Being, discloses it for the first time in the constitution of its Being, and, after thus arriving at the structures within it, makes these available to the positive sciences as transparent assignments for their inquiry (*SZ* 10).

The sciences require their corresponding grounding disciplines, their appropriate regional ontologies. But, in turn, the regional ontologies themselves require a grounding by means of a discipline in which the question of the meaning of Being is taken up:

> Ontological inquiry is indeed more primordial, as over against the ontical inquiry of the positive sciences. But it remains itself naive and opaque if in its researches into the Being of beings it fails to discuss the meaning of Being in general (*SZ* 11).

Regional ontologies need to be grounded in fundamental ontology. It is thus that the task of grounding, intrinsic to the character of scientific research, points back to the task of taking up the question of the meaning of Being.

(D) DASEIN

The issue of section 4 is the priority of Dasein—that is, Heidegger here undertakes to show that Dasein has a priority among beings such that it is capable of serving as the exemplary being for the question of Being. Dasein is that being which we ourselves are (a being characterized by "mineness") and which can question—which, to retain the generative context, can question about Being. The latter of these two characters provides the point of departure for exhibiting the priority of Dasein: Dasein is to be considered primarily in terms of its *questioning comportment* toward Being. The exhibition of the structure of this comportment involves two major stages. The comportment is to be exhibited in relation to Dasein's comportment to itself and in relation to Dasein's comportment to beings other than itself.

It is of crucial importance that Dasein's comportment with respect to itself is not a comporting of one being toward another being with which it is or becomes identical. On the contrary, Dasein's comportment with respect to itself is a comportment with respect to its Being. Heidegger offers a series of characterizations of this comportment.

First, it is said that Dasein is distinctive among beings (i.e., ontically distinctive) by the fact "that for this being in its Being this Being itself is at issue [*daß es diesem Seienden in seinem Sein um dieses Sein selbst geht*]" (*SZ* 12). This says: Dasein is such that its Being is at issue. In other words, it is such as to comport itself to its Being *as* something at issue and such that the comportment itself is permeated with the peculiar character of being "at issue." But anything which is at issue is thereby problematic, questionable in the most concrete sense. Dasein's comportment to its Being is a questioning comportment—not in the sense that Dasein continually raises explicit questions about its Being but rather in the sense that the questionableness of its Being is continually being lived through, regardless of the extent to which it gets taken as a basis from which to raise explicit questions.

Second, Dasein is said to be such "that in its Being it has a relationship of Being toward this Being [*daß es in seinem Sein zu diesem Sein ein Seinsverhältnis hat*]" (*SZ* 12). This says: Dasein's Being is not something which it merely *has* (in some more or less indefinite sense of "possession"), but rather in its comportment to its Being there is a peculiar duality. Dasein is not merely *in* its Being, but rather *in* its Being it also, on the other hand, *relates itself to* that Being. More precisely, Dasein is not merely established in a certain determinacy, i.e., does not merely *have* certain determinations (for example, in the way that a thing has color, shape, texture); but rather, in being established in a certain determinacy, it also relates itself to that being-so-established, i.e., relates itself to the *having* of the determination. Furthermore, Dasein relates itself to its Being (i.e., to its being-established, to its having of certain determinations) in such a manner that its Being is *held at issue* for it. Further still, this relating itself (comportment) to its Being is "a relationship of Being" (*Seinsverhältnis*); this means that the comportment itself belongs to the Being of Dasein, that the comportment belongs to that toward which it is a comportment. Hence, not only is Dasein's Being distinct from that of things—that is, to venture an example, one is not courageous in the same way that a couch is yellow but rather in such a way that one's being-courageous is something constantly at issue in every decision—but also it is such as to resist the operation of the logic governing things' having properties.

Third, it is said that "Dasein understands itself in its Being in some manner or other and with some degree of explicitness [*Dasein versteht sich in irgendeiner Weise und Ausdrücklichkeit in seinem Sein*]" (*SZ* 12). Thus, Dasein's comportment to its Being, its "having" that Being as something at issue for it, is named "understanding." It is important to observe what understanding, thus defined, *is not*. It is not an affair specifically of thought or conceptual knowing, if for no other reason than that the "distance" which such would require is here lacking. Furthermore, understanding is not a relation of knowing between two beings but rather a relation (comportment) between a being (Dasein) and its Being. Yet, even this allows too much distance; understanding is not something stretched, as it were, between Dasein and its Being so as to join them but rather is Dasein's way of being its Being. Dasein is in its Being understandingly.

Fourth, it is said that "it is characteristic of this being that with and through its Being this [Being] is disclosed to it [*Diesem Seienden eignet, daβ mit und durch sein Sein dieses ihm selbst erschlossen ist*]" (*SZ* 12). Dasein's understanding its Being, its comportment toward its Being, its having its Being as something at issue for it—all these are a matter of disclosedness (*Erschlossenheit*), of Dasein's having its Being disclosed to it. Yet, this multiple articulation of the matter indicates that such disclosedness is not to be identified as a sheer unproblematic presence, on the side of what is disclosed (Being), or as an untroubled gazing on, on the side of that being (Dasein) to which it is disclosed. With and through Dasein's way of being its Being, that Being is disclosed; more precisely, Dasein's way of being its Being is identical with that Being's being disclosed to Dasein. Dasein is in its Being disclosingly. Dasein is the *place* (the "*Da*") where its own Being (*Sein*) is disclosed.

Thus, Dasein's relatedness to its Being has been characterized in four ways: (1) as Dasein's questioning comportment to its Being, (2) as Dasein's having its Being as something held at issue for it, (3) as Dasein's understanding its Being, and (4) as Dasein's having its Being disclosed. All these characterizations serve to establish the priority of Dasein; they exhibit Dasein as the *place* of a prephilosophical (1) questioning about Being, (2) having Being at issue, (3) understanding of Being, and (4) disclosure of Being. Thus, Heidegger says that Dasein is ontically distinctive by the fact that it is *ontological,* or, more precisely, *preontological*—that is, by the fact that it sustains prephilosophically a peculiar comportment to Being, by the fact that it *is* (preontologically) *as* an understanding of its Being. This entails that, insofar as questioning about Being is specifically a questioning about the Being of Dasein, it is something already *prefigured* in Dasein itself *as* questioning comportment to *its* Being. Explicit philosophical questioning about the Being of Dasein is merely a "developed" form of that comportment which Dasein always already has to its own Being.

At this point it first becomes possible to clarify the curious title that Heidegger gives to section 4: "The Ontical Priority of the Question of Being." The title is curious because it seems not to designate what section 4 actually establishes, namely, the priority of Dasein (and not that of the question of Being). What, then, is the character of the priority to which reference is made in the title? The priority is again (as with the ontological priority of the question of Being) a priority in the order of grounding: The question of Being grounds questioning as such. But now the grounding is of an *ontic* sort, that is, a grounding pertaining to beings, a grounding in which the ground exhibited is a being. What kind of ontic ground does questioning presuppose? It presupposes a questioner, a being that is capable of questioning, i.e., Dasein. Yet, Dasein's fundamental comportment is precisely a questioning comportment to Being— that is, Dasein is as a prephilosophical questioning of Being—that is, Dasein is identical with the (prephilosophical) question of Being itself. Granted the distinctive priority of Dasein (which section 4 actually establishes), to say that questioning presupposes Dasein is to say that it presupposes the question of Being, not as the theme of an ontology but ontically, as the constitution of a being.[10]

Heidegger concludes the consideration of Dasein's comportment to its Being by focusing on one of the four characterizations: "Understanding of Being is itself a determinateness-of-Being of Dasein [*Seinsverständnis ist selbst eine Seinsbestimmtheit des Daseins*]" (*SZ* 12). Dasein has a certain ontological determinateness, and it is precisely this determinateness that all four characterizations present. The crucial point is that this determinateness is not a matter of determinations in the sense of properties or definite characteristics; Dasein's essence is not a matter of its possessing a determinate character (a "what") or certain determinate features. Dasein's proper determinateness is neither the determinateness of substance (e.g., as "a thing which is in such a way that it needs no other thing in order to be"[11]) nor the determinateness of subject (e.g., as "that whose Being [essence] consists simply in the fact that it posits itself as being"[12]). Rather, the essence of Dasein lies in its peculiar comportment to its Being, in the fact that "it has its Being to be." That Being to which Dasein so comports itself, the Being of Dasein, Heidegger calls "existence" (*Existenz*); the essence of Dasein lies in its existence.

The relatedness expressed by saying that Dasein exists, its relatedness to its Being, proves to be in a sense the focal point for the entire Analytic of Dasein, the kernel from which in the course of that Analytic everything will be unfolded. Even at the outset Heidegger indicates something of the complexity of this relation, of its resistance to traditional concepts and traditional language. Such an indication is perhaps most pointedly traced in the following statement, to part of which attention has already been drawn:

But then it belongs to the constitution of Dasein's Being [*Seinsverfassung des Daseins*] that in its Being it has a relation-of-Being [*Seinsverhältnis*] to this Being.

In this statement the word *Being* occurs four times; in each occurrence its function is different. These different functions can be clustered around the question: What is Dasein's Being?—even though the impropriety of such a question is readily apparent, even though that impropriety is in a sense precisely what is at issue. In each occurrence of the word *Being*, this question is answered differently.

There is reference, first of all, to a state regarding which one could say: Dasein is "in its Being." Dasein would be in its Being in actually being something or other. Accordingly, Dasein's Being would consist simply in what Dasein in a particular instance *is*. But, second, Dasein is said to be related "to this Being"—that is, in its Being, Dasein sustains at the same time a relatedness to its Being. In this respect, then, Dasein's Being would be that to which Dasein has such a relatedness—one term, so to speak, of the relation, over against Dasein as the other term. Yet, third, that relation is designated as a relation-of-Being (*Seinsverhältnis*). In this regard, Dasein's Being would, then, consist precisely in its relating itself to its Being; more pointedly, Dasein's Being would be the relation itself. The point is, then, that Dasein's Being involves all three of these connections: Dasein is in its Being in such a way as to sustain to its Being a relatedness in which its Being consists. These three connections, expressing in a very preliminary way the three ecstases of temporality (having-been, future, and present, respectively), are gathered up in the remaining occurrence, the first one in the statement, the reference to "the constitution of Dasein's Being." This gathering is precisely what the Analytic of Dasein is to work out.

Yet, the Analytic of Dasein is directed not merely to the Being of Dasein but to Being *as such*, even if in that Analytic Dasein is to serve as the exemplary being. It is thus necessary, at least, that from Dasein's comportment to its own Being there be unfolded a comportment also to the Being of beings other than Dasein. Only the very briefest indication of this direction is given in the introductory discourse.

Heidegger writes: "Being in a world belongs essentially to Dasein" (*SZ* 13). For anything to belong essentially to Dasein requires that it be essentially connected with that determinateness which Dasein is; and for being in a world to belong essentially to Dasein requires that in comporting itself disclosedly toward its own Being, Dasein also comports itself to a world—to such an extent that the latter comportment belongs integrally to the former. Being in a world is not something added on alongside Dasein's comportment to its Being; but rather, in comporting itself to its Being (i.e., in being Dasein), it is already in a world.

Heidegger elaborates:

> Thus Dasein's understanding of Being concerns equiprimordially the understanding of something like "world" and the understanding of the Being of the beings which become accessible within a world (*SZ* 13).

Dasein's understanding of Being is, hence, not an understanding merely of its own Being but also of the Being of beings within the world, of beings whose constitution is other than that of Dasein. Thus, questioning about the Being of beings other than Dasein is no less rooted in Dasein's preontological understanding than is questioning about the Being of Dasein. To the extent that these two moments form a unity, Dasein's preontological understanding is of Being as such; and ontology as such is just a "development" of that questioning comportment which Dasein is:

> But then the question of Being is nothing but the radicalization of an essential tendency-of-Being which belongs to Dasein itself, the preontological understanding of Being (*SZ* 15).

Dasein is the place of the disclosure of Being as such. An analytic of Dasein, an existential analytic, is consequently not just a preliminary step toward taking up the question of Being but is, rather, itself already a taking-up. The existential analytic is not merely preparatory for "fundamental ontology" but is already fundamental ontology; as Heidegger stresses, fundamental ontology must be sought in the existential analytic.

Where does *Being and Time* begin? It begins at that place where we already are, that place which Dasein is, the place of the understanding of Being. But in the beginning this place is a fragile unity, for it remains to be shown how Dasein's understanding of its own Being belongs together with its understanding of the Being of beings whose constitution is other than that of Dasein. At most, it is clear that Dasein's comportment with respect to itself and its comportment with respect to other beings are not to be explicated—neither separately nor in their way of belonging together—in certain philosophically familiar ways. Dasein's comportment with respect to itself is neither a self-positing nor a self-consciousness; it is not any kind of relationship between one being and another being with which it would be or would become identical; it is not even the turning upon itself of a self-identical act.[13] As a result, the question of how Dasein's comportment with respect to itself belongs together with its comportment with respect to other beings cannot be identified with, for instance, the question of how knowledge of self (self-consciousness) belongs together with knowledge of objects. What is crucial is that Dasein's comportment with respect to itself is a comportment toward its *Being,* for this prevents Dasein's turning from being regarded as a turning back into the establishment of self-identity; Dasein's unrest is more radical than any that could be attributed to a subject. In turn, the question of how Dasein's comportment with respect to itself belongs together with its comportment with respect to other beings is prevented from issuing in the demand for conformity of object to subject. Even in its beginning *Being and Time* has, as Heidegger later says, already left behind "all subjectivity."[14]

But how, then, do the two items belong together? How is it that, in comporting itself to its own Being, Dasein comports itself to the Being of other beings? The clue lies in that other item which Heidegger introduces alongside the Being of beings other than Dasein—namely, *world.* Because Dasein's comportment toward its own Being is essentially connected to the structuration of world as that within which beings are accessible in their Being, that place which Dasein is proves to be a unity.[15] The task is to exhibit Dasein as Being-in-the-world (cf. *SZ* 41).

Where does *Being and Time* begin? It begins at the place of the disclosure of Being, that place which Dasein is. It begins by coming into the circle, by engaging in the circling intrinsic to the question of Being itself. What is this beginning? What is the way into the circle? It is a projecting which takes its directives from the traces of the question—a projecting of the place of the beginning. It is a projecting of Dasein as the *place* of prephilosophical questioning about Being, having Being at issue, understanding of Being, disclosure of Being. The beginning of *Being and Time* is a projecting of the place where it begins—a projecting of Dasein in its appropriateness as the place of beginning. *Being and Time* begins by measuring out the place of contention regarding Being.

In a text first published in 1966 under the title "The End of Philosophy and the Task of Thinking," Heidegger writes of his

> attempt, undertaken again and again since 1930, to give the questioning in *Being and Time* a more originary [*anfänglicher*] form. This means: to submit the beginning of the question in *Being and Time* to an immanent critique.[16]

Heidegger's thought does not move away from *Being and Time* but rather back to its beginning—in order to attempt a more originary beginning.

NINE

Into the Clearing

Today we are perhaps beginning, belatedly, to understand what an immanent critique of *Being and Time*[1] might require—belatedly, for Heidegger himself, having undertaken again and again since 1930 "to subject the *Ansatz* of the question in *Being and Time* to an immanent critique," finally indicated in the mid-1960s that through this undertaking "the name of the task of *Being and Time* gets changed." Changed into what? Heidegger answers the question with a question, these two questions serving to enframe "The End of Philosophy and the Task of Thinking": "Does the title for the task of thinking then read instead of 'Being and Time': clearing and presence [*Lichtung und Anwesenheit*]?"[2] But here it is a matter not simply of a change *from* the text *Being and Time*, but rather of an immanent, i.e., radicalizing, critique set upon bringing into the open something already in play, inconspicuously, perhaps even concealedly, in *Being and Time* itself. Let us focus on a moment of the text in which such first stirrings are unobtrusively inscribed.

(A)

A circling within the text is completed at that juncture where the analysis of Dasein comes to be directed specifically to "Being-in" (Division I, chap. 5). For the "preliminary sketch" (*Vorzeichnung*) of the constitution of Dasein as Being-in-the-world was drawn by way of a preliminary, orientational characterization of this moment (*SZ* 12); and following the preliminary sketch, a rigorous (though of course only "preparatory") analysis was provided for the other two moments, world and self, leading finally back to Being-in as a theme for rigorous analysis. It is at the point of return to "Being-in" that the word *clearing* comes decisively into play (*SZ* §28).

For what purpose? As an interpretive name for Being-in itself, as interpretively synonymous with the names "there" ("*Da*") and "disclosed-

Originally published in *Heidegger: The Man and the Thinker,* ed. Thomas Sheehan (Chicago: Precedent Publishing, 1981).

ness" ("*Erschlossenheit*"). That Being-in is a constituent of the Being of Dasein means: Dasein is always its "there," Dasein is its disclosedness, Dasein is a clearing. Later another synonym will be added: Dasein is its truth. The first connection, however, is more immediate: a clearing (the paradigm: a clearing in a forest) is a place that can be lighted up whenever the sun's rays, the light, shine down through the opening above—or, more pointedly, a clearing must always be there already in order that the light break through so as to light up whatever stands there in the clearing. In *Being and Time* the difference between light (*Licht*) and clearing (*Lichtung*), manifestly in play metaphorically, is still precarious because of the attachment of the issue of clearing to "the ontically figurative [*bildlich*] talk about the *lumen naturale* in man" (*SZ* 133). Explicitly, to say that Dasein "is 'illuminated' ['*erleuchtet*'] is to say: cleared [*gelichtet*] in itself *as* Being-in-the-world, not through another being, but rather in such a way that it *is* itself the clearing."[3] The text is unequivocal here: rather than confounding light (illumination) and clearing, it is a matter of recovering for the issue of clearing what is really at issue in that ontically figurative (and traditional) way of talking about the *lumen naturale*, of detaching the issue from the metaphor of light, placing it on the other side. And so, immediately following, the difference is openly traced: "Only for a being that is existentially cleared in this way does what is present-at-hand [*Vorhandenes*] become accessible in the light, hidden in the dark" (*SZ* 133).

With the return to the analysis of Being-in, it is, then, a matter of exhibiting those moments, those "existentials," by which Dasein is itself the clearing—that is, of analyzing the existential constitution of the "there," of the clearing. This return, it turns out, completes another circle, one at a deeper stratum of the text—or, rather, at this deeper stratum, several circles. For in the analysis of the existential constitution of the clearing, it turns out that a major constituent is understanding and that understanding is fulfilled in interpretation; it suffices, then, to recall that at the outset (*SZ* §7) interpretation was already identified as the specific procedure of the analysis to come: The analysis (interpretation) has become an analysis (interpretation) of interpretation, and in this interpretation of interpretation it circles in a new way, back upon itself, reflexively. Even though the analysis is limited to inauthentic interpretation—this limitation being prescribed by the horizon of the entire preparatory analysis, everydayness—the reflexivity reaches far enough to allow that "preliminary sketch" of Being-in-the-world to be recognized as a moment of that specific fore-structure which belongs to the existential interpretation; and thus the previous, merely procedural circle is attached to the circle reflected from the matter itself.

The reflexivity intrinsic to the interpretation of interpretation is not, however, the only kind that breaks out in the return to "Being-in."

Another is exhibited in the analysis (*SZ* §29) of disposition (*Befindlich-keit*). The relevant characteristic of disposition is that according to which it discloses Dasein in its thrownness—that is, in the "facticity of its being delivered over" (*SZ* 135). To what is Dasein delivered over? It is "delivered over to the Being which, in existing, it has to be" (*SZ* 134); it is "delivered over to the 'there'" (*SZ* 135). Dasein's thrownness is a thrownness into the "there," into the clearing which it has to be, into disclosedness. Accordingly, disposition is such that in it "Dasein is brought before its Being as 'there'" (*SZ* 134)—that is, Dasein's thrownness into disclosedness is disclosed—that is, disposition is that mode of disclosedness in which is disclosed Dasein's character as disclosedness. This reflexivity within disposition, that it is disclosive of disclosedness, is the source of that primordial disclosive power which, intensified in anxiety, will later be exploited for the sake of a more primordial access to the Being of Dasein. How can the existential analysis exploit the reflexivity of disposition? How can it avail itself of the disclosive power of moods without thereby abandoning itself to them and disclaiming itself as a theoretical affair? There is only one way: Taking its "distance" from the dispositional disclosure, it must with appropriate reticence attend to that disclosure, accompanying it "only in order existentially to raise to a conceptual level the phenomenal content of what has been disclosed" (*SZ* 140).

The reflexivity of disposition points beyond the preparatory analysis (Division I) to the development of a more primordial access to Dasein (Division II); a third reflexivity points to Division III, to its question, the question of the entire work, the question of the meaning of Being. For the analysis of interpretation leads to a determination of the concept of meaning, and the text explicitly reflects this determination back upon the question of the meaning of Being. Granted the determination of meaning as that from which something becomes understandable, the question of the meaning of Being is correspondingly determined as a question about that from which Being becomes understandable to Dasein.

Thus, in the return of the analysis to "Being-in," a threefold reflexivity breaks out—reflexivity of such extent as to reach out to the entirety of *Being and Time*. It is little wonder that this return is announced by that word which when the name of *Being and Time* eventually gets changed, displaces *Being*: *clearing*.

(B)

I narrow the range, focusing now on one constituent of the clearing: understanding (*Verstehen*). A retracing of the existential analysis of understanding (*SZ* §31) will provide an opening onto those first stirrings in behalf of "clearing" and "presence."

As Dasein is no subject, so understanding is no immanent representational activity of a subject. Rather, understanding is to be taken up existentially, i.e., in connection with Dasein's comportment to its Being, a comportment which, distinct from blind relatedness between mere things, is fundamentally a matter of disclosure. The analysis begins by indicating the major terms in the relevant disclosive structure:

> In the for-the-sake-of-which [*Worumwillen*], existing Being-in-the-world is disclosed as such, and this disclosedness we have called understanding. [Reference is made to §18.] In the understanding of the for-the-sake-of-which, the significance which is grounded therein is disclosed along with it (*SZ* 143).

This says: The structure of understanding, as a kind of disclosedness, is such that in and through something, something else gets disclosed. Two items get disclosed: existing Being-in-the-world and significance. In and through what? The "for-the-sake-of-which"—identified in the analysis of worldhood (*SZ* §18) as a potentiality-for-Being (*Seinkönnen*), a possible way to be, a possibility in that sense which, not yet positively delimited, is to be distinguished from mere logical possibility, from the contingency of things present-at-hand, and from "free-floating" possibility in the sense of the "liberty of indifference." "Significance," determined in that same earlier analysis, is identical with the worldhood of the world, i.e., the referential totality by which a concrete world is structured. "Existing Being-in-the-world": This says simply "Dasein," with emphasis on its comportment to possibilities.

So, on the one side, the for-the-sake-of-which discloses existing Being-in-the-world—that is, those possibilities to which Dasein comports itself serve to disclose Dasein. But how is it that Dasein can be disclosed by possibilities?

> Dasein is not something present-at-hand which possesses its potentiality for something by way of an extra; it is primarily Being-possible. Dasein is in every instance that which it can be, and in the way in which it is its possibility (*SZ* 143).

Dasein is not something at hand which then, as a supplement, has a comportment to possibility; rather, its comportment to possibility determines what it is and how it is in any given instance. Even further: "Possibility as an existential is the most primordial and ultimate positive ontological determination of Dasein" (*SZ* 143f.). Dasein is disclosed in and through its possibilities, *from* those possibilities, because it is determined by its comportment to those possibilities, because "it is in every case what it can be" (*SZ* 143).

On the other side of the disclosive structure, the for-the-sake-of-which discloses significance—that is, a possibility prescribes what must be done to actualize it (an "in-order-to"); this, in turn, requires that something be done (a "toward-this"), etc.; and in each case what is to be done prescribes that with which it can be done. The possibility of providing oneself with adequate shelter prescribes securing the shingles against wind and rain; this, in turn, prescribes nailing them down properly; and this one does with a hammer. Within a given context a possibility delineates with a certain degree of determinacy a referential totality; it structures a world.

The analysis becomes more precise through the thematizing of understanding as projection (*Entwurf*). What does Dasein project in understanding? Does it project possibilities? Not primarily. What does it project primarily? It projects itself upon possibilities.

> Dasein has, as Dasein, always already projected itself; and as long as it is, it is projecting. As long as it is, Dasein always has understood itself and always will understand itself from possibilities (*SZ* 145).

The primary sense of projection is Dasein's self-projection, its projection of itself upon possibilities. *From* those possibilities Dasein is, in turn, given back to itself, disclosed to itself. Dasein does not disclose the possibilities (by projecting upon them) so much as the possibilities, being projected upon, disclose Dasein. Yet there is a sense in which Dasein may be said to project possibilities:

> Furthermore, the character of understanding as projection is such that understanding does not grasp thematically that upon which it projects—that is, possibilities. Grasping in such a manner would take away from what is projected its very character as a possibility and would reduce it to the given contents which we have in mind [*zieht es herab zu einem gegebenen, gemeinten Bestand*]; whereas projection, in throwing, throws before itself the possibility as possibility, and lets it *be* as such. As projecting, understanding is the kind of Being of Dasein in which it *is* its possibilities as possibilities (*SZ* 145).

This says: In projecting (in the primary sense: projecting itself), Dasein projects possibilities *as* possibilities. It does not create or invent them but lets them be as possibilities.

Another side has now to be added. For Dasein's self-projection is not a projection *only* upon possibilities:

> With equal primordiality it projects Dasein's Being both upon its for-the-sake-of-which and upon significance as the worldhood of its current world (*SZ* 145).

Dasein's projection is two-sided, a projection upon possibilities and upon significance (worldhood). Because this two-sidedness belongs to it, "pro-

jection always pertains to the full disclosedness of Being-in-the-world"
(*SZ* 146). But how can one and the same projection have these two sides?
Where is the unity? It lies in the connection between those two items on
which Dasein projects: A possibility opens up significance, i.e., prescribes, delineates a referential totality; and significance opens onto
possibility, for, in engaging oneself in a world, one tacitly submits oneself
to a certain range of possibilities connected with the structure of that
world. The unity of possibility and significance gives unity to the projection: One and the same projection is a projection upon both.

In turn, there is a certain analogous doubling of that self-disclosure
that is correlative to Dasein's self-projection. Dasein is to some degree
disclosed to itself, not only from possibilities, but also from significance.
And thus, globally considered, projective understanding can assume two
forms:

> Understanding *can* devote itself primarily to the disclosedness of the world;
> that is, Dasein can, proximally and for the most part, understand itself from
> its world. Or else understanding throws itself primarily into the for-the-sake-
> of-which; that is, Dasein exists as itself. Understanding is either authentic,
> arising out of one's own self as such, or inauthentic (*SZ* 146).

These two forms, authentic and inauthentic understanding, derive from
the fact that one or the other side can be dominant.

A final moment of the disclosive structure constitutive of understanding is added in §32. It involves extending to beings other than Dasein a
disclosive connection analogous to that of Dasein: They, too, get projected upon possibilities and significance, though of course they do not
project themselves:

> In the projecting of understanding, beings are disclosed in their possibil-
> ity. . . . Beings within-the-world generally are projected upon the world—
> that is, upon a whole of significance . . . (*SZ* 151).

As Dasein is projected upon possibilities and significance and thus disclosed, so beings other than Dasein get projected, generally upon significance, and disclosed therefrom. When such beings have been thus disclosed, they may then be said to have meaning.

What is meaning? Its determination is grounded on the analysis of
understanding:

> Meaning [*Sinn*] is that wherein the understandableness [*Verständlichkeit*] of
> something maintains itself. . . . *Meaning is the upon-which* [Woraufhin] *of a
> projection from which something becomes understandable as something* . . . (*SZ* 151).

Meaning is that upon which something is projected and from which it
becomes understandable: possibility or significance, as the case may be—

in any case, an item entwined in that total disclosive structure that constitutes understanding. But understanding is one of the major constituents of the "there," of the clearing, and its structure is accordingly entwined in that total structure by which the clearing itself is delimited. Meaning has been brought into the clearing. And, setting the relevant reflexivity into play, the question of the meaning of Being is likewise brought into the clearing. The analysis of understanding, by grounding the determination of "meaning," inscribes the question of the meaning of Being within the sphere of the clearing, gathers the issue of Being and time into the ἀληθείη εὐκυκλής (cf. Parmenides, Fr. 1).

(C)

But how does the analysis of understanding bring also into play the issue of presence? Within the text there is only one indication, an indirect one: a reference appended to the analysis, almost as though it were a passing remark, a reference to traditional ontology. The reference follows a more extended passage devoted to Dasein's "sight" (*Sicht*). Understanding is identified as what makes up Dasein's sight, and the passage serves to extend the analysis of understanding, just completed, back to the earlier analyses of Dasein's various modes of sight: circumspection (*Umsicht*), that sight with which Dasein in its concernful dealings with equipment holds the equipmental totality in view; and considerateness (*Rücksicht*) and forbearance (*Nachsicht*), those modes of sight which serve analogously in Dasein's solicitous dealings with others. To this appropriation of the issue of sight to that of understanding is then added the reference to traditional ontology:

> By showing how all sight is grounded primarily in understanding . . . , we have deprived pure intuition [*puren Anschauen*] of its priority, which corresponds noetically to the priority accorded the present-at-hand [*Vorhandene*] in traditional ontology (*SZ* 147).

The reference is far-reaching and decisive.

Intuition is deprived of its priority. What priority? A text of lectures contemporaneous with the redaction of *Being and Time* is explicit: Intuition is accorded priority in the sense that knowledge is taken to be primarily intuition. By whom is it accorded such priority? The lecture text answers: by the entire tradition. And that same text exhibits the ways in which that priority was granted by Hegel, Kant, Leibniz, Descartes, Aquinas.[4] Throughout the tradition, knowledge is taken as primarily intuition—that is, intuition is the paradigm in such fashion that all knowledge, to the extent that it is not simply intuition, is charged with compensating for what it lacks in intuition. Knowledge is ideally the sheer beholding of what is present, of what is merely there on hand present to one's gaze. Thus it is that the priority of intuition is correlative to the priority of the present-at-hand, a priority equally accorded by the tradition, a priority called into question almost from the outset of *Being and Time*.

The analysis of understanding culminates in a destruction of the priority heretofore accorded sheer intuitive presence to what is openly present to one's gaze. It constitutes, thus, a radical break with the tradition. But the text of *Being and Time* signals another break, too: "Even the phenomenological 'intuition of essences' [*Wesensschau*] is grounded in existential understanding" (*SZ* 147). The lecture text marks the break unmistakably, citing Husserl's "principle of all principles" (from *Ideas* §24): "that whatever presents itself originarily to us in intuition (in its bodily actuality, as it were) is simply to be accepted as that as which it gives itself but only within the limits in which it there gives itself." The principle enjoins one to attend to things as they show themselves *in intuition*. And thus it attests to Husserl's solidarity with the tradition: Taking over the traditional priority of intuition, Husserl elevates it to the rank of an explicit methodological principle.

How is intuition to be deprived of its priority? By showing that all sight is grounded in understanding. How does the grounding of sight in understanding serve to deprive intuition of its priority? Because intuition is itself a kind of sight, which, if grounded in understanding, relinquishes its priority to the latter. Actually, this priority is already relinquished in the earlier analyses of sight to which that of understanding gets referred back, most notably in that of circumspection (*Umsicht*): Since an item of equipment can show itself (as what it is in itself) only from out of an equipmental totality, that "sight" to which it is "given" is grounded in the sight by which the totality is held in sight—that is, Dasein's concernful dealing with an item is grounded in a prior, holistic sighting (cf. *SZ* §15).

Correlatively, that same earlier analysis also deprives being-present-at-hand (*Vorhandensein*) of its traditional priority by exhibiting its subordination to being-ready-to-hand (*Zuhandensein*)—a subordination that gets confirmed in the development initiated by the analysis of understanding (cf. *SZ* §33). This subordination bears decisively on the issue of presence. How? By displacing presence—that is, by replacing the sheerly present thing with a thing for which absence is constitutive. Under ordinary circumstances an item of equipment is not sheerly present in a self-contained positivity. On the contrary, it is extended beyond itself into the referential totality by which it is essentially determined; it is "elsewhere," beyond itself, not sheer self-contained presence. Furthermore, such an item is of such a character that when it shows itself most primordially as what it is (e.g., a hammer in hammering), it is never grasped thematically (i.e., as sheerly present) but rather remains withdrawn, holds itself back in a certain inconspicuousness in favor of the work for which it is in use. An item of equipment is "in itself" by withdrawing into itself, by being absent (cf. *SZ* §15). Drawn back into itself, drawn forth beyond itself—both modes of absence serve to determine the characteristic presence of equipment, a presence which, thus determined by absence, is distinct from the sheer presence which, as the correlate of intuition, is accorded priority by metaphysics and phenomenology.

The grounding of sight in understanding completes what the earlier analyses initiated. It refers intuition, displaced into concern, grounded already in circumspection, back to understanding itself. In understanding, Dasein projects itself upon possibilities. It *is* its possibilities—that is, it too is extended, extends itself, beyond itself so as to escape all self-contained positivity. And by its manner of projecting upon them, Dasein lets its possibilities be *as* possibilities, granting them that reserve of absence which prevents their crystallizing into the sheer presence of a given content. Possibilities disclose significance; and Dasein, projecting upon possibilities, projects also upon significance in such a way as to let it be as such, to let a referential totality take hold, to let a world take shape. But this shape is still more withdrawn than those items of equipment that come to presence within it. Something exceptional, some disruption, is required for it to become even minimally thematic (cf. *SZ* §16); its peculiar presence is even less the sheer presence correlative to intuition, is even more a presence essentially determined by absence. It is little wonder that traditional ontology, according priority to the sheer presence of intuition, completely passes over the phenomenon of world.

The grounding of sight in understanding gathers the entire analysis of Being-in-the-world into the issue of clearing. More decisively, it gathers into that issue the destruction of sheer presence accomplished by that analysis, the collapse of sheer presence into the play of presence and absence. In the gathering of this play into the clearing one hears the first stirrings within the *Sache* of *Being and Time*.

TEN

End(s)

Der Tod ist der Schrein des Nichts, dessen nämlich, was in
aller Hinsicht niemals etwas bloß Seiendes ist, was aber
gleichwohl west, sogar als das Geheimnis des Seins selbst.
Der Tod birgt als der Schrein des Nichts das Wesende des
Seins in sich. Der Tod ist als der Schrein des Nichts das
Gebirg des Seins.
—Martin Heidegger,
"Das Ding"

Beginning with a bit of pretense, as one always does when merely
beginning, let me presume that a discourse about philosophy is still
possible (if ever it was), a discourse about philosophy *as such*. Let me
simulate such a discourse, proceeding as though that sense that would
orient the entire discourse and guarantee its coherence were still intact
(if ever it was), as though the sense of sense were unquestionable. Let me
pretend that the "as such" has not itself become questionable, that it has
not become questionable *as such*, withdrawing thus from the very questioning, the very putting in question, threatening the coherence of the
theme of the discourse. Let me pretend—if only in order to begin
prefiguring such transgression—that one could outline coherently the
end of philosophy and perhaps even the task, the end, of a future
thinking.

(A)

Philosophy is not only word but also deed, is word which as such is deed,
is performative in its peculiar manner. Especially since deed comes to be
understood as end-directed, as teleological, as receiving its λόγος from its
τέλος, philosophy, too, is oriented to an end. And yet, no deed is an
absolute beginning, no word the first word, and in orienting itself to an
end, philosophy resumes something already begun, resumes it already in

Originally published in *Research in Phenomenology*, vol. 13 (1983).

the very name "philosophy," in thus naming itself. It resumes an already constituted orientation to an end, to end(s) already projected. The structure of the resumption is quite complex. It is not only a matter of philosophy's measuring itself against the end(s) but also, inseparably, an interpretation which reanimates, which to that degree (re)constitutes the end(s). It is a matter of both appropriation of tradition and distancing from it. Philosophy achieves self-understanding—and, inseparably, its (self-)constitution—precisely in drawing the lines of this configuration.

In almost every case, one can discern to some extent the divergence of the end(s). One can to some extent measure the distance between the (re)constituted end(s) and the end(s) taken over—even though such measuring usually, perhaps even inevitably, proceeds by simplifying the configuration, by abstracting from certain complexities in the constitution of tradition. And yet, it is precisely my intention to call attention to a case in which any such measuring would border on the unthinkable, a case in which not just the end(s) but the very sense of end, hence the very sense of sense, λόγος and τέλος *as such,* are brought into question. Or, rather, I want to resume the stance, to take up the movement, of a philosophical project elaborated at the threshold of such questioning. The project is that of Heidegger's *Being and Time* as elaborated in the lecture course of 1927 entitled *The Basic Problems of Phenomenology.*[1]

Let me, then, set the project at the threshold by anticipating the opening toward which it is in motion. Or, rather, let me refer to a much later text in which Heidegger glances back toward that threshold. That text, "The End of Philosophy and the Task of Thinking," first published in 1966, is prefaced by an identification of its own larger context:

> It is the attempt undertaken again and again ever since 1930 to shape the questioning [*die Fragestellung*] of *Being and Time* in a more primordial fashion. This means to subject the beginning [*Ansatz*] of the question in *Being and Time* to an immanent critique.[2]

The opening is an attempt at a critique of the beginning of *Being and Time,* an attempt at a more primordially shaped beginning, an attempt in play throughout Heidegger's later texts, from 1930 on. Presumably, however, it is not yet in play—at least not in the same way—in the lecture course of 1927, delivered a few months after the publication of *Being and Time.* The text of this course, *The Basic Problems of Phenomenology,* can be thus situated, at least provisionally: The text lies in the gap, the interval, between the end of *Being and Time* and the beginning of the critique of its beginning. The text stands at the threshold.

What is the end of *Being and Time?* What are its ends, in the two senses which most obtrude in the polysemic play of the word, end as τέλος and as termination? Let me begin with these senses even if they will not for long remain intact, much less independent. Recall, then, the goal of *Being and Time* as initially projected: It is to work out concretely the question of the meaning of Being by means of an interpretation of time as the horizon for all understanding of Being (*SZ* 1). With the projection of Being upon time, *Being and Time* would reach its goal, would come to its end. And yet, this is, of course, precisely what the work does not do; it merely stops, terminates, breaks off, short of this end. The end of *Being and Time* remains outstanding—something like an unpaid debt, or perhaps like the end of an unripe fruit prematurely plucked from the vine.

In *Being and Time* the (re)constitutive interpretation of the end(s) animating philosophical tradition is already in play, much more even than might appear on the surface of the text. Here already, in undertaking a *Wiederholung* of that questioning with which philosophy began in Plato and Aristotle and by which it has been continually, if ever more forgetfully, sustained—here already there is an appropriation of the end of philosophy, a convergence of the (projected) end of *Being and Time* with the end of philosophy as such.

Much later, in one of his final texts, the one that I have cited already, Heidegger explicitly delimits—not without a bit of pretense—the sense of end operative in his discourse about the end of philosophy, operative in that text itself, in its title "The End of Philosophy and the Task of Thinking":

> What is meant by the talk about the end of philosophy? We understand the end of something all too easily in the negative sense as a mere stopping, as the lack of continuation, perhaps even as decline and impotence. In contrast, what we say about the end of philosophy means the completion of metaphysics [*die Vollendung der Metaphysik*].[3]

This passage could, of course, sustain a thoroughly classical reading, one in which it would be taken as executing a decision in favor of one sense of end rather than another, end as τέλος rather than end as termination (in its various subordinate senses: stopping, lack of continuation, decline, impotence). But the suggestion of such a reading is precisely the bit of pretense. Immediately Heidegger corrects such a reading:

> However, completion [*Vollendung*] does not mean perfection [*Vollkommenheit*] as a consequence of which philosophy would have to have attained the highest perfection at its end.

Rather, the end of philosophy, its completion, is a place, a place of gathering:

> The end of philosophy is the place [*Ort*], that place in which the whole of philosophy's history is gathered into its most extreme possibility [*in seine*

äußerste Möglichkeit]. End as completion means this gathering [*Versamm-lung*].[4]

The end of philosophy is a matter of its being gathered into an end, not an end in the classical sense of τέλος, end as perfection, but rather end as extreme possibility. This text—one might be tempted to call it Heideg-ger's final retrospective text—thus announces a displacement of the very sense(s) of end, one which, if extended and followed up, would even-tually produce a displacement of the very sense of sense, would disrupt the securing of λόγος by τέλος. But what I want especially to note is that the displacement of end announced in this text corresponds quite pre-cisely to a displacement that is already produced in *Being and Time*, in Heidegger's analysis of the end of Dasein. Death, too, is called an *extreme possibility* (*äußerste Möglichkeit*) (*SZ* 250). The end of Dasein, the end of philosophy—in both instances it is a matter of a possibility that cannot be outstripped, of a possibility that withdraws all possibilities, that closes off decisively the opening to a future. It is a matter of an end to which closure and withdrawal belong, an end in which they replace, displace, openness and perfection.

(B)

Pretending that one could hold this end in view, let me now come back to the threshold, or, rather, advance from *Being and Time* to it. The text of the lecture course of 1927, *The Basic Problems of Phenomenology*, does more than merely announce the convergence of the end of *Being and Time* with the end of philosophy. It shows specifically and in detail how certain traditional theses about Being serve, when deepened by phenom-enological critique, to generate those four groups of problems which are regarded as "constituting the whole of the basic problems of ontology" (*GP* 321). These four groups of problems, viz., those of the ontological difference, of the basic articulation of Being, of the possible modifica-tions of Being, and of the truth-character of Being, are "the basic problems of phenomenology" (*GP* 21).

It is not, however, merely a matter of convergence of specific problems but also a matter of a fundamental orientation, a way of questioning about Being, that animates all specific problems, whether they take the form of traditional theses about Being or the more radical form of the basic problems of phenomenology. Heidegger exposes this fundamental orientation in the course of his phenomenological critique of Kant's thesis that Being is not a real predicate. The crux of the critique involves showing how the Kantian equation of existence with perception must be radicalized by a regress to intentionality and ultimately to the disclosed-ness of Being [*Erschlossenheit des Seins*] that is ingredient in the full structure of intentionality. The orientation is thus one which, in order to develop the question about Being, regresses to the subject. Heidegger insists that such regress is characteristic not only of modern philosophy but equally of premodern thought, e.g., as regress to λόγος as a basic comportment of the ψυχή: "All philosophy, in whatever way it may view the 'subject' and place it in the center of philosophical investigation, returns to the soul, mind, consciousness, subject, ego in clarifying the basic ontological phenomena" (*GP* 103f.). In developing the question of Being by way of an ontology of Dasein, *Being and Time* would, then, resume in a radical way that return to the subject characteristic of all philosophy. Hence, it is "clear that the ontology of Dasein represents the latent goal and constant and more or less evident demand of the whole development of Western philosophy" (*GP* 106). To this degree the end of *Being and Time* coincides with the end of philosophy: Both undertake to question Being by way of a regress to the subject. By carrying through the regress more radically, *Being and Time* would accomplish that end to which the entire philosophical tradition was directed; it would bring philosophy to its completion.

The convergence, the appropriation, is at the same time a distancing, and indeed only because of its distancing from the tradition, its divergence, can the Heideggerian project set about to complete what it has resumed. Specifically, Heidegger's phenomenological critique of the traditional theses about Being serves to expose a certain difference between the return to the subject as executed throughout the philosophical tradition and that same return as carried out in *Being and Time*. Throughout the history of philosophy and most conspicuously in ancient thought, the return to the subject is (according to the Heideggerian critique) carried out most fundamentally as a regress to production. By production (*Herstellen*) is meant that mode of comportment in which something whose look is imagined in advance is formed, actualized. In other words, production is the activity of forming or shaping products using an image, the anticipated look of the product, its εἶδος, as the guide and standard (cf. *GP* 149ff.). Ancient ontology's regress to production has two especially decisive consequences. First of all, it serves to generate the distinction between essence and existence, to accord that distinction universality, and to grant to the distinction the status of something unquestionable, self-evident. Heidegger's intention, on the other hand, is to destroy the alleged self-evidence of the distinction and to restrict drastically its range of validity: hence the displacement which he produces by declaring in *Being and Time* that "the 'essence' of Dasein lies in its existence" (*SZ* 42). The second consequence of the ancient ontological regress to production corresponds to the position accorded to sight in the concept of production: Sight, the anticipatory sighting of the product, of its look, is no mere appendage to production but, as guiding it, belongs at the center of its structure. The consequence is, then, that in ancient ontology a privileged status is given to pure seeing, to pure intuition, and correspondingly to what is purely and simply present to such intuition. In this regard, too, Heidegger's intention is to disrupt the allegedly self-evident priority—hence the displacement which he announces in *Being and Time* at the conclusion of the analysis of understanding: "By showing how all sight is grounded primarily in understanding . . . , we have deprived pure intuition of its priority, which corresponds noetically to the priority of the present-at-hand in traditional ontology" (*SZ* 147). If one can say that in this sense Heidegger displaces the metaphysics of presence, it must also be said that he does so because its underlying regress to production serves ultimately to conceal that understanding with which the subject comports itself to Being.

To the extent, then, that Heidegger would inhibit the regress to production, he would diverge from the direction of traditional ontology. And yet, this divergence is in service to a more radical convergence with the end of philosophy, a solidarity so constituted as to make the Heideggerian project the completion of the traditional ontology that it resumes. The moment of solidarity is expressed most directly in Heidegger's reflections on Plato in *The Basic Problems of Phenomenology*. To inquire about the meaning of Being is to inquire about that upon which Being is to be projected, i.e., understood. It is to inquire beyond Being, ἐπέκεινα τῆς οὐσίας—that is, in the same way and direction by which the Platonic Socrates was led in the *Republic* to speak of the ἰδέα τοῦ ἀγαθοῦ. For Heidegger no less than for Plato, this "beyond" is the end of philosophy; it is an end which is also the beginning, "the beginning and the end of philosophy" (*GP* 402), the coincidence of τέλος and ἀρχή. And so: "We, too, with this apparently quite abstract question about the conditions of the possibility of the understanding of Being, want to do nothing but bring ourselves out of the cave into the light . . ." (*GP* 404).

And yet, there is a moment of divergence, even if ultimately subordinate. This moment is expressed in Heidegger's reflections on Hegel in *The Basic Problems of Phenomenology*, his reflections on Hegel's thought as constituting the end, the completion, of philosophy:

> In Hegel, philosophy—that is, ancient philosophy—is in a certain sense thought through to its end. . . . But there exists just as much the legitimate demand to start anew, to understand the finitude of the Hegelian system. . . . Hegel saw everything that is possible. But the question is whether he saw it from the radical center of philosophy, whether he exhausted all the possibilities of the beginning so as to say that he is at the end (*GP* 400).

Philosophy has come to completion in Hegel; and Heidegger, starting anew, would complete it again, a second time, but now from its radical center. Now it is a matter of going beyond Being to—temporality. Now it is a matter of going beyond to the subject as temporality, a matter of going beyond Being by regressing to Dasein.

The end of *Being and Time*, which one tends to regard as a goal merely projected, as something which a subject sets before itself as directive end of its deed, which as the end of philosophy would then be projected by the entire tradition—this end, these convergent ends, now proves to be anything but a mere project in that metaphysical sense that I have just outlined. Rather, the end of *Being and Time* converges with that end by which is first made possible any projection whatsoever; the end of *Being and Time* is constituted precisely in its adherence to what would be the end of all ends. Heidegger outlines this adherence by defining the basic act of the constitution of ontology as the projection of Being upon its "beyond," upon temporality (*GP* 459). This projection, this end of philosophy and of *Being and Time*, is, in turn, to be regarded as the final term of a series of projections: understanding of beings, projection upon Being, understanding of Being, projection upon time (*GP* 437). Philosophy is precisely the movement of traversing this series of projections toward its end. This end is also the beginning (ἀρχή) in the sense that it generates the entire series, that is, makes possible all the other projections; it is the source which overflows toward them. Indeed, the preontological understanding that informs Dasein's everyday comportment is simply a matter of perpetually drifting along in the flow from this source. Philosophy, on the other hand, requires that one turn against the flow and swim upstream. With one notable exception (cf. *GP* 466), all the dangers to which Heidegger shows philosophy to be exposed result from the single danger of being reversed, of being drawn back into the flow of everydayness.

The solidarity between the end of *Being and Time* and the end of philosophy is reflected in the utterly classical character of this image that I have let take shape from Heidegger's text. It simply transposes into another metaphorical system that image which remains operative in philosophy from beginning to end, whether as the Platonic image of the cave or as the Hegelian image of the inverted world.

(C)

The specific orientation of *The Basic Problems of Phenomenology* to the end of *Being and Time* is straightforwardly announced by the footnote which at the very outset identifies it as "a new elaboration of Division 3 of Part I of *Being and Time*" (*GP* 1). The lecture course is directed toward the same end as *Being and Time* and is an attempt to achieve what the text as published in 1927 failed to achieve. *The Basic Problems of Phenomenology* is an attempt to bring *Being and Time* (and hence philosophy itself) to completion. It would fill the place of the missing third division, the place of the turning (*Kehre*) from "Being and time" to "time and Being."[5] To what extent does it succeed in filling this place? And what does its attempted filling of that place, the limits of its effort to fulfill an end which (as the much later text indicates) is the place of a gathering—what does this make manifest regarding the displacement of end(s)?

In *The Basic Problems of Phenomenology* the turning is carried out. The regress to the subject, the recovery of Dasein as temporality, gives way to a new movement: the explication of Being on the basis of temporality, the movement from time to Being. This new movement, the movement of "time and Being," occurs in the analysis of praesens (*Praesenz*) which Heidegger offers in that section of the final chapter entitled "Temporality [*Temporalität*] and Being."

The analysis proceeds from a discussion of equipment along lines quite similar to those developed in *Being and Time*. The question has to do with the understanding of Being that must be ingredient in all circumspective concern with equipment. How is it that in dealing with the ready-to-hand (*das Zuhandene*) Dasein already has an understanding of Being-ready-to-hand or readiness-to-hand (*Zuhandensein, Zuhandenheit*), that is, of the way of Being of the handy? The analysis proceeds by identifying readiness-to-hand as a specific variation of a single basic phenomenon which may be designated as presence and absence (*Anwesenheit und Abwesenheit*) or in general as praesens (*Praesenz*). The problem is: How does an understanding of praesens enter into Dasein's dealing with the ready-to-hand? How does such an understanding enter in such a primordial manner that it first makes possible any such dealings?

The analysis focuses on the relation between praesens and time. First, Heidegger ascertains that praesens is not identical with the "now"; the "now" pertains to the intratemporal, to the ready-to-hand rather than to readiness-to-hand as such. Praesens is a more original phenomenon than the "now," which, according to the analysis in *Being and Time*, originates in and through the self-interpretation of primordial temporality. It is, then, at the level of primordial temporality that the connection is to be sought. Specifically, Heidegger seeks the connection in that specific ecstasis of the present that belongs to the temporality of circumspective concern, viz., *Gegenwärtigung* (making-present, enpresenting). What, then, is the connection between praesens and enpresenting (as the specific present ecstasis of circumspective concern)? Heidegger insists that they are not identical. Rather: "*Enpresenting . . . projects that which it enpresents, that which can possibly confront us in and for a present, upon something like praesens*" (*GP* 435). What is the connection? Enpresenting projects upon praesens. But what kind of projection is this? And what, more precisely, is the connection corresponding to it?

At this point in the analysis, Heidegger introduces one of the most

significant results of the analysis of primordial temporality developed in
Being and Time (cf. *SZ* §69c): To each ecstasis of primordial temporality
there belongs a "whither," a horizon, or what Heidegger, alluding to the
Kantian schematism, calls a horizonal schema. This designation of the
"beyond" belongs to the very structure of an ecstasis as a throwing/being-
thrown out beyond. Resuming this analysis, Heidegger proceeds in *The
Basic Problems of Phenomenology* to characterize praesens as such a horizonal schema:

> As the condition of possibility of the "beyond itself," the ecstasis of the
> present has within itself a *schematic predesignation* of the *where out there* this
> "beyond itself" is. That which lies beyond the ecstasis as such, due to the
> character of the ecstasis and as determined by that character, or, more
> precisely, that which determines the *whither of the "beyond itself"* as such in
> general, is *praesens as horizon*. The present [*Gegenwart*] projects itself within
> itself ecstatically upon praesens. Praesens is not identical with present, but,
> as *basic determination of the horizonal schema of this ecstasis*, it joins in constituting
> the complete time-structure of the present (*GP* 435).

This is the crux of Heidegger's analysis and represents the major contribution that the lecture course makes toward filling the place of the
missing third division of *Being and Time*. Here Heidegger focuses upon
the complex structure that is exhibited by primordial temporality even
when one restricts attention to a single ecstasis. That structure includes
not only the ecstasis proper (e.g., enpresenting) but also the horizonal
schema (e.g., praesens). Furthermore, within the temporalizing of the
ecstasis, as a central moment of that temporalizing, the ecstasis proper
projects upon the horizonal schema. Thus, within the very temporalizing
of temporality there is a primordial projecting, a kind of proto-understanding that comes to pass as, for example, a projecting of enpresenting
upon praesens: "Enpresenting is the ecstasis in the temporalizing of
temporality which understands itself as such upon praesens" (*GP* 435f.).
It is by virtue of this proto-understanding that Dasein always understands the Being of beings antecedently to its dealing with them, that, for
example, it understands readiness-to-hand (as a specific variation of praesens) antecedently to its dealings with the ready-to-hand: "As removal
to . . . , the present is a being-open for *beings confronting us*, which are
thus *understood antecedently upon praesens*" (*GP* 436). In exposing this
proto-understanding intrinsic to the very temporalizing of the ecstases of
primordial temporality, Heidegger's analysis has arrived at the understanding of Being on the basis of time: "*Accordingly, we understand Being
from the original horizonal schema of the ecstases of temporality*" (*GP* 436). In
exposing this proto-understanding, Heidegger's analysis has arrived at
an end which is also the beginning from which arises the understanding
of Being; it has reached that point which, as with the Platonic ἰδέα τοῦ

ἀγαθοῦ, is both end and beginning. To the extent that the analysis genuinely and fully reaches this point, it brings *Being and Time* and philosophy itself to their common end, their completion.

But of course Heidegger's analysis, confined to a few pages in the final sections of *The Basic Problems of Phenomenology*, does not, even by the most mundane measure, fully reach this end-point. Even the determination of readiness-to-hand remains quite incomplete, as Heidegger notes: "The primarily praesensial schema belonging to readiness-to-hand as to a specific mode of Being requires a more particular determination with regard to its praesensial content" (*GP* 439). The analysis actually goes no further than to show in general how the proto-understanding intrinsic to the temporalizing of temporality is the place in which the ontological difference is first opened up. The lecture course stops short of those other three groups of basic problems for which the way has been pre-pared through Heidegger's phenomenological critique of the traditional theses about Being. *The Basic Problems of Phenomenology* remains quite incomplete. By no means does it fill the place of the missing third division of *Being and Time*.

Its limitation is not, however, merely a matter of such incompleteness, not merely a matter of its failing to fill out through specific analyses the end-place which it exposes. There is a more radical kind of limitation, too. Heidegger indicates this limitation by referring to the series of projections: understanding of beings, projection upon Being, under-standing of Being, projection upon time. He says:

> The series . . . has its end at the horizon of the ecstatic unity of temporality. We cannot establish this here in a more primordial way; to do that we would have to go into the problem of the finitude of time (*GP* 437).

The limitation lies, then, in the fact that Heidegger's analysis in *The Basic Problems of Phenomenology* does not establish the end-place *as end*, does not exhibit it in such a way as to show that it is the end of the series of projections. That would require, says Heidegger, taking up the problem of the finitude of time—that is, showing how it is that primordial tem-porality is an enclosed end-place in contrast to the traditional representa-tion of time as an infinite sequence of now-points. Why not take up this problem? Heidegger says: "It is not possible to go into further detail here on the finitude of time, because it is connected with the difficult problem of death, and this is not the place to analyze death in that connection" (*GP* 387).

Being and Time does, however, offer such an analysis (§65). In that analysis Heidegger shows that the finitude of temporality does not refer to some stopping of time; rather, such finitude is determined by the peculiar negativity of death, that is, by the character of death as unsurpassable, as taking away all possibilities. The finitude of temporality is constituted by Dasein's Being-toward this possibility and hence lies in the ecstatical character of the future. What is of utmost decisiveness is that Heidegger expresses this ecstatical character *in terms of a closing* (*Schliessen*): "The ecstatical character of the primordial future lies precisely in the fact that the future closes one's potentiality-for-Being, that is, is itself closed . . ." (*SZ* 330). At the very core of Dasein's authentic disclosedness there is radical closure, a closing which is itself closed. At the very core of that temporalizing of temporality in which Dasein would, preeminently, open up the ontological difference, there is radical closure.

The analysis begun in *The Basic Problems of Phenomenology* could be radically extended and the end of the series of projections exhibited as end only if the closure which constitutes the finitude of temporality were shown to be already installed within that end-place in which the ontological difference has been shown to open up. But is the analysis of the finitude of time and the installation of closure to which it leads merely something missing in *The Basic Problems of Phenomenology*, merely a lack, a gap, that could be filled without affecting the massive solidarity with the history of philosophy proclaimed so openly in this text? Or would the installing of radical closure in that place beyond Being perhaps set this text moving against itself, against that solidarity it so openly proclaims? Would such installing of closure in the end of all ends perhaps set that text moving across the threshold—toward the beginning of the critique of the beginning of *Being and Time*, toward the beginning of the displacement of end(s)?

ELEVEN

Heidegger/Derrida—Presence

METAGRAM

Now, afterwards, transposing the event, textualizing it so as to indicate that it served as the point of reference for the texts that follow. The event was a symposium announced under the title "Heidegger/Derrida."[1] A text was written in advance of the event and in order to provide a certain preparation for it. That text, a program, was published some weeks before the event took place.[2] Another text was written for the event itself, a text that was then read aloud upon that occasion, an epigram replacing the program that by then had become, for essential and structural reasons, unreadable at that event.

PROGRAM

Two authors are named. Neither will be present—though one could be—at the event for which the title "Heidegger/Derrida" serves as an announcement, the event for which this text—which I, a third author, have signed in advance—is to provide a certain preparation. The concern, of course, will be, not with those two authors themselves, but with the texts that bear their signatures, with what is usually called—quite carelessly, no doubt—*their* texts. And so, in the title the names represent, i.e., substitute for and hence announce, certain texts. Or, alternatively, they represent, either directly or through the signed texts, a certain theoretical matter (*Sache*), what is usually called—quite carelessly, no doubt—the *meaning* of the texts. Recall the opening sentence of Heidegger's *Nietzsche*:

> "Nietzsche"—the name of the thinker stands as the title for *the matter* [*die Sache*] of his thinking.[3]

The substitutional (representational) function thus traces the relation of author to text and, perhaps less obtrusively, the relation to what is meant by the author in the text: author/text/meaning.

Let me focus for now on the first of these relations, on the way in

which the understanding of it has been prepared, most decisively though
not exclusively, beginning with Aristotle's *On Interpretation* (16a). What is
written (τὰ γραφόμενα) is taken to refer to (to be a symbol of: σύμβολα)
what is spoken (τὰ ἐν τῇ φωνῇ); and speech is to be understood by
reference to the subject who speaks, as an activity of the speaking subject.
An author would perhaps reduce this schema by repressing or merely
enacting speech silently; but the relation would remain fundamentally
the same, the author producing the text through his activity, expressing
in it what is already intact within himself (τὰ ἐν τῇ ψυχῇ παθήματα),
originating it so as to be entitled to authority over it. Such is, in the
merest sketch, the ordinary, i.e., traditional, conception which the texts
"of" Heidegger and Derrida serve *to bring thoroughly into question,* both in
what they say and often also in their very form of saying, both in word
and in deed. Most directly, these texts disrupt the traditional conception
by showing how it is inseparable from that metaphysics of subjectivity
whose transgression these texts would broach. Thus, in the Heideggerian text language proves irreducible to the activity of a speaker,
requiring, rather (to put it in the very briefest formula), a listening to
something said in advance of its sounding in human speech.[4] To this
extent language is withdrawn from the subject, the author dispossessed
of what he would otherwise have taken simply as *his* text. Much the same
displacement is released, though from quite a different direction, by
certain Derridean texts, for example, by the critique which *Speech and
Phenomena* brings to bear upon the Husserlian propensity to conceive
expression, meaning, signification, in reference to the τέλος of intuitive
fulfillment and thereby to compromise that very originality or ideality of
meaning which the *Logical Investigations* was set upon establishing. The
conclusion is that signification is essentially capable of functioning independently of all intuition, whether it be that of the sensibly present
object or of the self-present subject. The operation of signification, the
functioning of language, does not require the presence, even the mediated presence, of the subject; the text is unaffected by the death of the
author.[5] In this sense—though only and precisely in this sense—nothing
is to be gained by the presence of the author, not even if he were to read
his texts aloud, feigning even an originary dictation.

What is put at issue most immediately by the title is not, however, the
chain of substitutions linking author to text and to meaning but rather
the opposition between the two chains designated by the names of the
two authors. Let me focus, then, on the slash. It functions as a kind of
punctuation mark, as one of those nonphonetic elements that appear to
distinguish writing, to mark it off from speech. If I were to pronounce
the title "Heidegger/Derrida" aloud—for example, at the event for
which this text is to provide a certain preparation—if I were to use this
text as a pretext for speech, for purposes of that feigning of speech that

occurs in reading, then it would be necessary to insert the mark in speech by some kind of artifice, for example, by a gesture that would trace it or by the substitution of a word such as "slash," which would then be functioning in a way quite different from its straightforward semantic function. In living speech, present to its self-present author, this mark, this trace of writing, cannot be simply *presented*; it remains outside that speech, thus requiring therein its representative, its substitutive gesture or word. And so, the very way in which this mark functions mirrors what will prove to be at issue between those two authorial chains between which the mark is drawn: the issue is presence, or, more precisely, withdrawal of, withdrawal from, presence.

Ordinarily this mark—which I have already begun calling by substitution a "slash," translating this artifice back into the written text—is taken as marking some kind of opposition. And yet, a primary strategy of the Heideggerian and Derridean texts is precisely to deconstruct binary opposition. Thus, Heidegger's *Nietzsche* proposes, in view of such founding oppositions as intelligible/sensible, an inversion of "Platonism" in which philosophical thinking would also twist free of it[6]—what the Derridean text will designate as the two operations of reversal and displacement. It is a matter of opposites that can be neither reduced to unity nor stabilized hierarchically nor dialectically sublated into a third term. Under the title *Dissemination* it is a matter especially of displacing the three of ontotheology, of destroying the trinitarian horizon, of adding a fourth, self-effacing term which, like *différance*, displaces synthesis, opening the triangle on a fourth side, reinscribing it as an open square.[7]

And so, it is here a matter of preparing such an opening from the opposition of the two authorial chains, in this way preparing for that event to which this text—which I, a third author, have signed in advance—is directed. Or, rather, it is a matter of relinquishing this point, this apex, and of beginning to write a fourth text, feigning a preface.[8] It goes without saying that here it can be a matter *only* of beginning, of merely locating the site for a deconstructive geometry.

"Everything starts with the dyad,"[9] and so in order to begin, it is necessary to return to the opposition Heidegger/Derrida. And yet—remaining for now within the classical conceptuality, e.g., of German Idealism—opposition is never simply such, never opposition as such; even if absolute in form, opposition is never absolute in content but presupposes a conditioning position. The opposition of opposites presupposes a common position, the slash conjoining before it can separate. It is from that position that one must begin.

Let us begin, then, from the positing of metaphysics as at its end, its limit, the delimitation of metaphysics in its closure, a positing of it for destruction (*Destruktion*) or—reproducing orthographically the necessary bond of the operation *with* metaphysics—the deconstruction of

metaphysics. This positing is governed by a certain exposure of metaphysics, an exposure of a positing common to metaphysics throughout
its history and warranting to this degree the phrase "metaphysics as
such." What is common to metaphysics is the positing of Being (*Sein*) as
presence, its self-positing as metaphysics *of presence*.

Hence, it is imperative to understand what "presence" means, to
understand how the meaning of presence is such that metaphysics of
presence is posed for delimitation, deconstruction. It is with the question
of the meaning of presence that one can begin to construct the deconstructive square.

In *Being and Time* presence means predominantly, though not exclusively, *Vorhandenheit* (presence-at-hand, in the usual translation). This is
to be understood in its correlation with pure seeing, with νοεῖν,[10] with
intuition (*Anschauung*): When something gives itself to one's sheer gaze,
when it is simply there for one's looking, displaying itself before and for
apprehension, then it has the character of being present-at-hand. Such a
character is to be contrasted with that of things with which one deals
concernfully, when one manipulates things and puts them to use. The
contrast between *Vorhandenheit* and *Zuhandenheit* (readiness-to-hand, in
the usual translation) is well known, and the relevant analyses offered by
Being and Time need not be repeated or even summarized here. What
does, however, need to be stressed is the rigorous order that the phenomenological analyses of *Being and Time* (I, 3) establish with respect to
these two modes: Presence-at-hand is founded on readiness-to-hand,
and things come to show themselves as present-at-hand only when certain structures of readiness-to-hand get covered over or repressed. One
could say, then, that in the strict sense everything is ready-to-hand; or,
alternatively, that there is nothing purely present-at-hand. In what one
might take as present-at-hand—e.g., the hammer merely stared at—
there is always something else operative yet repressed, a concealed
operation of readiness-to-hand, a disregarded instrumentality. What is
decisive is the displacement of presence that this analysis produces.
There are no simply, sheerly present things; for everything is openly or
concealedly ready-to-hand, and what is ready-to-hand—the hammer
when one takes hold of it and uses it—is not sheerly present as a self-
contained positivity. Rather, it is extended beyond itself into the referential totality by which it is determined, its presence limited and yet rendered possible by its insertion in that totality. But the totality is one of
signifying references; it is *Bedeutsamkeit*, the operation of signification.[11]
There is no pure presence, for in whatever presents itself there is already
in play the operation of signification. Presence is delimited—limited and
yet rendered possible—by the operation of signification.

The Derridean text, too, is addressed to a delimitation of presence, of
that sheer perceptual presence that would be correlative to the stratum

of preexpressive experience that Husserlian phenomenology would rigorously separate from the operation of signification. It is on the most elementary level that *Speech and Phenomena* is focused: simple sensory presence (e.g., of a tone) in the living present. That is, it is a matter of deconstructing the phenomenology of internal time-consciousness, bringing fully into play the Husserlian analyses of retention and protention in precisely such a way as to show how that phenomenological text works against itself, withdrawing that very self-identical present, the living present, that, on the other hand, it would preserve as the non-displaceable center, the living core, of time. Both the Husserlian and the Derridean analyses are well known and need not be repeated here. It is in a sense only a matter of stress, of stressing that the connection of the present to the immediate past and future is an essential, i.e., constitutive, connection. It is not as though there is first a present "now" which then comes to be connected to past and future; rather, these connections belong to its very constitution as a present "now"—which is to say that there can be no simple self-identical present. The peculiar complexity of the "now" is elaborated in *Speech and Phenomena* by means of the concept of repetition. The point is that the "now" essentially involves a possibility, structure, or movement of repetition in two senses. First, the present "now" includes repetition of the previous "now," namely, in retention. In other words, the present "now" must be constituted in such a way that it is possible for the past "now" to be repeated in it; its constitution must be such as to include such possibility of repetition. Secondly, the present "now," the *form* of presence, is itself ideal and hence infinitely repeatable, its return ad infinitum being "inscribed in presence itself."[12] Thus, the present "now" essentially involves the possibility, structure, movement of repetition both *of previous "nows"* in itself and *of itself* as the ideal form of presence.

This figure of repetition may be called the *trace*. It is , as it were, the figure into which the phenomenological figure of closed-off presence gets deconstructed:

> Such a trace is—if we can employ this language without immediately contradicting it or crossing it out as we proceed—more "primordial" than what is phenomenologically primordial.

Or again:

> In all these directions, the presence of the present is thought of as arising from the bending back of a return [*du pli du retour*], from the movement of repetition, and not the reverse.[13]

This operation of the trace, this bending back of a return by which the presence of the present is constituted—to employ still, under erasure, the language of phenomenology—also is called *différance*. Or, it may be called the operation of signification, taking the latter in the most deconstructively (not phenomenologically) primordial way. As in the Heideggerian text, presence is delimited—limited and yet rendered possible—by the operation of signification. The latter is not a matter of presence, not even necessarily of presence to or of an origin, a speaker; like writing, its function is independent of the absence, even the death, of the author. Or, rather, this operation of signification is writing in that form in which it emerges from the application of the double operation of reversal and displacement to the metaphysical opposition speech/writing. As *archi-écriture* it is "at work at the origin of sense," delimiting presence.[14]

In conclusion, three issues:

(1) Though in *Being and Time* presence means predominantly *Vorhandenheit*, this is not the only meaning of presence in play. In fact, an entire chain of meanings is introduced at the outset (§6), only to be provisionally abandoned in the published portion of the text. But beginning with the 1927 lecture course *The Basic Problems of Phenomenology* and still more openly in later texts, a system of meanings of presence is developed along various, not easily reconcilable directions. A note in the Derridean text that is itself characterized as a note on a note from *Being and Time* calls attention to this issue, this problem of translation:

> The following pages may be read as timid prolegomena to a problem of translation. But who better than Heidegger has taught us to think what is involved in such a problem? Here, the question would be the following: how to transfer into, or rather what transpires when we transfer into the single Latin word *presence* the entire differentiated *system* of Greek and German words, the entire *system of translation* in which Heideggerian language (*ousia, parousia, Gegenwärtigkeit, Anwesen, Anwesenheit, Vorhandenheit*, etc.) is produced? . . . Above all, how to transfer into the single word *presence*, both too rich and too poor, the *history* of the Heideggerian text which associates or disjoins these concepts in subtle and regular fashion throughout an itinerary that covers more than forty years?[15]

(2) On the other hand, the question is whether the Heideggerian text, moving in the system of translations of presence, succeeds in delimiting presence as such:

> The Heideggerian de-limitation consists sometimes in appealing to a less narrow determination of presence from a more narrow determination of it, thereby going back from the present toward a more original thought of Being as presence (*Anwesenheit*), and sometimes in questioning this original determination itself, and giving us to think it as a closure, as *the* Greco-Western-philosophical closure. . . . In the first case the displacements would remain within the metaphysics of presence in general.[16]

Does this first case really "occupy *almost* the entirety of Heidegger's text"? Or, on the contrary, is there perhaps always in play in the Heideggerian text that directedness, announced in the 1927 lecture course,[17] the directedness ἐπέκεινα τῆς οὐσίας, beyond to an order that is not a matter of Being, of presence, beyond to the meaning, the truth, the clearing of Being, beyond to that which delimits Being as presence?

(3) Finally, it is necessary to disrupt a web of assumptions that I have left undisturbed hitherto, most pointedly the assumption that in asking about the meaning of presence one is asking simply for one or several positive senses. It is necessary to disrupt this assumption of straightforwardness, because meaning "has never been conceivable, within the history of metaphysics, otherwise than on the basis of presence and as presence"[18]—as, to take the exceptionally revealing Husserlian case, presence to eidetic intuition. To ask straightforwardly about the meaning of presence is already to assume what presence means, to assume it in the very question of meaning.

But then, is not the Heideggerian question itself caught in this web of assumptions and as a result held firmly within the closure of metaphysics? If the question of Being is determined as a question of meaning, as the question of the meaning of Being, then is it not in its very formulation a question of presence, a question directed toward a recovery of presence? Indeed this would be so, *were it not the case that* the Heideggerian text, from *Being and Time* on, engages ceaselessly in a deconstructive reduction, a delimitation, of meaning, its reduction to the *Woraufhin des Entwurfs,*[19] its referral to world, i.e., signification, and eventually to ἀλήθεια. Meaning as presence becomes, is reduced to, the meaning of presence, the latter taken, not straightforwardly, but as that which delimits presence. The Heideggerian text, thus releasing the torsion in the question of the meaning of presence, twists it free of metaphysical closure.

Is it not in this way, through such distortion, that the Heideggerian text could be twisted together with the Derridean text, the authorial chains intertwined in a new contortion which, broaching the delimitation of what one would like to call presence *as such,* would form the site of the opposition Heidegger/Derrida? Or, rather, would not such a figure trace out the space within which one could inscribe an open square in place of the opposition Heidegger/Derrida?

EPIGRAM

We are present here today for a discussion of certain texts. Among the texts of which we are to speak, some were written for this event, written in advance and in order to provide a certain preparation for it. Some of these texts have been published already, including the one bearing my signature.

Suppose I were now to read that text here at this event, for which it would, then, have provided a certain preparation, or, rather, a kind of introduction. Suppose I were to read the text aloud, feigning even an originary dictation, pretending almost that that text had not been written in advance, much less published, but was being spoken for the first time. In fact, I have in a sense just read from it, or, rather—let me say in order to mark the very distance at issue here—I have just cited that text, quoted from it, quoted the words (which now I quote a second time) "feigning even an originary dictation." And yet, the problem is that I cannot really feign in living speech this text that was written in preparation for the present event. The difficulty stems, on the one hand, from its peculiar temporality, its way of stationing itself as a present in relation to which this event lies in the future, the event which is now present so that the text is decisively past, not only written in the past but written as a text that will have become past. There is also another difficulty, one to which the text refers in anticipating the event in which it might be taken as a pretext for speech, the difficulty that the title of the text, indeed the title of this event itself, cannot be spoken except by recourse to some kind of artifice, inserting into speech, for example, certain gestures or the names of punctuation marks.

Let me, then, forego feigning an orginary dictation and grant the present divergence from the text published prior to this event in preparation for it. Now in speaking it is a matter of taking up—from a distance that precludes sheer coincidence—the text that was written previously. But which text is that? Is it the text as printed and distributed prior to this event? Is that the text that I have written? Is that the text that could be called—even if a bit carelessly—*my* text? Certainly it is not the only one, that is, here too, in the identity of the written text, there is divergence; or, rather—let me say in order to stress at least the multiplicity—there is dispersion of the written text. And not just in the sense of multiple copies of (as we say) the *same* printed text, a multiplicity that one would immediately render ineffective by positing the ideality of the text. Rather, a multiplicity that would range from the printed text across various proofs, typescripts, etc. to the handwritten text. Which of these is the text? Which of these is *my* text? Or does it make any difference? Is this dispersion, this virtual dissemination, at all effective when I, the author of the text, take up the text? Does it affect the character of such authorial practice and the structure therefore of such an event as we are engaged in here today?

Let me turn to a recently published text by Heidegger, the text of his lecture course of 1942–43 entitled *Parmenides*. At a point in this text where Heidegger takes up some verses from Pindar, he addresses the issue of practice, i.e., πρᾶξις—or, more precisely, πρᾶγμα, which he translates as *Handlung* in a sense that is prior to the division between things and practices exercised upon those things. The translation is meant to enforce an essential connection, that of practice, πρᾶξις, πρᾶγμα, with the *hand*. One acts by means of the hand, says Heidegger's text, to such an extent that

> the hand is, along with the word, the essential mark of man. Only a being which, like man, "has" words (μῦθος) (λόγος) also can and must "have" hands.[20]

Heidegger's text thus marks out a second, even more remarkable connection: between hand and language. Language empowers man's possession of hands; no animal, says Heidegger's text, has a hand. But also, because man is τὸ ζῷον λόγον ἔχον, he not only can but also, Heidegger says, *must* have hands. It is this necessity that is most remarkable; and though I cannot here even begin to expose the immense range of the metaphysical oppositions that are profoundly disturbed by it, some gauge can be given by a single immediate reference, namely, to the disturbance of the opposition between the logical (or, to risk the translation, the rational) and the manual. And yet, what is the character of the connection such that it is one of necessity? How is it that word and deed are necessarily conjoined? How is the necessity generated?

A decisive indication is given by Heidegger's characterization of the word "as the essential domain [*Wesensbereich*] of the hand."[21] The sense is that the word provides, grants, sustains, that space, that open expanse, within which the hand can be operative in its appropriate way. What is its appropriate operation? What does the hand do, and what kind of space does it require? Most of all, it deals with surrounding things, takes hold of them and uses them—in short, handles them. More precisely, citing now Heidegger's text, it handles things "insofar as they come to presence as present-at-hand and ready-to-hand in the domain of the 'hand.' "[22] In short, the hand handles what is present-at-hand and ready-to-hand in the domain of the hand.

But what is this domain? It is precisely that which, in one or another respect, is named by all the existentials of *Being and Time*. It is that which is most directly analyzed under the titles: *Da* of Dasein, Being-in-the-world, disclosedness (*Erschlossenheit*), clearing (*Lichtung*), ἀλήθεια. In the very briefest formula, it is that open expanse in which things present themselves and out into which Dasein is extended, standing out (eksisting) in such a way that it can handle things as they come and go. Coming from under cover, coming to be uncovered and returning whence they came, engaged, then, in the round of becoming unconcealed and concealed, the round of presence, within a domain that can, then, be called that of unconcealment and concealment (*Entbergung-Verbergung*). It is only a matter of stressing now, in the 1942–43 lecture course, that this domain is the domain of the hand, that, in Heidegger's formula, "the hand is as hand only where there is unconcealment and concealment." Or, more extensively:

> There is a "hand" only where beings as such appear unconcealedly and man comports himself unconcealingly to beings. The hand, like the word, secures the bearing [*Bezug*] of Being to man and thereby the relation [*Verhältnis*] of man to beings.[23]

Because both word and hand, even if in different ways, secure this domain, both may be said to belong to the essence of man—essence, not as pure or originary presence, but rather as indicated by the formula that identifies the truth of essence as the essence of truth, i.e., as ἀλήθεια. Thus Heidegger's text refers to the essential belonging-together of hand and word (*die Wesenszusammengehörigkeit der Hand mit dem Wort*). This belonging-together comes to a certain fruition, reveals itself concretely, when the peculiar *zeigen/zeichnen* of the hand coalesces with that of the word, when the manual complex of pointing-showing-drawing-signing draws in the word, installing its showing in a sign. This occurs in and as *writing*. Hence: "Writing [*Schrift*] is in its essential origin handwriting [*Handschrift*]."[24] The withdrawal of writing from the hand is therefore, Heidegger concludes, nothing less than momentous.

It is perhaps, then, a bit less easy simply to dismiss the dispersion in the identity of the written text, passing over the difference between, for instance, the printed text and the handwritten text. Does this difference, then, make a difference? In a certain sense, perhaps not. That is, insofar as the sense of the text, what it means, becomes the sole focus, that meaning posited in its ideality would seem effectively to cancel the dispersion of the written text. But suppose that the situation is such that the focus is not exclusively on a complex of meaning transcending the text; suppose that a certain divergence supersedes upon the situation, as when an author takes up a previously written text, takes it up even, perhaps, first of all, in the most literal sense, with his hand. Then there is, perhaps, a difference not immediately cancelled by the reference to ideality.[25] For what the printed text then bespeaks, especially at the very moment when one takes it up manually, is nothing less than the withdrawal of writing from the hand. One could perhaps begin to analyze this authorial situation by referring to the trace of the hand in the text, the trace that would be borne by the handwritten text but canceled on the way to publication. And one might, furthermore, reflect this dispersion back upon the author himself, distinguishing, then, from the various deficient modes the operation of one who finds the trace of his hand in the text that he takes up. There would be a dispersion of the authorial I corresponding to that of the written text.

This manual dispersion, as one might call it, is not the only kind which an authorial I undergoes. Even within the text, without the author's externally taking it up, within, for example, the text that I have written in preparation for the present event in which I am to take it up, there is dispersion, various scatterings, of the authorial I. Let me mention only the most obtrusive. The I speaking in that text speaks sometimes in its own name, as a third author, but at other times, when quoting, paraphrasing, summarizing, in the name of one of the other two authors, that is, in such a way that almost no incoherence would arise were Heidegger's signature or Derrida's, as the case may be, to be attached to the relevant portion of the text. Also, the I speaking in its own name in the text comes at certain points to speak its own name, introducing a reflexivity, as when, almost at the beginning, there is reference—and here I take up, quote my text—to "this text—which I, a third author, have signed in advance."

Of course, one might still undertake to reduce these differences, to cancel the dispersion, by positing a subjective ideality under which all could be regathered. One might recall that move that has virtually governed all of modern philosophy and insist that the I—whether specifically authorial or not—is precisely that which remains in all these connections one and the same. And yet, one could call upon this leap to self-identity only at the cost of passing over the very questionableness that the Heideggerian and Derridean texts have recovered from the metaphysical theory of the I as self-identity posited in and through self-presence. In short, since Nietzsche exposed, i.e., dispelled, the lightning that grammar had kept positing behind the flash,[26] the I has proved ever less capable of securing itself against all that would draw it forth and withdraw its self-presence, for example, the words it must speak and the hands it must use.

In this regard one can begin to understand why the hand, linked to the present-at-hand and ready-to-hand, is in a sense privileged by Heidegger. It is preeminently in handling things that one is drawn forth into an exteriority that is irreducible to self-presence. The I, using its hands, the manual I, if you will, is never simply mirrored back to itself from an object present to it, for nothing is ever simply present, everything being (in the strict sense) to-hand, ready-to-hand, which is to say—here I take up my text again—"extended beyond itself into the referential totality by which it is determined, its presence limited and yet rendered possible by its insertion in that totality." In this withdrawal of presence, the I is drawn along, extended. The analytic of Dasein becomes, then, an analytic of extendedness as such, of that dispersive stretching-out that in its full structure coincides with primordial temporality.

Here I have wanted, then, to indicate—though ever so briefly and all too abstractly—something of what I take to be the more radical dimension broached in Heidegger's texts, the dimension which, it seems to me, it is especially Derrida's virtue to have recognized and taken up, in contrast to other developments stemming from Heidegger. To be more precise, it is a matter of a dimension that one would want to designate as radical, were it not precisely such as to call into question the very value of the *radix* that such a designation would assume.

But let me be outspoken here today about one issue that I took up in my text written in preparation for this event. It is the issue of that entire text and also of all that I have been saying here today, but focused on the question of the closure of the Heideggerian project. The question is whether that project in its initial orientation toward the *meaning* of Being does not continue to be governed by the very metaphysical privilege that it would put in question, the privilege of presence. The point is that such closure might be operative were it not that *Being and Time* carries out a decisive opening toward another determination of meaning. In the question of the meaning of Being, it is not only a matter of displacing meaning from presence but also in a sense a matter of redetermining the meaning of Being precisely as that displacement. This is why—if I may put it all too cryptically—the meaning of Being is time.

But "time" is only a first name, and in the lecture course of 1942–43 Heidegger says openly that "time" is the first name (*der Vorname*) for ἀλήθεια.[27] Ἀλήθεια, even more obtrusively, is not synonymous with presence, and the Heideggerian transgression can virtually never be read as a matter of appealing to a less narrow determination of presence from a more narrow determination of it. One might, then, want to maintain certain reservations when Derrida, whom I have just requoted, feigns to capture the Heideggerian move in such a trap. And yet, it is precisely by his having feigned to mark such limits, by his having attempted, as he once said, "to locate in Heidegger's text . . . the signs of a belonging to metaphysics,"[28] that we here today can—if we are equal to it—come a bit nearer sustaining what, for want of a proper word, I shall call—writing under erasure—a radical reading of Heidegger.

But let me be still more outspoken. Ἀλήθεια is not a determination of presence but its delimitation. One could say—and every such formulation is by the very nature of the case open to objection—that ἀλήθεια is what not only makes possible but also limits presence. It is the limit, perhaps, that needs now to be stressed, that is, it would seem, already stressed when in the Heideggerian analysis of truth everything turns on the transition to untruth—literally, as confirmed by that marginal note in Heidegger's copy of *On the Essence of Truth* which locates precisely in that transition "the leap into the . . . turning [*der Sprung in die . . . Kehre*]."[29] The same stress occurs in the 1942–43 lecture course where the discussion that begins with the goddess ἀλήθεια (from Parmenides, Fr. 1) makes its final return only after the long detour through the Platonic underworld of λήθη. One of the things that comes to light on that shadowy way is that λήθη (Heidegger translates: *Vergessenheit, Vergessung*) does not relate only to the past, that ἀλήθεια—to this extent, at least—does not, then, bespeak a nostalgia for a lost age of presence.

But it does bespeak withdrawal of the originary, not of an original that would be pure presence but rather of the word that would grant the domain of the hand. This is why indeed I cannot but have been feigning all along an originary dictation, repeating always at a distance, repeating in a sense that is decisively not temporal except insofar as time is the first name of ἀλήθεια. To repeat in this way is to submit to the withdrawal that, drawing one along, draws one into dispersion, scattering the authorial I.

And you will, of course, have noticed that all along I have been reading from a written text, another one, different from the text published in advance of this event. A further dispersion, of course. But also perhaps something of an enactment at a distance, allowing me finally to say that in both word and deed I have been all along—and I quote now for the last time—"feigning even an originary dictation."

TWELVE

Reason and Ek-sistence

I would have spoken of the crisis of reason if there were such a Heideggerian discourse. That there is no such discourse may be presumed to stem from the peculiar circumstance that such a discourse, one organized by the concept of crisis, would fall within that very state that one would be seeking to expose and analyze as crisis and somehow to overcome. How could one ever thematize, much less resolve, a crisis of reason by simply appealing to reason and to concepts built upon that of reason, concepts such as that of crisis?

On the other hand, the depth of what one might otherwise call the crisis of reason is repeatedly invoked in Heidegger's texts. For example, in certain of the polemics in the *Letter on Humanism*, Heidegger charges that precisely those who conduct a certain defense of logic, who oppose thus the degradation of reason, turn out to be ruled by irrationalism, by a denial of *ratio*.[1] Defense of reason becomes its denial—that is, the very opposition rational/irrational is disrupted. Is this not tantamount to what one would like to call a *crisis* of reason?

Let me, then, call it that—translating the word, however, back into Greek, so as to divert it away from that metaphysical concept of reason on which it is otherwise built, or at least back toward the origin of that concept. Let me, then, call it: κρίσις, from κρίνειν, meaning to separate, divide, put apart, hence literally to decide and so to judge, as in the case of a contest. So, it is a matter of the *separation* of reason—on which there is, in fact, a Heideggerian discourse, a strand in the fabric of the *Letter on Humanism*. This discourse not only analyzes the crisis of reason as separation but also lays out a way by which that crisis would be resolved, a way by which the separation of reason would be overcome, reason's condition of separation surpassed, exceeded, and reason thus gathered. As gathered, reason is called ek-sistence, and it is to ek-sistence that thinking must become accordant if it is to enter into a *Verwindung der Metaphysik*.

My concern is, then, to take up this Heideggerian discourse in such a manner as to retrace the way from reason to ek-sistence, the way of the gathering of reason. And yet, the discourse on the separation and gathering of reason is only a strand to be disentangled from a much richer discourse. The characterization of its way as stretching from reason to ek-sistence is therefore incomplete, provisional. Two respects in which this formulation is provisional need to be marked at the very outset.

First of all, the formulation suggests a kind of sequencing that ought not to be merely presumed. Specifically, the formulation suggests that it is a matter of first exposing the crisis and of then responding to it in a way aimed at overcoming it; that is, the sequence would be, first, to get it in view *and then* to set about doing something about it. The problem is that such a sequencing would reproduce, within what one might want to call theoretical activity, one of those types of separation at issue in the crisis of reason, namely, the separation between theoretical and practical. In other words, such a sequencing would remain within that very crisis that it would be aimed at overcoming. It is imperative, therefore, to suspend all such sequencing, leaving in abeyance the question of how the two moments are interrelated, that is, of how the exposure of the separation of reason belongs together with the gathering of reason by which that separation would be overcome. In this connection one could refer to those lines from Hölderlin that are cited by Heidegger at certain critical junctures:

> But where danger is, grows
> The saving power also.[2]

It is for this intertwining that the space must be left open.

Something else, too, is to be left in abeyance, a certain reflexivity. For that strand of the discourse of the *Letter on Humanism,* tracing the way of gathering, is itself in some sense an operation of that very regathered reason to which that way leads. Indeed, Heidegger explicitly calls attention to such reflexivity near the end of the *Letter on Humanism*: "But just now an example of the inconspicuous deed of thinking manifested itself" (*HB* 362).

With these two provisions, let me now venture to outline four stretches on the way from reason to ek-sistence.

The first is that of the determination of reason, its metaphysical determination. But caution is required from the outset, caution against taking for granted a certain linearity, another sequencing. For it is not as though metaphysics is first constituted as such and then brought to bear upon reason so as to produce a metaphysical determination of reason. On the contrary, the very determination of metaphysics occurs in and through the determination of reason; that is, the beginning of metaphysics, its delimitation, coincides with the delimitation of reason.

Let me focus on two determinations. The first determines reason as θεωρία. In this determination what is decisive is the relation to ποίησις in the sense of τέχνη, i.e., to production (*Herstellen*). What is the relation of reason to production? What is production? Heidegger's analysis of production—more precisely, his account of the Greek analysis—is already intact in his Marburg lectures, for example, in *The Basic Problems of Phenomenology*:

> Whatever is shaped [*Das Geprägte*] is, as we can also say, something formed [*ein Gebilde*]. The potter forms a vase out of clay. All forming [*Bilden*] of things formed [*Gebilden*] is effected by using an image [*Bild*], in the sense of a model [*Vorbild*], as guide and standard. The thing is produced by looking to the anticipated look of what is to be produced by forming, shaping. It is this anticipated look of the thing, sighted beforehand, that the Greeks mean ontologically by εἶδος, ἰδέα.[3]

The point is that in making something one looks to a model, one envisions the look (εἶδος) of what is to be produced; this vision is, then, what governs the entire process of production; it is what constitutes, as it were, the center of the structure of production. Θεωρία is, then, determined as precisely such a vision carried out, however, independently of production. The determination of reason as θεωρία thus determines it as pure vision of the sheer look of something, envisagement of the εἶδος.

This is the connection in which to read Heidegger's discussion of θεωρία at the beginning of the *Letter on Humanism*. There Heidegger refers to "the technical interpretation of thinking," i.e., the interpretation of it as in service to τέχνη, or, more generally, to πρᾶξις and ποίησις. According to this ancient interpretation, thinking taken for itself is *not practical*—that is, it is determined by a lack and thus exposed to a certain demand that its lack be overcome. Hence, the characterization of thinking as θεωρία "is a reactive attempt to rescue thinking and preserve its autonomy over against acting and doing" (*HB* 314).

The second determination is more openly linked to the beginning of metaphysics. Here the pure envisagement of the εἶδος comes to be determined as a vision of the Being of beings. The envisagement of the εἶδος becomes thus a holding of Being in view in such a way that beings are represented in their Being, referred back to it, set back upon it as ground. But such representing of beings in their Being is what constitutes metaphysics as such.

Such is, then, the first stretch on the way, a kind of starting point, recalling the determination of reason as theoretical representation, the beginning of metaphysics as such.

Let me now, secondly, extend this determination toward a separation of reason, specifically outlining the separation of reason from what Heidegger calls its element. To this end, observe, then, that in the determination of metaphysics, i.e., of reason as theoretical representation, there is operative a decisive limit. The limit serves to delimit metaphysics, to open up and demarcate its proper space; and yet, at the same time, it serves to close metaphysics off from whatever might fall beyond that limit. Heidegger's introduction of the determination of metaphysics, i.e., of reason, as representation is followed immediately by an identification of this limit:

Metaphysics does indeed represent beings in their Being and so thinks the Being of beings. But it does not think Being as such, does not think the difference of both. Metaphysics does not ask about the truth of Being itself (*HB* 322).[4]

Another passage clarifies the matter further:

But when thinking represents beings as beings, it no doubt relates itself to Being. In truth, however, it always thinks only of beings as such; precisely not, and never, Being as such. The "question of Being" always remains a question about beings (*HB* 331).

One could say that metaphysics, i.e., reason, circles between Being and beings. In that circling a limit is operative, a limit that Heidegger's text outlines in several different ways. The limit consists, first of all, in the failure of metaphysics to think the difference between Being and beings—that is, its failure to think the very space in which it would circle. Thus, second, it never genuinely thinks Being as such but only beings as such. Failing to think the difference, it cannot but turn Being into a being, for instance, into God or some cosmic ground. Its circling is thus even less extensive than would be presumed: Because its movement from beings toward Being would involve at the same time a turning of Being into a being, it would be always already caught up in a circling back toward beings and would never stretch even so far as Being. And so, third, the limit of metaphysics consists in its failure to ask about the truth of Being itself. Instead of asking about Being itself, it turns Being into a being.

It is in this connection that Heidegger's text enacts the following counter-turn, asking about and reserving Being itself:

Yet Being—what is Being? It "is" It itself. The thinking that is to come must learn to experience that and to say it. "Being"—that is not God and not a cosmic ground (*HB* 331).

And yet, it is not simply Being itself that goes unquestioned but the *truth* of Being, i.e., the space in which the difference opens, the openness that must always already give way (in both senses) to the opening of difference, the clearing (*Lichtung*) into which illumination can stream, lighting up beings in their Being, allowing beings and their Being to shine in such a way as to show themselves.

The limit of metaphysics, of reason, is its failure to extend to the truth of Being and consequently even to Being itself in its difference from beings. And yet, though confined to circling between beings and Being (turned, in turn, into a being), reason moves nevertheless within the orbit of the opening, of the truth of Being, taking it—quite literally—for granted, even though the very determination of reason is such as to render that dimension inaccessible as such, beyond the limit of reason. It is thus that Heidegger writes:

> The truth of Being as the clearing itself remains concealed for metaphysics. However, this concealment is not a defect of metaphysics but a treasure withheld from it yet held before it, the treasure of its own proper wealth (*HB* 331f.).

And it is in this sense that reason is separated from its element, fallen out of it, fallen into crisis, set homelessly wandering—separation, fallenness, crisis, homelessness belonging to reason in its very constitution, belonging to the very constitution of metaphysics.

Overcoming the separation of reason, resolving the crisis of reason, would require, then, that the limit be exceeded, that reason be stretched beyond the circle, extending into the clearing, being gathered to its element. But to exceed the limit in the direction of the truth of Being would be to exceed reason itself, since the limit is generated by the very determination of reason. It would be a matter of surpassing reason as pure envisagement of the Being of beings, of extending it beyond Being. And it would be a matter—though only and precisely in this sense—of a destruction, or, if you will, a deconstruction, of reason. Stretched beyond Being, reason would no longer be reason. Thus extended, Heidegger calls it: *ek-sistence*.

In this stretch of the way, the primary task is to think the "beyond" of Being. More precisely, what is required is a thinking that would accord with ek-sistence in such a way as to let become manifest the "beyond" into which ek-sistence stands out, "the dimension of the ecstasis of ek-sistence" (*HB* 334). This is the dimension toward which the formulation of the question in *Being and Time* was already oriented, its formulation as the question of the *meaning* of Being, of the horizon from which, within which, Being can be, and indeed always already is, disclosed. *Being and Time* was to have shown that the meaning of Being is time, not *Zeitlichkeit*, which as ecstasis is the way of thinking what comes to be called ek-sistence, but rather *Temporalität*, the time of Being. It is again the meaning of Being, its "beyond," that Heidegger undertakes to think after *Being and Time* as the truth of Being. Thus, in the *Letter on Humanism* ek-sistence is characterized as "an ecstatic inherence [*Innestehen*] in the truth of Being" (*HB* 325), as "standing out into the truth of Being" (*HB* 326), or, alternatively, as "standing in the clearing of Being" (*HB* 323). Or, again, referring back to *Being and Time,* Heidegger identifies what was there called world with the dimension that the *Letter on Humanism* calls more often the truth of Being:

> "World" is the clearing of Being into which man stands out on the basis of his thrown essence. "Being-in-the-world" designates the essence of ek-sistence with regard to the cleared dimension out of which the "ek-" of ek-sistence essentially unfolds (*HB* 350).

It is, then, a matter of extending reason into that "beyond" of Being that is variously called world, truth, clearing—that is, of thinking it ecstatically, as being-outside-itself, as being what it is only *from* that "beyond"—that is, as the being whose essence is ek-sistence.

Such is, then, the second stretch on the way from reason to ek-sistence, a stretch which in a sense runs the entire way, a stretching of the ecstatic way beyond Being.

The third stretch on the way does not extend farther but rather cuts across a certain division that has marked reason from the beginning, its separation into theoretical and practical. This separation is linked to the so-called technical interpretation of thinking: Thinking is taken primarily to be in service to ποίησις and πρᾶξις, interpreted as *practical* reason in a broad sense. Theoretical reason, pure θεωρία, is then posed over against technical-practical reason, and an attempt made to shore it up in its autonomy over against the practical. And yet, in a sense it is never really autonomous but rather from the outset is too exclusively determined by opposition to the practical, i.e., all too determined as the mere negative of the practical. Theoretical reason is from its inception threatened by crisis (in every sense).

But the plight of reason is not simply the outcome of a misconception of the theoretical, of a conceiving of it as too dependent negatively on the practical. Rather, this very opposition, the separation installed classically between theoretical and practical, was, according to Heidegger's analysis, built upon an insufficient determination of the practical. The practical, i.e., the essence of action (*das Wesen des Handelns*), has not been pondered decisively enough, either in the beginning of metaphysics or still today. Action has been regarded only as causing an effect (*als das Bewirken einer Wirkung*), not as essentially accomplishment (*Vollbringen*) in the sense of unfolding something into the fullness of its essence (*HB* 313). It is only thus that the separation was and remained installed.

What happens to this separation when reason comes to be regathered to its element? Is a thinking that extends beyond (to) Being to be called theoretical? Or practical?

> The answer is that such thinking is neither theoretical nor practical. It comes to pass [*ereignet sich*] before this distinction (*HB* 358).

Extended beyond (to) Being, thinking at the same time stretches back to a point anterior to the separation of reason into theoretical and practical, thus exceeds that opposition, displacing what has already been inverted, deconstructing it. Heidegger elaborates:

> But now in what relation does the thinking of Being stand to theoretical and practical behavior? It exceeds all viewing [*Betrachten*], because it cares for the light in which a seeing as theoria can first sustain itself and move. Thinking attends to the clearing of Being in that it puts its saying of Being into language as the home of eksistence. Thus thinking is a deed [*ein Tun*]. But a deed that also exceeds all praxis. Thinking towers above action and production [*Handeln und Herstellen*] . . . (*HB* 361).

Regathered to its element, thinking is anterior to theoria. It is not a mere seeing, not even of Being, but rather an attending to the very opening, the space, in which lighting and seeing can take place. As such it is also anterior to praxis as classically determined—anterior, first of all, in the same way that it is anterior to theoria, namely, as an attending to the very opening within which all causing of effects can take place. Thinking, regathered to its element, exceeds praxis in another way too, namely, by extending back from action as classically determined to action as essentially accomplishment (*Vollbringen*). Or, rather, thinking becomes accomplishment, i.e., a matter of unfolding something into the fullness of its essence. What does thinking come to unfold or to let unfold? Nothing less than *essence itself*—essence no longer determined, however, as εἶδος for a pure θεωρία but rather determined now from ekstasis, from the stretching beyond (to) Being, determined now as the truth of essence which coincides with the essence of truth, i.e., as the truth of Being. Thinking is in deed engaged in the unfolding of the clearing.[5]

In all respects, then, the excess of thinking, its stretching back behind the theoretical, behind the practical, behind the very separation of theoretical from practical, is a matter of its engagement in the unfolding of the clearing, the place of all shining and showing, the abode, too, of man. It is thus that thinking is an originary ethics:

> If the name "ethics," in keeping with the basic meaning of the word ἦθος, should now say that ethics ponders the abode [*Aufenthalt*] of man, then that thinking which thinks the truth of Being as the primordial element of man, as one who eksists, is in itself the original ethics (*HB* 356).

It is only in attending to this abode which the truth of Being is for man that one could begin to ponder what might become law and rule for man. Otherwise, Heidegger insists, "all law remains merely something fabricated by human reason" (*HB* 361)—that is, by reason separated from its element, by reason in perpetual crisis.

Such is, then, the third stretch of the way, stretching from the separation of reason into theoretical and practical back to ek-sistence as the extension of man into the clearing, into his abode.

The fourth stretch also cuts across a certain division, not, however, one within reason, but rather one within man as such, namely, that separation of animality from reason that is broached by the determination of man as rational animal.

What happens to this separation when man comes to be regathered into his abode? What happens to it when reason comes to be extended into ek-sistence? Can a being of such extended reason still be regarded as a specific kind of living creature, i.e., as an animal? Heidegger's answer is, in a sense, guarded—that is, it guards against venturing a definitive statement regarding non-human beings, marking its reservation with such remarks as: "For as far as our experience shows, only man is admitted to the destiny [*Geschick*] of ek-sistence" (*HB* 324). Regarding man, on the other hand, there is no reservation, no reserve of human being this side of ek-sistence:

> Therefore ek-sistence can also never be thought of as a specific kind of living creature among others. . . . Thus even what we attribute to man as *animalitas* on the basis of the comparison with the "animal" is itself grounded in the essence of ek-sistence. The human body is something essentially other than an animal organism (*HB* 324).

As ek-sistence, man is not simply a specific kind of living creature. He is not simply a being among others, because, stretched beyond (to) Being, he exceeds beings in the direction of the truth of Being—not just exceeds but *is* that very exceeding. He is always in excess of beings, stretched beyond them, and hence is not to be grasped as one among them. Even what most persistently presents itself as a reserve this side of ek-sistence, as a certain *animalitas* within the *humanitas*—even this, man's bodily being, is essentially grounded in ek-sistence. The human body, too, is ek-sistent.

Such is, then, the last stretch of the way that I proposed to outline. It is a matter of exceeding the separation installed in man as rational animal, a matter of regathering the human body to reason, but to a reason that is itself regathered to its element, reason become ek-sistence. The human body, too, would be stretched beyond the all-too-human, beyond (to) Being, and the way thus prepared for a humanism for which "the essence of man consists in his being more than merely human . . ." (*HB* 342).

THIRTEEN

Meaning Adrift

> For language plays with our
> speech—it likes to let our
> speech drift away into the more
> obvious meanings of words.
> —Heidegger,
> *Was Heisst Denken?*

But for the slightest twist, Nietzsche would be just the last metaphysician.

The story is at least twice-told. Once in Heidegger's text "The Will to Power as Art": the story of how Nietzsche set out to overturn Platonism, to invert it, to stand it on its head, of how, according to a familiar schema, he could not but be caught within that which he would invert, remaining ensnared in it almost to the end, twisting free of it only at the last moment:

> During the time the overturning of Platonism became for Nietzsche a twisting free of it, madness befell him.[1]

At the end, the slightest twist, setting one from that moment adrift from the logic of opposition, adrift in a certain oblique opposition to logic. Twisting, turning, drifting—into what? Into the end? Into a beyond? Into madness?

Yet Heidegger only retells—with a certain twist—a story that Nietzsche himself told during his final year. The story is, of course, that of "how the 'true world' finally became a fable."[2] By now the story has perhaps been too often retold, has perhaps become all too familiar. Who cannot recite its six great episodes, the history of metaphysics from Plato to Nietzsche condensed to just over a page! The most fitting preface to every contemporary discourse that wants to be done with metaphysics, that thinks it can be done with metaphysics, every discourse that in addressing the end of metaphysics would fancy itself securely installed in a present perfect, if not a past perfect.

Originally published in *Heidegger Studies*, vol. 1 (1985).

The story ends with high noon:

Noon; moment of the slightest shadow; end of the longest error; high point of humanity; . . .

What happens in this final moment, this end told of at the end of the story, in the sixth, the final episode? The earlier episodes tell of a certain drift of the "true world," a certain drifting away in which that "world" becomes unattainable for now, then unattainable as such, and eventually unknown. In the end, this drift is what serves to expose the "true world" as an error, as due to be abolished. And yet, the abolition of the "true world" is not what occupies the final moment, at least is not what is told of in the last episode. It is, rather, the penultimate episode that tells of how the "true world" was done away with, of how well before noon it was thoroughly dismantled, at the coming at bright day, at breakfast, to the cheers, the infernal noise (*Teufelslärm*) of all free spirits. The final episode begins, then, with these words: "The true world we have abolished: . . ." So, when it begins, the "true world" has already been abolished; presumably, it is thus that the words no longer need be enclosed in those quotation marks which, in the fifth episode and in the title of the entire story, serve to mark a certain impropriety. When the final episode begins, the true world has drifted utterly out of sight, and, thus effaced, has been abolished, done away with. And that would be the end of it. The end of the supersensible, the end of Platonism, the end of metaphysics. That would be the end of it, were any of these such as could end once and for all. But do they indeed have—could they have—an end beyond which one would simply be done with them? Do they simply end? Is it not rather precisely because there is no simple end that a final episode is required? The final episode does not, then, tell of something after the end, of a "beyond" in which the end of metaphysics would have been left behind. Rather, it continues the story of the end, tells of something else that cannot but have been done in and through the abolition of the true world, something which, though done at the same time, comes to be realized only after a certain lapse. The end is not a moment but an interval. It extends from daybreak to noon. At least to noon.

Thus extended so as to encompass (at least) both the twilight of the idols and the high noon of humanity, the end is anything but simple. Not only in its extension but also in its textuality; for it is, to adapt Nietzsche's words, a "question mark so black, so monstrous [*ungeheuer*], that it casts shadows upon the man who puts it down."[3] How, then, does the end cast shadows upon its very inscription? The end is the end of a story, the story of how the true world finally became a fable, of how it finally turned into a story, of how in the end it proved to be nothing more than a story, not only something told about but something posited only in the telling, in the story. What story? The story told by Nietzsche, perhaps for the first time in its full compass, certainly for the first time *as a story* and not as the history of being, as the "history of an error"[4] and not as the history of truth. The story is, then, on the one hand, a story about the true world, about its drift and eventual abolition, its drifting into abolition; and yet, on the other hand, the story is that which the true world becomes, the story into which it turns. In short, the story is about the true world becoming finally just the story itself. It is the story of the true world becoming the "true world," words inscribed within and extending into the story itself. It is, then, a story from which that of which it tells cannot be simply set apart. It is the story of how the true world, drifting away into abolition, drifts into the very story of the drift into abolition. It is a story whose very meaning is set adrift in language.

It is thus appropriate that the story begins and ends as it does, enclosing the drift of the true world between two instances of writing. At the beginning, when the true world assumes its least remote, its simple, convincing guise, it is literally the translation of a sentence—a "transcription [*Umschreibung*] of the sentence 'I, Plato, *am* the truth.'" Product of a rewriting, the true world and its drift could never have been distinct from the drift in language, the drift of the story, which thus also ends by telling of a writing:

INCIPIT ZARATHUSTRA

Another story, beyond the story of the end, or, rather, a story that would extend the end.

The extension, the opening of the end, is produced, or at least decisively prepared, by what is told of in the sixth episode of Nietzsche's story. What is it, then, that happens at the end, disrupting the simplicity of the end, extending it not only from daybreak to noon but even, perhaps indefinitely, beyond? What is it that cannot but have been done in and through the abolition of the true world?

> The true world we have abolished: What world has remained? the apparent one [*die scheinbare*] perhaps? . . . But no! *with the true world we have also abolished the apparent one.* [The punctuation and italics are Nietzsche's.]

The true world has drifted utterly out of sight, has disappeared once and for all; and in the end one has now only to proclaim that disappearance. The point of the final episode is that this proclamation does not leave simply intact the other world, the apparent world, that has always (i.e., since the beginning of metaphysics) been simultaneously both opposed and subordinated to the true world: With the true world we have also abolished the apparent one.

And yet, there is a critical difference. What is proclaimed in the abolition of the true world is the utter disappearance of that world. What is proclaimed in the abolition of the apparent world is not its disappearance; for those things that have previously been consigned to the apparent world have by no means disappeared, but rather, whatever the story told, whatever the proclamation, they continue stubbornly to appear, to show themselves. What has been abolished is not that world that has always been understood as apparent but rather the possibility of continuing to understand it in that way prescribed by the metaphysical opposing of it to a true world. What has been abolished is any understanding of the apparent by reference to the true, by reference of the apparent thing to its meaning in the most rigorous determination; for the drift of the true world is the drift of meaning, and meaning set adrift can be, for metaphysics, hardly more than the sheer dissolution of meaning, its disappearance. What disappears is not the apparent world but its meaning; and the abolition of the apparent world is the proclamation of its meaninglessness, moment of the slightest shadow.

One could, of course, say—and it has often been said—that, once the true world has vanished, then the apparent one loses the character of apparentness, ceases to be appearance *of* the true, much less its mere semblance or even its dissemblance. What then would be required would be an understanding of the things of that world *from themselves* rather than one that would proceed by referring them to the true, to the intelligible, to meaning. And yet, things can be understood from themselves only by being taken as they show themselves, as they appear—that is, only by continuing to be taken (though now in a different way) as apparent, as appearances, if not as appearances *of* something exceeding the world of appearances. The things of *die scheinbare Welt* are to be taken as they shine forth in their self-showing. It is a matter of letting them show themselves.

It is, then, toward such a hermeneutics that the end of metaphysics opens. Afternoon. The shadows begin to lengthen; now in the opposite direction.

It is, then, upon phenomenology that the end of metaphysics opens. Rigorous openness—that is, engagement in the things themselves, in their self-showing, and, simultaneously, reticence before them.

One could say, then, that the end of metaphysics is phenomenology. This would not be the same as saying (as has now often been said) that phenomenology is the end of metaphysics—that is, that phenomenology in the end only repeats, even if most rigorously, the founding gestures of metaphysics. The difference could perhaps be marked—though not without beginning to disfigure the schema—as that between an end that opens out and one that closes off.

It all depends on how the things themselves are taken, for metaphysics too, from Plato to Hegel, appeals to τὸ πρᾶγμα αὐτό, measuring its rigor by its adherence to this injunction. In any case, to take the things themselves as they show themselves is never—whether in metaphysics or in phenomenology—simply to suppress all reference beyond the things; it is never simply to turn the thing upon itself (though such a turning does become a moment in the metaphysics of the subject); nor is it ever simply a turning of one thing toward another, a reference of one being to another. It is never a matter of forsaking the γιγαντομαχία περὶ τῆς οὐσίας for the sake of telling stories merely about beings.[5] It is not movement within every field of reference that is—or can be—suppressed at the end of metaphysics but only movement within that field constituted by the metaphysical opposition between true and apparent, between intelligible and sensible. What must be inhibited in the face of the things themselves as they show themselves is the reference to an essence, an εἶδος, a meaning (in its classical determination). Otherwise, one ends up reconstituting metaphysics within phenomenology—that is, closing off phenomenology within the end of metaphysics.

Need it be said that *Being and Time* opens another field of reference, a field other than that in which appearing things would be referred to an εἶδος and thus understood from that εἶδος? *Being and Time* opens a field that is both other than the metaphysical field and in a founding way inclusive of that field, which is thus, in a sense, made possible by the phenomenological field.[6] *Being and Time* opens a field in which appearing things, things as they show themselves, can be understood without the metaphysical opposition between true and apparent being reconstituted, without the story of the true world having to be retold.

Let it suffice to recall the phenomenological opening in the most schematic terms. The field opened by the phenomenological analyses in *Being and Time* is not, as with the metaphysical field, one that would lie between appearing things and something else to which, as to a true world, they would be referred. Rather, the reference through which things would come to be understood would be a referral of them to this field, a certain dispersion of them into the field, in no case a referral beyond the field. The phenomenological field is, of course, what Heidegger calls—at least in the initial analyses—*world*. To understand something by reference to world is not to refer it to something else that would shine through it, expropriating its self-showing, but rather to refer it to an open system of references to which, in its very self-showing, it is already referred. To understand something in this manner is to understand it *from itself*, to take it *as it shows itself*; for what the initial analyses of *Being and Time* demonstrate is that self-showing is always, first of all, a showing from out of a system of references, from out of an environing world. Those same analyses, accordingly, also set about determining intraworldly reference as meaning (*Bedeutung*), hence broach a redetermination of meaning that would differ radically from the metaphysical determination.[7] In place of meaning posited over against self-showing things in such a way as to expropriate their showing, in place of meaning as it has drifted away out of sight when the true world finally becomes a fable, Heidegger's phenomenological analyses redetermine meaning as nothing less than the very *drift of the world* from out of which things show themselves.

Meaning a drift, meaning adrift—as the very site of self-showing. To be in the world is, then, to mean this drift, to look ahead into it so as to let things show themselves from out of it. Being-in-the-world is being adrift in meaning a( )drift.

Meaning, thus redetermined, is not simply to be set over against language as something utterly autonomous that language would only express. Even in *Being and Time* any such utter separation is already undermined, at least by the inclusion of discourse (*Rede*) as one of the constituent moments of the *Da* of *Dasein,* that is, of the disclosive opening of the world, of what Heidegger calls simply: disclosedness (*Erschlossenheit*).[8]

He calls it also truth, the primordial phenomenon of truth, ἀλήθεια. Thus, the phenomenological analyses of *Being and Time* issue in a redetermination of truth, one which does not metaphysically oppose truth to appearances, true world to apparent world, but rather displaces that opposition: truth as the opening/openness of the very site of self-showing. It is precisely for the sake of enforcing this displacement that Heidegger insists on distinguishing between truth as ἀλήθεια and truth as correctness (ὀρθότης), even if finally at the cost of relinquishing the word *truth.*[9] This displacement, in turn, produces a displacement of the relation between truth and meaning, dissociating them only then to set meaning adrift in truth, to redetermine it as the very drift of truth. A( )drift, too, in language.

This double displacement could provide a context for a careful reading of the recently published text of Heidegger's lecture course of 1942–43 entitled *Parmenides.*[10] For that entire text, beginning with the Parmenidean words on/of the goddess truth, is addressed single-mindedly to the question of truth, perhaps most notably to recovering the meaning of truth and of untruth and to retelling the most momentous story told by the Greeks about truth and untruth, the μῦθος told at the end of Plato's *Republic.* One could perhaps even characterize the text *Parmenides* as an assembling of the elements of the double displacement.

Let me limit my reading to a single short passage. It occurs near the beginning of the text. Heidegger has introduced ἀλήθεια and proposed the translation: *Unverborgenheit*—let us say: unconcealment. The word itself contains two indications, points in two directions in which *Unverborgenheit* can be investigated: 1) to *Verborgenheit* (concealment); and 2) to an overcoming of *Verborgenheit,* a kind of strife with concealment. These indications suffice to allow Heidegger to propose that truth is never simply present in and of itself but rather is something contested in strife with concealment, from which it must be wrested. Truth has—one might say—always already drifted away into untruth. The third direction thus indicated is that of truth as standing in "'oppositional' relations" ("'gegensätzliche' Beziehungen").[11] It is a matter, then, of asking about the counter-essence (Gegenwesen) of ἀλήθεια. Or, rather, of asking about the *word* for the counter-essence of ἀλήθεια. Almost immediately the interrogation has drifted into language.

An interrogation of ληθές and of ψεῦδος commences, a discussion of the fundamental meaning (Grundbedeutung) of each. But the discussion is abruptly broken off, or, rather, it is interrupted, and before resuming it on the following page, Heidegger inserts two very remarkable paragraphs.[12] It is to this passage that I want especially to call attention.

The passage begins:

> In the attempt to trace the fundamental meanings of words and expressions, we are, to be sure, not infrequently guided by an inadequate conception of language as such, from which then arise the familiar erroneous judgments concerning the investigation of fundamental meanings. We ought not think that the words of a language initially possess pure fundamental meanings and that with the passage of time the latter get lost and become deformed. The fundamental and root meaning remains quite concealed [verborgen] and appears only in what one calls the "derivative."

Words are not like coins which with the passage of time, with the passage from hand to hand, get so effaced that their inscriptions become more and more difficult to discern. Words do not, in this sense, get worn out, used up; the very model of use and wear arises from an inadequate conception of language. The fundamental meanings of words do not get effaced in the course of time, through use or perhaps misuse, but rather are always already effaced, concealed, apparent only in what is already derivative. The root appears only in the stem.

The passage continues:

> But this designation is misleading, because it presupposes that somewhere there is for itself a "pure fundamental meaning," from which others are then "derived." These erroneous conceptions, which even today still govern the science of language, have their source in the fact that the first reflection on language, Greek grammar, was developed under the guidance of "logic," i.e., of the theory of the saying of assertion [vom Sagen der Aussagen], as the theory of the proposition [als Satzlehre]. According to this theory propositions are composed of words, and words designate "concepts." The latter indicate what is represented [vorgestellt] universally along with words. This "universal" of the concept one then regards as "the fundamental meaning." The "derivatives" are particularizations of the universal.

An erroneous conception, still in force today, has arisen from the Greek reflection on language, from the reflection on language carried out both within and then under the guidance of Greek philosophy, preeminently the philosophy of Plato and of Aristotle, that is, at the beginning of metaphysics. That reflection proceeds according to the theory of the proposition as composed of words, the latter designating concepts or universals—that is, meanings as classically defined, fundamental meanings in distinction from the more particular meanings that can derive from and even serve to conceal the fundamental meanings.

It goes almost without saying that this reflection on language, setting meaning over against word, over against language, is inseparable from the metaphysical tale of the true world over against the world of appearing things. And equally, that this reflection is precisely the one that—now that the true world has finally become a fable—the phenomenological analyses of *Being and Time* radically displace by demonstrating that assertion is a derived (*abkünftig*) mode of interpretation; and that the apophantical "as," according to which the proposition would be assembled from words designating meanings already detached from the world of appearances, is secondary in relation to the hermeneutical "as" and a corresponding speech that would be attuned to meaning adrift in the world.[13]

But what is the erroneous conception that has arisen from the Greek, i.e., metaphysical, reflection on language? Heidegger is explicit: It is the supposition that somewhere there is for itself such a thing as fundamental meaning. Somewhere—not only beyond derivative meanings, but, more critically, beyond the designating words, beyond in a subsistence for themselves, independent of those words, capable even of drifting away behind the cover of "derivative" meanings, of having always already begun drifting away, of drifting away just as, according to that history of an error told by Nietzsche, the true world has drifted away out of sight, beyond recall. Something to be abolished.

The passage concludes:

> Yet, when in connection with our investigation we think about fundamental meaning [*auf die Grundbedeutung hindenken*], we are guided by an entirely different conception of the word and of language. To think that we are pursuing a so-called "word-philosophy," which sorts out everything on the basis of mere word-meanings, is, to be sure, a very comfortable opinion, but also one so superficial that it cannot even any longer be designated as a false opinion. What we call the fundamental meaning of words is that about them that is originary [*ist ihr Anfängliches*], which never appears at first but only in the end, and even then never as a detached and prepared structure [*als ein abgelöstes und präpariertes Gebilde*] that we could represent for itself. So-called fundamental meaning holds sway concealedly in all the ways that words have of telling [*in allen Sageweisen der jeweiligen Worte*].

Once meaning has—as the true world—drifted away out of sight, it comes—unless understood outside the classical definition—to be mere word-meaning, virtual meaninglessness; and nothing could be more superficial than to sort out everything on the basis of such word-meanings, except perhaps to mistake for such a "word-philosophy" an attentiveness to the meaning of words as that which is originary in them. Fundamental meaning, displaced from the metaphysical opposition that has always determined it, is, then, that which is originary about words, that which, invoked by them, housed in them, lets things originate, come forth into self-showing. The originary in language is nothing other than world, ἀλήθεια, the open site of self-showing. It is also what lets metaphysics itself originate, enclosing the founding oppositions of metaphysics so as to delimit and yet withhold itself from metaphysics, remaining inaccessible, never appearing at first, in the beginning, in the origination, but only in the end, only when the drift of the true world finally transgresses the limit. It is not something detached that can be represented for itself, not only because all representing is already drawn along into its drift but also because it is itself drawn into the drift of language, holding sway in the ways that words have of telling.

Suppose that the originary, which can be called truth and world, were now to be called the true world. And suppose that one were to tell then of how the true world drifts along in the drift of language, in the ways that words have of telling, in their *Sageweisen,* or—letting the translation itself now drift ever so slightly—in the styles (*Weisen*) in which a fable (*Sage*) can be told. One would then have begun again to tell—though with an ever-so-decisive twist—the story of how the true world finally became a fable.

IV.
ARCHAIC CLOSURE

FOURTEEN

At the Threshold of Metaphysics

> Die Schwelle ist der Grundbalken, der das
> Tor im ganzen trägt. Er hält die Mitte,
> in der die Zwei, das Draussen und das
> Drinnen, einander durchgehen, aus. Die
> Schwelle trägt das Zwischen.
> —Heidegger, *Unterwegs zur Sprache*

> Alle Metaphysik . . . spricht die Sprache Platons.
> —Heidegger, "Das Ende der Philosophie
> und die Aufgabe des Denkens"

> Auch wir wollen mit der scheinbar so
> abstrakten Frage nach den Bedingungen
> der Möglichkeit des Seinsverständnisses
> nichts anderes, als uns aus der Höhle
> ans Licht zu bringen. . . .
> —Heidegger, *Die Grundprobleme
> der Phänomenologie*

The threshold of *Being and Time* is of Platonic origin. It is inscribed on
the untitled first page of that text, excised from the middle of the *Sophist*:

> For manifestly you have long been aware of what you mean when you use
> the expression "being" [ὄν—Heidegger translates: *seiend*]. We, however,
> who once thought we understood it, have now become perplexed.[1]

This passage marks the beginning of *Being and Time,* or, rather, the way
to that beginning: Echoing the voice of the Eleatic Stranger, it invokes
the perplexity (*Verlegenheit*) to which in the Platonic dialogue he ironically attests, perplexity about the meaning of Being.

In a certain sense this moment of perplexity can be regarded as the
transition to metaphysics. It is the moment of transition *from* telling

---

A portion of this text appeared in French as "Au Seuil de la métaphysique," in *Heidegger,*
ed. Michel Haar (Paris: L'Herne, 1983).

stories about beings (242c) (determining "beings as beings by tracing them back in their origin to some other beings, as if Being [*Sein*] had the character of a possible being"—*SZ* 6) *to* developing the question of what Being means and engaging thus in a γιγαντομαχία περὶ τῆς οὐσίας (246a; *SZ* 2). It is the moment of turning from beings to Being and as such forms the threshold of metaphysics. Because *Being and Time* sets out to recapture this movement, to renew this turning at the threshold of metaphysics in order to embark upon a repetition (*Wiederholung*) of the beginning of metaphysics, it can appropriately invoke as its threshold the Platonic attestation to that moment.

The project of repetition is broached from the outset, repetition as recovery of a level of questioning long since covered over:

> Yet the question we are touching upon is not just any question. It impelled the researches of Plato and Aristotle, only to become silent from then on *as a theme for actual investigation.* What these two men achieved persisted through various displacements and "retouchings" [*Verschiebungen und "Übermalungen"*] down to the *Logic* of Hegel. And what was once wrested from the phenomena with the utmost effort of thinking, fragmentary and incipient though it was, has long since become trivialized (*SZ* 2).

It is because of this concealment that it is necessary today "to raise anew the question of the meaning of Being" and, first of all, "to reawaken an understanding for the meaning of this question" (*SZ* 2)—that is, to recover that perplexity to which the words of the Stranger attest. It is because of the concealment wrought by metaphysics itself that it is necessary to return to the threshold and to repeat the beginning of metaphysics.

And yet, the concealment is not totally extrinsic to that beginning. On the contrary, the very presuppositions that support the concealment, that foster the opinion that questioning about the meaning of Being is unnecessary, "have their roots in ancient ontology itself" (*SZ* 2–3). From its very inception, metaphysics, in raising the question of Being, also implants near the center of the question the seeds of concealment. Mere repetition is thus out of the question. What is called for is rather a repetition which, exposing the duplicity broached in the very beginning of metaphysics, displaces itself accordingly. *Being and Time* is not just a repetition of the beginning but rather its supplement.

Thus, the exposure of the duplicity of metaphysics—that is, its destruction—belongs intrinsically to the project of raising again the question of the meaning of Being. Though *Being and Time* (in its incomplete state) stops short of such destruction, its positive phenomenological analyses, gathered into the analysis of truth (§44), do suffice to indicate the domain in which the duplicity can most effectively be exposed, namely, that of the problem of truth (*SZ* 225). This indication is given through that phenomenological analysis which draws the lines of a fundamental ambiguity in the concept of truth, recovering, on the one hand, the primordial phenomenon of truth and demonstrating, on the other hand, the way in which the ordinary (i.e., sedimented metaphysical) concept of truth originates; and which then sketches the duplicity of metaphysics as a movement within this ambiguity. Yet, these lines and this sketch are drawn only within the limits proper to it as a phenomenological analysis—that is, not as destruction.

It is in *Plato's Doctrine [Lehre] of Truth*² that this destruction is undertaken as such. Here Heidegger's explicit intention is to expose what remains unsaid in the Platonic text, and it is precisely this "unsaid" that is denoted by the word *Lehre*. At the very outset Heidegger identifies this "unsaid," this *Lehre*: It is "a change in the determination of the essence of truth" (*W* 203). Limiting his reading to the so-called allegory of the cave, Heidegger thus undertakes to show that two different concepts of truth are operative in that text and that a change from one to the other is under way. More precisely, Heidegger undertakes to read this Platonic text as the covert inscription of that moment of transition in which both terms, both determinations of the essence of truth, remain in play and in which consequently the dynamic ambiguity of the Greek concept of truth can become manifest.

Let me outline, ever so briefly, Heidegger's reading of those all-too-familiar pages of the *Republic*. The reading focuses primarily on the way in which the two determinations of the essence of truth are operative in that tale.

The story is one of παιδεία. Insisting that this word cannot be translated, Heidegger ventures only to approximate it with the German *Bildung,* taken in the older sense; a similar approximation could be ventured with the English *education,* likewise taken in its older sense. However, these substitutes hardly even allude to the Platonic determination: παιδεία is a turning-around of the human soul in its entirety (περιαγωγὴ ὅλης τῆς ψυχῆς; Heidegger translates: *Umwendung des ganzen Menschen*). It is a turning-around which is at the same time a movement, a displacement, from the domain of man's ordinary dealings with things to another domain in which things show themselves as they properly are, in their "look," their "outward appearance" (*Aussehen*), i.e., in their εἶδος, their ἰδέα. It is a movement toward unconcealment (*Unverborgenheit*), a movement through a series of domains in which the unconcealment of things is successively and positively transformed. The movement of παιδεία is thus governed by the modalities of unconcealment and the domains of things unconcealed that correspond to these modalities. Unconcealment, said in Greek, is ἀλήθεια, the word usually translated as "truth." The original Greek concept of truth, truth as ἀλήθεια, as uncon-cealment, is thus operative in the Platonic text as governing the move-ment of παιδεία. Each of the modalities of truth determines a distinctive stage of that movement.

The first stage is that of men chained in the cave and completely occupied with things as most immediately presented, as shadows cast upon the wall of the cave. This mode of unconcealment, this revelation of things only through the shadows they cast, defines this stage of παι-δεία, though its deficiency, and hence its relation to παιδεία, can come to light only after one has broken with it. The prisoners, on the other hand, "would hold that the unconcealed [τὸ ἀληθές] is nothing other than the shadows of things" (515c; *W* 219).

The second stage is that of release from the chains. Looking around at the things which cast the shadows, the former prisoner is now "nearer to being" (515d)—that is, the things previously revealed only through their shadows are now more unconcealed. But again, the relation of this state to παιδεία, its character as an advance toward unconcealment, can only come to light subsequently. The one who has just turned around is so blinded and confused by what he sees that he will "believe that what was seen previously is more unconcealed [ἀληθέστερα] than what is now shown."

At the third stage, the liberated prisoner emerges from the cave. And though again he is initially so blinded by the excess of light that he is "unable to see even one of the things now said to be unconcealed" (516a), he comes eventually to gaze upon things in their proper "look," in that ἰδέα which appears in all appearing things and makes them accessible and which consequently is the most unconcealed (τὸ ἀληθέστατον—cf. 484c). At this stage, corresponding to the most unconcealed, man under-goes genuine liberation.

Though in a sense παιδεία reaches its fulfillment in the orientation to the most unconcealed, there is nevertheless an additional stage. This final stage is prescribed by the essential reference which παιδεία has back to its privation (ἀπαιδευσία, *Bildungslosigkeit*). Because παιδεία is also a continual overcoming of this privation, because education is also a con-tinual overcoming of ignorance, the story concludes with the return to the cave. Again it is a modality of unconcealment that determines the stage. This modality derives from the essential connection to conceal-ment: To unconcealment belongs a continual overcoming of conceal-ment—that is, the unconcealed must not only be somehow brought to appear but must be torn away from concealment. The α-privative in ἀ-λήθεια says: Truth originally meant what is wrested from concealment. Only in that modality of unconcealment in which this essential connec-tion is appropriated does παιδεία reach its genuine fulfillment. In deed the allegory itself appropriates this connection, appropriates it through the textual deed of presenting the way of παιδεία as a movement out of and back into a *cave,* that is, an open space enclosed by the earth.

Although the original Greek concept of truth as unconcealment remains operative in the story of the cave, there is also another determination of truth at work there. The priority which this other concept of truth comes to have is reflected in the way the story is shaped: Its force does not derive from the image which it presents of enclosedness (*Verschlossenheit*) inside the cave and openness outside it—that is, its force does not derive from the image which it presents of the unconcealment and concealment that constitute the original Greek concept of truth. The force of the story derives, rather, from the role of the fire, of its light and the shadows cast by it, of the brightness of the day, of the sunlight lighting up things, of the sun. In other words, what figures prominently in the story are the things inside and outside the cave and especially the light which lights up these things, *not* the enclosed openness which is named in the concept of truth as unconcealment, named as that within which any lighting can first take place, as that which any lighting hence presupposes. In another text, where he identifies the original concept of truth as clearing (*Lichtung*), Heidegger formulates the issue quite succinctly:

> No look [*Aussehen*] without light—Plato recognized this. But there is no light and no brightness without the clearing. Even darkness needs it.[3]

In the story of the cave, however, the awareness of this need recedes into the background. Although the story both names and enacts the determination of truth as unconcealment, it has as its central theme the ἰδέα and the lighting that pertains thereto. Shifted thus to the center, the ἰδέα is no longer regarded as a foreground offered by ἀλήθεια but rather as the ground which makes ἀλήθεια possible (cf. W 234). Unconcealment and the unconcealed are accordingly assimilated to the ἰδέα: The unconcealed gets identified as what is apprehended in the apprehension of the ἰδέα, and unconcealment gets reduced to being nothing more than the shining of the ἰδέα (W 225f.).

Such is the change in the determination of the essence of truth, i.e., Plato's *Lehre,* his unsaid: The ἰδέα becomes master over ἀλήθεια, to such an extent that it can be said that the highest ἰδέα "is itself sovereign in that it grants ἀλήθεια [= unconcealment] and apprehension [of the unconcealed]" (517c; W 230). Ἀλήθεια comes under the yoke of the ἰδέα, and consequently the essence of truth comes to be determined in reference, not to unconcealment, but to the ἰδέα:

> If in all comportment to beings it is a matter of the ἰδεῖν of the ἰδέα, of looking at the "look" ["*Aussehen*"], then all effort must be concentrated on

making possible such a seeing. . . . Everything depends on the ὀρθότης, the correctness, of the looking. . . . As a result of this approximation of the apprehension as an ἰδεῖν to the ἰδέα, there is a ὁμοίωσις, a correspondence of knowing with the thing itself. Thus arises from the priority of the ἰδέα and the ἰδεῖν over ἀλήθεια a change of the essence of truth. Truth becomes ὀρθότης, correctness of apprehension and of assertion (*W* 230f.).

This change of the essence of truth from unconcealment to correctness also effects a change of the locus of truth: Truth is shifted from the domain of beings to the human comportment toward these beings.

Such is the beginning of metaphysics as exposed by the Heideggerian destruction: a turning toward Being as ἰδέα, which precisely because it takes this direction brings about simultaneously a change in the essence (and locus) of truth. And if both determinations of truth remain in play in Plato and in Aristotle, from then on the determination of the essence of truth as correctness becomes "authoritative for the whole of Western thought" (*W* 232).

Still more significantly, the destruction shows that it is precisely through this change in the essence of truth that the seeds of concealment are implanted in the metaphysical way of raising the question of Being. The bringing of ἀλήθεια under the yoke of the ἰδέα and the consequent redetermining of truth as correctness constitute in effect a concealing of ἀλήθεια, a concealing of unconcealment. Being, determined as ἰδέα, assimilates that unconcealment from which the ἰδέα was previously taken to stand out; with this reductive assimilation, the way is, then, prepared for that obliteration of the ontological difference that eventually makes it come to appear unnecessary even to question about the meaning of Being. The duplicity of the beginning of metaphysics and the change in the essence of truth are constituted in one and the same gesture.

The destruction, thus exposing the concealment broached in the beginning of metaphysics, prescribes the supplementary character of the repetition announced in *Being and Time*. The repetition, added to the Platonic beginning as a raising anew of the question of Being, would also replace that beginning, replace it by displacing it. The repetition would return to the threshold of metaphysics, to that moment of perplexity regarding Being, and would venture a recovery of ἀλήθεια; it would venture a certain step back from the threshold in order eventually to cross it in a different way.

According to Heidegger, the themes developed in *Plato's Doctrine of Truth* go back to his lecture course of 1930–31 entitled "*Vom Wesen der Wahrheit.*" The text was written in 1940 and first appeared in *Geistige Überlieferung* in 1942. It first appeared as an independent publication (together with "Letter on Humanism") in 1947.

Critical response soon followed. The most notable of those responses was that by the Plato scholar Paul Friedländer, who in preparing a second edition of his monumental three-volume work on Plato included in volume 1 an entire chapter devoted to a critical examination of *Plato's Doctrine of Truth*.[4] Friedländer advances two major criticisms. First, he contests Heidegger's thesis that among the pre-Platonic Greeks the α- of ἀλήθεια functioned privatively, that the original sense of ἀλήθεια was thus unhiddenness or unconcealment. Friedländer argues that, for example, in Hesiod ἀλήθεια, even when used in this sense, refers to persons who do not forget, not to the hiddenness and unhiddenness of being. He argues, furthermore, that in Homer ἀλήθεια and ἀληθής almost always occur in connection with verbs of assertion; ἀλήθεια does not mean unconcealment but rather the genuine, the coherent, the correct. Friedländer's second major criticism is a rejection of the "construction" based by Heidegger on the thesis that originally ἀλήθεια meant unconcealment:

> Heidegger's historical construction . . . is untenable: the Greek concept of truth did not undergo a change from the unconcealment of being to the correctness of perception.[5]

In particular, such a change does not occur in Plato; at most, it may be said that there is a certain "two-sidedness" in Plato's doctrine of truth.

Heidegger's first response comes in 1958 in his lecture "Hegel and the Greeks." He mentions that in Homer ἀλήθεια occurs in connection with verbs of assertion. Then, referring explicitly to Friedländer, he says:

> From that it has been concluded rashly enough [*voreilig genug*] that unconcealment is "dependent" ["*abhängig*"] on the *verba dicendi*.

Heidegger inverts the order of dependence, at the same time putting in question the very sense of dependence:

> It is not that unconcealment is "dependent" on assertion [*Sagen*], but rather that every assertion requires already the domain of unconcealment (*W* 443).

Heidegger's definitive response to Friedländer's criticisms is found in his lecture "The End of Philosophy and the Task of Thinking," written in 1964, published in French translation in 1966 and in German in 1969. Remarkably, the response passes in silence over all that is vulnerable in the formulations and developments of the criticisms, most notably Friedländer's naive employment of the very kind of metaphysical concepts and distinctions (e.g., reality, being, epistemological/ontological) which the Heideggerian destruction calls radically into question. Rather, his response is to the criticisms that succeed in reopening the question.

The response properly begins at that point in Heidegger's lecture where in reference to Plato he draws the distinction (cited above) between the light which lights up things and the clearing (*Lichtung*) within which any lighting can first take place. Even if the clearing remained unthought even among the Greeks, it was nevertheless named when Parmenides spoke of ἀλήθεια. Heidegger immediately translates ἀλήθεια as "unconcealment." It is precisely this translation that is the primary object of Friedländer's critique.

Heidegger indicates what he considers the positive ground of the translation. It is not etymological: "If I stubbornly translate the name ἀλήθεια as unconcealment, it is not for the sake of etymology but on account of the *Sache* that is to be thought" (75f.). The positive ground of the translation is provided not by philology but rather by an attentiveness to what is named in the words of Parmenides, to what (as the entire lecture undertakes to show) is given as the *Sache* for thinking at the end of philosophy.

Heidegger insists that, if ἀλήθεια is thus translated, it cannot then also be translated as "truth." Insofar as truth is understood as correspondence of knowledge with things, even as correspondence of knowledge with Being (e.g., as ἰδέα), it is something utterly different from ἀλήθεια as unconcealment (i.e., clearing). This strict distinction presumably holds even if correspondence is understood in terms of intention and fulfillment, as Heidegger, following Husserl, understood it in *Being and Time*. Heidegger is thus not only introducing the distinction developed in *Being and Time* (§44) between the truth of expressions (e.g., "the picture on the wall is hanging askew") and the primordial phenomenon of truth as disclosedness (*Erschlossenheit*) but also is radicalizing that distinction to such a degree that the title "truth" is now withdrawn from the latter entirely. Heidegger does not disguise the self-criticism that this move involves:

> In any case one thing becomes clear: The question of ἀλήθεια, of unconcealment as such, is not the question of truth. Thus, it was inappropriate [*nicht sachgemäss*] and consequently misleading to call ἀλήθεια in the sense of clearing truth (*SD* 77).

Now, finally, Heidegger addresses himself directly to the criticisms. In a sense he simply grants the two major criticisms advanced by Friedländer. He concedes, first, that ἀλήθεια did not mean unconcealment among the early Greeks:

> The natural concept of truth does not mean unconcealment, not even in the philosophy of the Greeks. It is often and justifiably pointed out that the word ἀληθές is already used by Homer only for the *verba dicendi*, for assertions [*Aussagen*] and thus in the sense of correctness and reliability, not in the sense of unconcealment (*SD* 77).

But what, then, of that naming and experiencing of unconcealment that Heidegger so carefully and insistently traces in the fragments of the early Greek thinkers? And what of the power accorded to unconcealment, thus experienced, to grant, i.e., make possible, truth in the natural sense?

> Within the horizon of this question it must be acknowledged that ἀλήθεια, unconcealment in the sense of the clearing of presence, was forthwith and solely experienced as ὀρθότης, as the correctness of representations and statements (*SD* 78).

But then, if even among the early Greeks ἀλήθεια as unconcealment was experienced only as correctness, if even among the pre-Platonic Greeks truth already meant correctness, what is to be said of that change in the essence of truth that *Plato's Doctrine of Truth* would locate in the Platonic texts?

> But then the assertion of an essential change of truth, i.e., from unconcealment to correctness, is also untenable. Instead, one must say: ἀλήθεια, as clearing of presence and presentation in thinking and saying, comes forthwith under the perspective of ὁμοίωσις and *adaequatio*, i.e., the perspective of adequation in the sense of the correspondence of representing with what is present (*SD* 78).

Friedländer's second major criticism is thus also granted.

One might be tempted, then, to conclude that unconcealment was simply not experienced among the Greeks and that it was not in any sense named in sayings such as that of Parmenides which spoke of ἀλήθεια. But this is not Heidegger's conclusion. Rather, the fact that ἀλήθεια meant correctness and not unconcealment signifies for him that unconcealment was experienced by the Greeks only as (through, in the perspective of) correctness. Whatever the philological findings, the traces of the experience of unconcealment are too deeply cut in the texts of Greek thinking ever to be obliterated. One such trace is the Platonic story of the cave. It is, in a sense, even an exemplary trace. For though, in the face of Friedländer's critique, Heidegger can no longer locate in the Platonic text a change from unconcealment to correctness, he is not, on the other hand, at all obliged to expunge the ambiguity of the allegory, the interplay in it between unconcealment and correctness (truth). And, more generally, the effect of Heidegger's response to the critique is, in the end, to release precisely this ambiguity into the entire field of Greek thought, to extend it back throughout Greek thought. One could, then, say that in a sense metaphysics will always already have begun, that its beginning, the appearance of the ambiguity, will always already have been in play. Or, if one takes metaphysics, rather, to begin only when the ambiguity disappears in favor of the single determination of truth as correctness, then one will want to say that metaphysics will not yet have begun with Plato.

In a sense, it is to just such results that Friedländer himself comes in the later editions of his work, namely, in the third German edition (1964) and the second English edition (1969) based on it.[6] In these later editions there are very substantial revisions in the chapter devoted to Heidegger. On the one hand, Friedländer continues to oppose the "construction" according to which there would be in Plato a change from truth as unconcealment to truth as correctness:

> What stands unchanged is my criticism of Heidegger's historical construc-
> tion. For the result has become even more clear. It was not "first in Plato"
> that truth became the correctness of perception and assertion. This meaning
> was present much earlier, i.e., in the old epic.[7]

Friedländer's opposition on this point is thus based on his thesis that the sense of truth as correctness was already present in the early Greeks. This thesis and its consequence are also granted by Heidegger, in fact in the same year in which Friedländer's substantially revised edition appeared.

On the other hand, in the later editions Friedländer virtually retracts the other major criticism that had previously been advanced against Heidegger. The Preface to the later editions marks this shift:

> Yet, recent extensive analysis of the meaning of ἀλήθεια in the older litera-
> ture has more clearly brought out the various early meanings of the concept.
> It has become clear that the aspect of unhiddenness most stressed by Hei-
> degger was present very early . . . (*F2* vii).

Likewise, at the conclusion of the chapter devoted to Heidegger, the retraction is explicit:

> In my discussion with Martin Heidegger, I have learned that my earlier
> opposition to the interpretation of ἀλήθεια as unhiddenness was unjustified
> (*F2* 229).

And yet, though granting to Heidegger that truth as unconcealment is in play in the early Greeks, Friedländer continues nonetheless to insist that the other sense of truth, truth as correctness, was *also* already present there. And so, in Plato—but also earlier, also perhaps always already, from Homer on—there is in play an ambiguity in the essence of truth, or, as Friedländer prefers to say, a "two-sidedness" or "equilibrium":

> For Plato, there is in ἀληθής and ἀλήθεια an equilibrium between the
> revealing truth, the unhidden reality, and the truthfulness which measures
> that reality by this truth (*F2* 229).

For Heidegger the granting of the ambiguity provokes a further question: "How is it that ἀλήθεια, unconcealment, appears to man's natural experience and speaking *only* as correctness and dependability?" (*SD* 78). His answer: because man is turned only to what is present, not to its presence and not to the clearing in which it can be present. Ἀλήθεια remains concealed. The question is:

> Does this happen because self-concealing, concealment, λήθη, belongs to ἀ-λήθεια not just as an addition, not as shadow to light, but rather as the heart of ἀλήθεια? . . . If this were so, then the clearing would not be the mere clearing of presence, but the clearing of self-concealing presence, the clearing of self-concealing sheltering [*des sich verbergenden Bergens*] (*SD* 78).

Ἀλήθεια would always, at best, have been experienced only through ὀρθότης because of the ingredience of λήθη.

Let me return to *Plato's Doctrine of Truth* in order to measure somewhat more closely the extent to which the ambiguity in the Greek concept of truth is in play in that text. To what extent does ἀλήθεια as unconcealment remain securely in force at the very locus of what Heidegger would mark as the transition to correctness, as the beginning of metaphysics?

One could regard the Platonic discourse on τὸ ἀγαθόν, as well as Heidegger's own reading of that discourse (and even his reading of that reading), as concentrating precisely (on) that ambiguity; in other words, one could regard these as a series of superimposed discourses weaving between what in *Plato's Doctrine of Truth* Heidegger still calls the two determinations of the essence of truth. On the one side, ἡ ἰδέα τοῦ ἀγαθοῦ is the culmination of the development by which ἀλήθεια comes to be placed under the yoke of the ἰδέα. The Platonic text says explicitly that τὸ ἀγαθόν grants ἀλήθεια (514c); Heidegger cites the passage, translates it (rendering ἀλήθεια as *Unverborgenheit*), and then concludes immediately: "Ἀλήθεια comes under the yoke of the ἰδέα" (*W* 230). Τὸ ἀγαθόν is the highest idea, the idea of all ideas, that which enables the shining of all ideas and which thus makes possible all appearing, all coming to presence. It is the highest, the most elevated, idea, which, on the other hand, because it makes all showing possible, must be in view, must show itself, everywhere and constantly.

And yet, τὸ ἀγαθόν resists being totalized as something everywhere and constantly present. The Platonic text says that it is "scarcely to be seen" (μόγις ὁρᾶσθαι—517b). In *Plato's Doctrine of Truth* Heidegger cites and translates this passage; then, in a later reading of his text, Heidegger writes the following in the margin: "ἀγαθόν of course ἰδέα, but no longer coming to presence [*nicht mehr anwesend*], therefore scarcely visible" (*W*

227). But what of an ἰδέα that no longer comes to presence? Is this "no longer" intended to mark a contrast with some past? Could such a past ever have been present, a past-present in which the ἀρχή (cf. 511b) would be present, an absolute beginning? But let me postpone the leap to the final μῦθος of the *Republic* in order to pose now a more immediate question, a more immediately erosive question. Does not the very essence of an idea (i.e., essence as such, idea as such, etc.) consist precisely in its coming to presence, in its purely showing itself as the "look" that makes visible those things incapable of such pure self-showing, constituting their visibility in and through its own shining? What, then, of an idea that proves to be scarcely visible, that no longer comes to presence? What of an idea that grants all pure self-showing but does not purely show itself? Can one continue, confidently, even coherently, to call τὸ ἀγαθόν an ἰδέα if it is such as to withdraw itself from self-showing, to remain withdrawn from full presence? Without even entering into the complex (and finally deconstructive) metaphorics that governs the Platonic discourse on τὸ ἀγαθόν, one would need at least to say that there is operative in that discourse (and in the two Heideggerian discourses layered upon it) a certain erosion, a certain slippage of the determination of τὸ ἀγαθόν as ἰδέα, a slippage in the direction back toward an ἀρχή that would no longer be foreground, that would no longer issue in pure transparent self-showing, a slippage back toward an ἀρχή which, like ἀλήθεια, would, in its very empowering of the shining/showing of all things, hold itself back, withdrawn into the shadows.

Heidegger himself marks the ambiguity as it is in play in one particular passage in the Platonic text: "The ambiguity reveals itself with full clarity in the fact that [in the relevant passage: 517b–c] ἀλήθεια is dealt with and spoken about while at the same time ὀρθότης is meant and set as a standard—and all in the same train of thought" (*W* 231). In the passage the two determinations are thus interwoven; specifically, they are interwoven in the two phrases that Heidegger underlines in the passage, so that there is a peculiar kind of crossing between the two phrases. In both phrases what is at issue is ἡ ἰδέα τοῦ ἀγαθοῦ, considered as yoking together knowing with what is known. The first phrase determines τὸ ἀγαθόν as the cause of all that is correct (ὀρθά) and beautiful (καλά). The second determines it as the sovereign which grants truth (ἀλήθεια) and apprehension (νοῦς). Heidegger's text indicates that these two pairs, ὀρθά/καλά and ἀλήθεια/νοῦς, do not correspond, the first member of each pair belonging, rather, with the second member of the other pair, the two lines of affiliation corresponding to the two different determinations of truth.

The crossing could be traced out much more closely. In reference to the governing schema, viz., τὸ ἀγαθόν as the yoke joining knowing with the known, the alignments proposed by the two ordered pairs may be plotted either vertically or horizontally. Plotted vertically, the members of the first pair (ὀρθά/καλά) would represent what is known and would be aligned, respectively, with ἀλήθεια and νοῦς, the second pair thus representing the side of knowing. Plotted horizontally, on the other hand, one member of each pair would represent knowing, the other member representing what is known; thus, ὀρθά, as ὀρθότης, would be aligned as the knowing corresponding to καλά, and νοῦς aligned in the same way (though in the opposite direction) with ἀλήθεια.

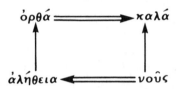

But neither set of alignments holds. Ὀρθά, the correct, does not, as that which is known, correspond to ἀλήθεια but rather to νοῦς: For the metaphysical determination of truth, everything hinges on correct apprehension. Furthermore, neither ὀρθά (as ὀρθότης) nor νοῦς (aligning with ὀρθά as correct apprehension) can be aligned with καλά, the beautiful, which in the *Phaedrus* is call τὸ ἐκφανέστατον, the most manifest, that which most shines forth; it is not, however, a matter of a pure showing that would be transposable from sensible visibility to an order of correct apprehension; rather, the beautiful is what shines forth in the midst of the visible, what preeminently draws the soul forth within the visible, not beyond its shadows.[8] Thus, καλά can only be aligned with ἀλήθεια. Hence the crossing:

Yet even this crossing does not resolve the tension in the configuration of the two pairs, especially not if the connection of the configuration with the governing schema is brought again into play. For while indeed the alignment of νοῦς with ὀρθά coheres perfectly with that schema, ἀλήθεια cannot, on the other hand, be aligned as a knowing to which would correspond καλά as the known. Ἀλήθεια can be assimilated neither to knowing nor to the known but rather cuts across this distinction, crossing in the direction of what would precede and yoke together knowing and the known, inscribing another cross in the configuration, a double cross against the sovereign, double-crossing what metaphysics will come to call "the good."

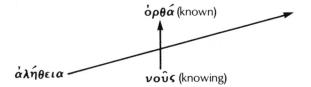

Such is the figuration of the ambiguity in the Platonic text.

But what secures the ambiguity? What forestalls the assimilation of ἀλήθεια to ἰδέα, its reduction to the mere shining of the ἰδέα? What serves to inhibit that inversion by which the foreground of ἀλήθεια would become its ground? What is it that thus withholds the Platonic text from metaphysics at the very moment when metaphysics is founded? What is it that holds the Platonic text at the threshold of metaphysics?

That which secures ἀλήθεια, and hence the ambiguity, in the Platonic text is none other than that which at the same time holds ἀλήθεια aloof, letting it appear to man's natural experience as correctness. What secures ἀλήθεια is λήθη, concealment (*Verborgenheit*).

In *Plato's Doctrine of Truth* Heidegger alludes, of course, to the way in which the question of λήθη is addressed by the story of the cave, most notably by its being a story of a *cave*, of an *enclosed* openness. However, it is in another text, that of his lecture course entitled *Parmenides* (1942–43),[9] that Heidegger most explicitly takes up the question of λήθη in relation to the Platonic text. Most of the lecture text is in fact devoted to a discussion of the counter-essence (*Gegenwesen*) of truth, i.e., to the concealment (*Verbergung,* λήθη) that belongs to unconcealment (*Unverborgenheit,* ἀλήθεια). The counter-essence, the "opposite" of truth, is, first of all, falsity; and so Heidegger begins with a discussion of the sense of the false (τὸ ψεῦδος), which he renders as *Verstellen*, disarranging, putting one thing in the place of another, hence obstructing, disguising, counterfeiting. For the Greeks, falsity does not pertain to the comportment of a subject but rather takes place, as it were, on the side of things. A situation in which, for example, a house blocks the view of the mountains exemplifies the initial and simplest sense of *Verstellen*, the sense of covering-up (*Verdecken*), blocking from view, obstructing the view of something. But covering-up, putting one thing in the place of another, can also serve to disguise. Heidegger's example is that of covering up a door in a wall by placing a chest in front of the opening; in this case it is not only a matter of putting the chest in place of the door, covering up the door, but also one of disguising, counterfeiting, distorting, in that the situation is made to allege that there is no door in the wall; the disarrangement makes it look as though the wall ran on continuously behind the chest (*Parm* 42–47).

Heidegger's primary concern, however, is not with this sense of concealment but rather with showing that among the Greeks there are also other senses decisively operative, senses which exceed *Verstellen*. Heidegger mentions several words that so attest: κεύθω, κρύπτω, καλύπτω, which he translates as *Bergen, Verbergen,* and *Verhüllen* respectively. He refers also to various passages in Homer, for example, that which says that Troy contains (*birgt*) rich treasures, or that which proclaims that Odysseus' ship contains (*birgt*) expensive wine. More decisive is that which declares that the earth shelters, contains, secures, conceals (all these senses in play in *bergen*) the dead. Perhaps most decisive of all is the discourse about Ἄϊδι κεύθωμαι, about being sheltered (contained, secured, concealed) in Hades; for in this connection there is broached a relation of concealment not only to earth and to what lies beneath the earth but also to death and to birth. In all these connections—and, as Heidegger insists, there can be no question of merely counting up species—what especially obtrudes is a form of concealment in which what gets concealed is not simply nullified and put aside but rather sheltered, secured, preserved. Such a form of concealment not only exceeds *Verstellen* but also carries virtually nothing of that negativity that belongs to the false (*Parm* 88–92).

And yet, all of this remained elusive for the Greeks. In the lecture text Heidegger continues to insist that, though the opposition between ἀλήθεια and λήθη was primordially experienced among the Greeks, neither λήθη nor even ἀλήθεια was explicitly and essentially thought through by them. What the lecture text adds, however, is that what had been experienced regarding the belongingness of λήθη to ἀλήθεια comes to be expressed in the completion that Greek thought reaches in Plato:

> The final word of Greek antiquity [*Griechentum*], which names λήθη in its essence, is that μῦθος with which Plato's dialogue on the essence of the πόλις concludes (*Parm* 140).

That μῦθος, the so-called myth of Er, is, according to Heidegger, a saga (*Sage*) about the essence of λήθη (*Parm* 155).

It is in this connection that Heidegger in the lecture text proceeds to a reading of the myth of Er. From his intricate and minute reading, let me simply extract three points. First, Heidegger stresses that the climax of the myth occurs when the souls that are about to be reborn arrive at the last of the sites through which they must pass in that demonic place. This final site is called: τὸ τῆς Λήθης πεδίον, the plain of concealment. This plain is, according to the Platonic text, "barren of trees and of all that naturally grows on earth" (621a). This barrenness signifies, according to Heidegger's reading, that the field, λήθη itself, is counter to φύσις, i.e., that as withdrawing and concealing, it counters all emerging into presence. Second, Heidegger's reading stresses that the only thing that the wandering souls find on this plain is a river, which is called Ἀμέλης, translated by Heidegger as *Ohnesorge,* carelessness. The water of the river can be held by no vessels, because it is sheer slipping-away (*Entgängnis*), withdrawal as such, which counters that care (*Sorge*) for unconcealment that would take care that beings remain in the sphere of the unconcealed. Finally, the drinking of this water—required of all except the one, Er, who is to save the tale—is taken to signify that each man, upon returning to earth, brings along an essential belongingness to the realm of concealment (*Parm* 175–78). On earth, too, and not only in Hades, λήθη belongs essentially to ἀλήθεια.

Even, for instance, in the πόλις, to which the entire discussion in the dialogue named accordingly is addressed. That much more reason for not isolating the myth of Er from the remainder of the discussion in the *Republic,* for letting the myth flow back, as it were, through the entire dialogue, inscribing concealment throughout yet perhaps most insistently in the opening deed ("I went down yesterday to Piraeus . . .") and in the story told, at the center, of the cave from which, as from the shadowy realm of Hades, one would ascend into the light and the clearing above. One might then also want to ask more insistently about what has always been called the body, to take seriously the sense in which, however ascendant, one never really leaves the cave but continues gazing at shadows, remaining far short of a pure apprehension of the εἴδη. One might then begin to wonder about a certain Heideggerian translation, namely, of ψυχή as *Mensch* (cf. *W* 217). One might then need to insist all the more on the play of the ambiguity in the *Republic,* throughout the *Republic,* even in the opening of the allegedly fundamental distinction between τὸ νοητόν and τὸ αἰσθητόν, the distinction by which the very sense of fundamental, of fundament, of ground—to say nothing of sense itself—is first determined.[10]

In the course of his lecture text *Parmenides,* Heidegger poses the following question: "Is the shadowness of Being in Hades connected with the essence of the Greek experience of beings and of their unconcealment?" (*Parm* 144). What if this question were to govern a reading of the *Republic?* Then it would be a matter of tracing in the dialogue the lines—or, rather, the shadows—of archaic closure, of the closure belonging to the ἀρχή, belonging within the origin at the origin, at the threshold of metaphysics.

FIFTEEN

Hades

(Heraclitus, Fragment B 98)

My concern is to engage in a thoughtful reading of a fragment of Heraclitean thinking. Any attempt at such a reading must contend with the distance at which the tradition, in running its course, has placed us. Yet we are prepared for this contention, opened to it in a unique way, insofar as we are thrown out of the tradition through its very ending and freed of that weight which we would otherwise bear to the beginnings of the tradition. In this respect, Fink's insight is decisive: "It is only as nihilists that we can speak with the Greeks"[1]—even if, on the other hand, the very self-insight of nihilism proceeds already from a bearing toward beginnings, from dialogue with Greek thinking.

(A)

Fragment 98 reads: "αἱ ψυχαὶ ὀσμῶνται καθ᾽ Ἅιδην." Diels translates: "Die Seelen atmen Geruch ein im Hades."[2] Burnet renders it in English: "Souls smell in Hades."[3] Freeman eliminates the ambiguity: "Souls have the sense of smell in Hades."[4] Cherniss eliminates any suggestion of mere passivity: "Souls employ the sense of smell in Hades."

This fragment is handed down only by Plutarch. It is quoted in his dialogue "Concerning the Face which Appears in the Orb of the Moon," specifically, in the course of the myth with which this dialogue concludes. The myth, told by an unnamed stranger, portrays the moon as inhabited by souls that have left their bodies after death on earth or have not yet been incorporated by birth into terrestrial bodies. Among these are certain souls who,

> resembling the ether about the moon, . . . get from it both tension and strength. . . . In consequence, they are nourished by any exhalation that

Originally published in *Heraclitean Fragments*, ed. John Sallis and Kenneth Maly (University of Alabama Press, 1980).

reaches them, and Heraclitus was right in saying: "Souls employ the sense of smell in Hades."[5]

Such is the context in which the fragment is handed down, a context in which it was placed by Plutarch more than five hundred years after the death of Heraclitus. It is a decidedly Hellenistic context, related back probably to Plato's *Timaeus*[6] but foreign to early Greek thinking. The early Greeks did not set Hades in the sky; nor could they have identified Hades with the source of night's illumination.[7] Hades was much too awesome.

One is thus obliged to take up Heraclitus' saying as a fragment in a dual sense: Not only does it lack its original context, but also it must be wrested from that context in which it has stood since Plutarch. To attempt a thoughtful reading requires, first of all, that one let the fragment be radically fragmentary.

So, I let the context drop away and attend to the isolated fragment. But, then especially, the paradox that the fragment seems to express comes to light. One wonders that souls can be said to have any senses whatever in the realm to which they pass after death, much less a sense so inferior as smell, so coarse and bodily, especially in comparison with sight.[8] Is not death precisely the separation of the soul from everything bodily and sensible—hence, from all senses and, most emphatically, from senses as bodily as smell? This teaching regarding death, extracted from the beginning of Plato's *Phaedo*, provided the basis for the traditional understanding of death (if not also of life), and it is only by utmost vigilance that one can be so nihilistic as not still to carry this teaching along. When one lets the context drop away, the danger is that one may then merely draw the fragment into that context which one carries along. Little is accomplished if the fragment is freed from the Plutarchian context only to be transposed to the context provided by a sedimented, traditional teaching, especially since the latter context serves only to render the fragment hopelessly paradoxical. It is only as nihilists that we can speak with the Greeks.

So, I grant the fragment its requisite distance from the traditional teaching regarding death and the soul. Instead of drawing it into our context, I undertake to set it back within the context of early Greek teachings regarding death and the soul. According to certain of these teachings, the soul is breath; when at death the soul is separated from the body, the other senses perish, so that souls in Hades neither see nor hear; but since soul is breath and since smell is inhaled with the breath, even the bodiless souls in Hades retain the sense of smell.[9]

Thus, without being accommodated to something alien, the fragment becomes understandable from this context—even though the puzzle remains as to how the sense of smell could be had by mere breath, i.e., without any organ of smell. However, in this way the fragment becomes understandable *only* as an affirmation and extension of popular opinion regarding the soul. One expects something more and, seeking to read thoughtfully this fragment of thinking, anticipates a dimension in which the fragment would become understandable in that radicalness which distinguishes all genuine thinking from popular opinion. There is reason for such anticipation, not only in the reports about Heraclitus' haughtiness and his disdain for common opinions,[10] but, more significantly, in the various fragments expressing the opposition between a hearkening to the λόγος and the many's mere semblance of understanding.[11]

But how is one to think the fragment back into the dimension anticipated? Perhaps by heeding the warning expressed in another fragment:

> You would not find out the limits of soul, even by travelling along every path: so deep is its λόγος (Fr. 45).

How is one to undertake to think the fragment back into its anticipated dimension? By proceeding not from soul but rather from the word with which Fragment 98 ends, *Hades*—that is, by regressing from the end of the sentence back toward its beginning, by reading the sentence backwards.

(B)

Hades (Ἀιδης) is not primarily the name of a place; in classical Greek it is, rather, the name of a god.[12] On the other hand, the god is closely connected with his domain and his character thoroughly determined by that connection. Thus, the extension of the name *Hades* to the domain of the god Hades is not without grounds.

Homer tells of the original assignment of the god's domain. In the *Iliad* he has Poseidon speak of how, when the world was divided into three parts, the three brothers, Zeus, Poseidon himself, and Hades, cast lots and of how each then received his own domain, sky being granted to Zeus, sea to Poseidon, and the dark underworld to Hades.[13] The name *Hades* already anticipates the allotment: It means "unseen." Hades and his domain are withdrawn from the light, from the light of the sun. They are withdrawn, not merely in the way that things are temporarily enclosed in the darkness of night, but rather in such a way that they never admit the light of the sun. This withdrawal is in part retraced by Heraclitus in Fragment 120. He names four directions: the limit of morning, that of evening, the bear, and (opposite the bear) the boundary mark of flashing Zeus. It is thus that the domain of the sun, including both day *and* night, is measured out.[14] Hades is set over against this domain, withdrawn from it into the "nocturnal abyss," into essential concealment. The domain of Hades is a λήθης δόμος, a place of oblivion, an abode of concealment.[15]

For Homer, Hades is not only the "unseen" god withdrawn from the domain of sun and light but also the ruler of the dead; the domain into which he is withdrawn is that to which all are withdrawn after death. It is the domain in which dwell, according to the *Odyssey*, "the unheeding dead, the phantoms [εἴδωλα] of dead men."[16] It is the abode where men, withdrawn by death, live on as εἴδωλα, as phantoms, as images. It is the abode in which men, withdrawn from the open life of the πόλις, reduced to mere images, are enclosed amidst shadows, in obscurity, in concealment.

In Fragment 27 Heraclitus poses death in its concealing power. "There await men after they are dead things which they do not expect nor opine." This says: Beyond death are things which in no way reveal themselves to living men, things which can in no way be foreseen, things radically concealed.[17] For living man, death is radical concealment, a veil on which shimmer only the faint images cast there by the poets. But how, then, does it happen that Heraclitus says: Souls employ the sense of smell in Hades?

Perhaps one should begin to wonder what the fragment says and especially whether it carries the claim of telling how things are *in* Hades. Also it should again be recalled that *Hades* refers to the god, not the place; and then one rightly wonders how souls can be said to be *in* Hades. In fact, the fragment does not say ἐν Ἅιδη but rather καθ᾽ Ἅιδην. What does καθ᾽, i.e., κατά, mean here? Certainly it may mean "in" (for instance, in the sense of "throughout"). But it has a wide range of other possible meanings. It may have the sense of direction toward a thing or purpose, the sense that would be expressed in such statements as: "Souls are on the scent of Hades" or "Souls employ the sense of smell for the sake of Hades." The preposition may also have the sense of fitness, conformity, accord. In this case the fragment would be rendered: "Souls employ the sense of smell in accord with Hades." Thus rendered, the fragment says: In the specific mode corresponding to the sense of smell, souls comport themselves in accord with Hades. Now the fragment has ceased being a proclamation of how things are after death. But what does it mean for souls to comport themselves in accord with the god Hades? What kind of comportment would this be? Both in his character as withdrawn from the sun's domain and as ruler of the dead, Hades is the god whose comportment is determined by concealment—no less than Zeus' comportment is determined by the unconcealing wrought by the lightning bolt he wields. Souls comport themselves to Hades precisely insofar as they are engaged in and by concealment. What is at issue in the fragment is not the state of dead men but rather living man's engagement in λήθη.

(C)

But why is that mode of comportment in which man comports himself to concealment identified as corresponding to the sense of smell? What does smell have to do with concealment? Does it perhaps serve to make phenomenally manifest man's comportment to concealment?

Another fragment regarding smell needs to be brought into consideration, namely, Fragment 7, which reads: "εἰ πάντα τὰ ὄντα καπνὸς γένοιτο, ῥῖνες ἂν διαγνοῖεν." In translation: "If all things were to become smoke, distinguishing would be by means of the nose."

This fragment has been frequently discussed and variously interpreted.[18] Almost invariably, however, interpretation has come down to a correlating of the fragment with an abstractly conceived relation between one and many. For example, the fragment has been regarded as ironical, specifically, as a criticism of man's tendency to find diversity while ignoring the unity of things. It is thus regarded as saying: Even if things turned to smoke so that their oneness became evident, men's noses would still smell out differences and concentrate on the diversity of things. However, the one (ἕν) of which Heraclitus speaks is not the mere outcome of a dissolution of all differences between things but is, rather, that which gathers all things (τὰ πάντα) and lights them up in their articulated differences, just as the lightning steers all things (Fr. 64) by flashing out in the night so as to light up things and let them be seen in their articulation.[19] For things to turn to smoke would thus hardly suffice to make evident their oneness but would rather serve to conceal their unity no less than their diversity. Another direction of interpretation regards the fragment as simply putting forward something that in a paradigmatic fashion is both one and many, in the sense that the smoke is one to sight but many to smell; but this interpretation also fails completely to retain the proper tension between one and many, that is, it regards the one as a mere result of dissolution of differences (in this case, differences for sight).

Nevertheless, it is important to bring into play the contrast between sight and smell in relation to the phenomenon of smoke. If all things were to become smoke, then one could not employ the means on which usually one relies primarily for distinguishing between things, namely, sight. At least as regards sight, smoke conceals.[20] Not only does it conceal whatever stands behind it, but also, as itself impenetrable to sight, it is peculiarly self-concealing. For all things to become smoke would mean that they become concealed from sight, not by something else that would come to stand in front of them, but rather by themselves, by their own self-concealing withdrawal from sight. What the antecedent clause of the fragment poses is concealment.

So, if all things were to become smoke, distinguishing would be by means of the nose, that is, by the sense of smell. Why? Because under this condition sight could not execute that distinguishing usually entrusted primarily to it. But then, the question is: How capable is the nose of taking over the work of the eyes? How capable is smell of laying out things in their distinctness? Later, Aristotle will contend that man's sense of smell is inferior in two respects, "inferior to that of all other living creatures and also inferior to all the other senses we possess";[21] in both respects, the inferior position of our sense of smell lies in its inferior capacity for distinguishing things.[22] Heraclitus also attests, though indirectly, to the inferiority of the sense of smell by speaking of the superiority of other senses, the senses that teach one something, the senses to which a teaching and learning (μάθησις) attaches: "I give preference to everything of which sight and hearing give knowledge."[23] But what, most of all, attests to the inferiority of the sense of smell is the phenomenon itself. For man, the sense of smell is hardly at all a matter of teaching and learning (μάθησις). For man, the sense of smell is, least of all the senses, capable of genuinely distinguishing things, of reenacting the lighting-articulation to which so many of the fragments are in one way or another addressed—the lighting-articulation which the one (ἕν) brings to all things (τὰ πάντα). Smell least of all is capable of embracing the distinct contours of things in such a way that they become manifest as they are. In utmost contrast to sight, the sense of smell lets things remain submerged in indistinctness, sunk in concealment.

Thus, there is a peculiar fittingness of the sense of smell to the smoke of which the fragment speaks. Whereas the antecedent clause poses concealment, the consequent clause poses that way of comportment toward things that is most subjected to the power of concealment, that is least capable of drawing things out of their withdrawal into self-closure and indistinctness. What the fragment poses as correlative to the concealment (of smoke) is human comportment to concealment.

Let me add, in passing, that another mode of comportment that is intrinsically linked to concealment is sleep. According to Hesiod, sleep is carried by night, has its home in the underworld, and, most significantly, is the brother of death.[24] It is in this connection that—if one accepts the testimony handed down by Sextus Empiricus[25]—one might understand the peculiarly privileged position that Heraclitus assigns to breath in sleep: In sleep, breath (and, hence, smell) is the only point of attachment that one retains with the surrounding. Within that reposing in concealment that one undergoes in sleep, there is a withdrawal from one's waking comportment with things into a passive retention of the one mode of that comportment that is most fitted to concealment.

(D)

A position has now been reached from which to read more thoughtfully the fragment with which we began: "αἱ ψυχαὶ ὀσμῶνται καθ᾽ ῞Αιδην." *Hades* names the god who withdraws from the domain of the sun and rules over the dead—the god whose basic comportment is determined by concealment, whose mythic deeds trace, as it were, the direction and movement of concealment. The fragment speaks of comportment in accord with Hades—that is, of comportment which accords with that of Hades by being itself a reenactment of the god's comportment, by being itself an engagement in the movement of concealment. This engagement Heraclitus makes phenomenally manifest by the reference to smell, that manner of comportment in which man is preeminently engaged by, drawn into, held within, the movement of concealment.

Thus read, the fragment is a tautology—that is, a sentence (λόγος) which says the same thing (τὸ αὐτό) over again. What it says is: engagement in concealment. But it says it in two quite different ways: phenomenally in the reference to smell, mythically in the reference to Hades.

Let me, then, displace the literal translation—the translation: "Souls employ the sense of smell in Hades." Or rather, let me expand it in such a way as to install within it the reading that has been attempted. Then it might be rendered: Souls, employing the sense of smell, are engaged in the movement of concealment. Or, still more expandedly: The soul's employment of the sense of smell exemplifies and makes phenomenally manifest the soul's engagement in the movement of concealment, in the withdrawal of things into self-closure and indistinction.

At this point the limit of the fragment begins to come into play, its limitation to engagement in concealment. This is a limit because in his comportment to things man's engagement is never solely an engagement in concealment—certainly not in his waking hours, not even in the night. For, to speak with the Heraclitean images of Fragment 26, in the night man kindles a light and even in sleep touches upon, thus lights up, death. The same issue is evident in Fragment 7—provided one attends carefully to what the fragment says phenomenally. Over against comportment to concealment, it poses concealment phenomenally as smoke. What needs to be noticed is very commonplace: Smoke accompanies—*fire*! It is, as Fink says, the "shadow of fire";[26] and yet its concealing power is such that it can even conceal that which it shadows. With smoke there is fire—that is, the one (ἕν), which Heraclitus also thinks as λόγος, as lightning, as sun. But how are they together?

At the limit of the fragment which I have attempted to read, at the point from which it speaks, its beginning—here one comes up against the issue from which perhaps all the fragments of Heraclitean thinking ultimately rebound—the issue, to say it phenomenally: How do fire and smoke belong together? One can also ask it mythically: Where lies the joint which joins the domain of the sun to that of Hades, Zeus' lightning to Hades' withdrawal into darkness, revealment to concealment? Where is that joint by which, as Heraclitus himself says (Fr. 15), Hades and Dionysus are held together in the unity of sameness?

This would also be the joint of the soul, the joint which, as λόγος sunk into the depths of the soul, gathers the soul into its limits. The sense of the warning that was heard in Fragment 45 is now clearer: It warns of the rebound from the issue of the togetherness of revealment and concealment. One direction in which the rebound may be sustained is that in which one is carried by taking up Heraclitus' saying in Fragment 32: "The one, alone wise, is not willing and is willing to be called by the name Zeus." ῝Εν is Zeus as the highest being, yet ῝Εν is not Zeus insofar as it is that which lets every being come forth into presence, be revealed.[27] Must one not say the same of Hades? The nocturnal abyss, set over against the sun's domain (over against the entire domain of ἕν-πάντα), is not willing and is willing to be called by the name *Hades*. The abyss is Hades as the lowest (deepest) being yet is not Hades insofar as it is that which withdraws every being back into self-closed absence, into concealment. Or, does the abyss of Hades, as withdrawing things into concealment, perhaps withdraw itself still more sternly from every attempt to call it by name?

In the course of the tradition since Heraclitus, the deepest thinkers have sought nevertheless to name what Heraclitus the obscure names Hades. The task remains—or, rather, if we are sufficiently capable of nihilism, it is posed for us with renewed force and clarity, posed as a task that could never be brought straightforwardly to completion without violating precisely that which the name would name, without thus unleashing again the strife between name and the self-closing withdrawal that the name would name. The task is, rather, to persevere in the difference and to let the strife between name and named be a reenactment of the primordial strife between Zeus and Hades (light and darkness), Dionysus and Hades (life and death). This strife of ἀλήθεια is the strife, the war (πόλεμος) which, in the famous words of Fragment 53, is the father of all things. But it is also a strife which is reflected, duplicated from afar, in the structure of every image, even the simplest—in that dual character by which revealment and concealment are conjoined in every play of images.

Notes

Ὁρισμός

1. Jacques Derrida, *Positions* (Paris: Editions de Minuit, 1972), 77. Also "Le retrait de la métaphore," *Poesie* 6 (1979): 110.

2. ". . . ihre unbedingte Herrschaft im Seienden selbst. . . ." *Vorträge und Aufsätze* (Pfullingen: Günther Neske, 1954), 71.

3. Ibid., 155.

1. IMAGINATION AND METAPHYSICS

1. *Kritik der reinen Vernunft*, ed. Raymund Schmidt (Hamburg: Felix Meiner, 1956), A 5/B 8–9.

2. *A Midsummer Night's Dream*, act 5, sc. 1, lines 12–17.

3. *Meditations on First Philosophy*, trans. Laurence J. Lafleur (Indianapolis: Bobbs-Merrill, 1960), 27.

4. Samuel Johnson, *The Rambler*, no. 125 (Tuesday, 28 May 1751). *The Yale Edition of the Works of Samuel Johnson*, vol. 4, ed. W. J. Bate and Albrecht B. Strauss (New Haven: Yale University Press, 1969), 300.

5. John Dryden, Epistle Dedicatory to "The Rival Ladies." *The Works of John Dryden*, general editor H. T. Swedenberg (Berkeley: University of California Press, 1962), 8: 101. Dryden's remark is directed specifically at "Imagination in a Poet" and is put forth in defense of rhyme, which "Bounds and Circumscribes the Fancy."

6. *A Midsummer Night's Dream*, act 5, sc. 1, lines 18–22.

7. *Phaedo* 99e.

8. Cf. *Being and Logos: The Way of Platonic Dialogue* (Pittsburgh: Duquesne University Press, 1975), chap. 5.

9. *Imaginatio* translates φαντασία, and *phantasia* renders φάντασμα. Cf. Murray Wright Bundy, *The Theory of Imagination in Classical and Medieval Thought* (University of Illinois, 1927), 193, 278.

10. Gianfrancesco Pico della Mirandola, *On the Imagination*, Latin text with English translation by Harry Caplan, *Cornell Studies in English*, vol. 16 (New Haven: Yale University Press, 1930), 25.

11. Ibid., 33.

12. Ibid., 29.

13. Ibid., 47.

14. Ibid., 29.

15. Pico refers this statement to Synesius (*De Insomniis*). Ibid., 37.

16. Cf. *The Gathering of Reason* (Athens: Ohio University Press, 1980), esp. chap. 7, sec. 2.

17. *Kritik der reinen Vernunft*, B 151.

18. F. W. J. Schelling, *System des transzendentalen Idealismus* (Hamburg: Felix Meiner, 1957), 227.

19. "Lecture on the Slave-Trade (June 1795)," in *Imagination in Coleridge*, ed. John Spencer Hill (Totowa: Rowman and Littlefield, 1978), 27.

20. *The Prelude*, bk. 14, line 192.
21. See especially the section entitled "Of the Typic of Pure Practical Judgment" in *Kritik der praktischen Vernunft*, vol. 5 of *Kants Werke: Akademie Textausgabe* (Berlin: Walter de Gruyter, 1968), 67–71.
22. Ibid., 42.
23. Pico, *On the Imagination*, 81.
24. *Republic* 510b.
25. Ibid., 533a.
26. To this sentence, written during the period of *Die Fröhliche Wissenschaft*, Nietzsche adds the following parenthetical comment: "(unfortunately made obscure [*verdunkelt*] by German philosophy—frosted glass)." *Gesammelte Werke. Musarionausgabe* (München: Musarion Verlag, 1920–29), 11: 284.
27. "Circles," vol. 2 of *The Collected Works of Ralph Waldo Emerson* (Cambridge: Harvard University Press, 1979), 179.

2. THE END OF METAPHYSICS: CLOSURE AND TRANSGRESSION

1. See especially *Die Fröhliche Wissenschaft*, vol. V/2 of *Nietzsche Werke: Kritische Gesamtausgabe*, ed. Giorgio Colli and Mazzino Montinari (Berlin: Walter de Gruyter, 1967ff.), 158–60; and in *Die Götzen-Dämmerung* the chapters entitled " 'Reason' in Philosophy" and "How the 'True World' Finally Became a Fable," vol. VI/3 of *Werke*, 68–75.
2. *Die Götzen-Dämmerung*, 75.
3. *Die Fröhliche Wissenschaft*, 145 (§ 108).
4. *Kritik der reinen Vernunft*, A 856/B 884.
5. Ibid., A xiii.
6. *Phänomenologie des Geistes*, ed. Hoffmeister (Hamburg: Felix Meiner, 1952), 12.
7. *System des transzendentalen Idealismus*, 298.
8. *Zur Sache des Denkens* (Tübingen: Max Niemeyer, 1969), 63.
9. *Sein und Zeit* (Tübingen: Max Niemeyer, 1960), especially § 50.
10. *Kritik der reinen Vernunft*, B 71–72.
11. *Nietzsche* (Pfullingen: Günther Neske, 1961), 2: 201.
12. Jacques Derrida, *La Voix et le phénomène* (Paris: Presses Universitaires de France, 1967), esp. chap. 5.
13. "Das Ende der Philosophie und die Aufgabe des Denkens," in *Zur Sache des Denkens*, 61–80.
14. *Sein und Zeit*, 132.
15. *Zur Sache des Denkens*, 71.
16. Ibid., 72.
17. *Émile*, vol. 4 of *Oeuvres Complètes* (Paris: Gallimard, Pléiade, 1959), 304f.

4. HEGEL'S CONCEPT OF PRESENTATION

1. *Jenaer Schriften* 1801–1807, vol. 2 of *Werke* (Frankfurt a.M.: Suhrkamp Verlag, 1970), 182.
2. *Phänomenologie des Geistes*, ed. J. Hoffmeister (Hamburg: Felix Meiner Verlag, 1964), 16f. Hereafter *Phän.*
3. *Jenaer Schriften*, 182.
4. Following the division given by Hoffmeister, which is based on that given in the table of contents of the first edition of 1807.

5. Within the Preface, see also the statements in sections 14–15, e.g., "scientific knowing, however, demands rather that one surrender to the life of the object" (*Phän.* 45).

6. Thus, near the end of the Preface Hegel satirizes those who take that "royal road to science" which consists in relying on common sense (i.e., refusing to undergo the inversion into philosophy) and in reading reviews of and *prefaces* to philosophical writings—a "vulgar road [which] can be taken in one's dressing gown" (*Phän.* 56f.), that is, which excuses itself from the "*Anstrengung des Begriffs.*"

7. For the purposes of this study, it will suffice to let the usage of *aufheben* and its derivatives be governed by the sense determined in the early stages of the *Phenomenology* and expressed thus in the chapter on Wahrnehmung: "Das Aufheben stellt seine wahrhafte gedoppelte Bedeutung dar, welche wir an dem Negativen gesehen haben: es ist ein *Negieren* und ein *Aufbewahren* zugleich" (*Phän.* 90). Hegel's more extended determination is given in *Wissenschaft der Logik,* ed. G. Lasson (Hamburg: Felix Meiner Verlag, 1967), 1: 93–5. No English word suitably translates *aufheben.* However, because of the stylistic difficulty of retaining the German verb with its separable prefix, resort will be had to the frequently used translation *sublate*—which makes it necessary to insist all the more that the sense of the word be taken from Hegel's explicit determinations and not from extraphilosophical preconceptions.

8. "Es kommt nach meiner Einsicht, welche sich [nur] durch die Darstellung des Systems selbst rechtfertigen muß, alles darauf an, das Wahre nicht als *Substanz,* sondern eben so sehr als *Subjekt* aufzufassen und auszudrücken" (*Phän.* 19). *Nur* was added in the revisions for a second edition, which Hegel began to prepare shortly before his death.

9. Part I. Definition 3.

10. Fichte, *Grundlage der gesammten Wissenschaftslehre,* vol. 1 of *Werke* (Berlin: De Gruyter, 1971), 120–22.

11. *Differenz des Fichte'schen und Schelling'schen Systems der Philosophie* (Hamburg: Felix Meiner Verlag, 1962), 75ff.

12. *Erste Einleitung in die Wissenschaftslehre: Werke,* 1: 440; *Zweite Einleitung in die Wissenschaftslehre: Werke,* 498.

13. Note added to the second edition of the *Grundlage* in 1802. *Werke,* 1: 98.

14. Hegel, *Differenz,* 48, 75.

15. In the *Differenz*-Schrift (77) Hegel uses this formulation ("Das Absolute selbst aber ist darum die Identität der Identität und der Nichtidentität") in showing how Schelling's thought goes beyond the limited standpoint (of subjective subject-object) to which Fichte remains attached. The formulation takes on added significance if contrasted with the corresponding formulation given in Schelling's *Darstellung meines Systems der Philosophie,* which was published the same year as Hegel's *Differenz-Schrift;* Schelling's formulation is: "Die absolute Identität *ist* nur unter der Form einer Identität der Identität" (*Sämmtliche Werke.* Abt. I/4: 121). In the section of the *Phenomenology* under consideration, Hegel's mention of "intellectual intuition" is presumably to be understood as a reference to Schelling (cf. *Differenz,* 92f).

16. Regarding the governing sense of *sublate,* see note 7 above.

17. Cf. Werner Marx, *Hegels Phänomenologie des Geistes: Die Bestimmung ihrer Idee in "Vorrede" und "Einleitung"* (Frankfurt a.M.: Vittorio Klostermann, 1971), 98.

18. The connection at issue here between self-consciousness and serious otherness can be clarified by reference to Fichte. In Fichte's work there occurs a

distinction which, granted certain fundamental differences, corresponds rather closely to Hegel's distinction between the true in itself and the true for itself. In the formulation given in Fichte's *Zweiter Einleitung* (1797), the relevant distinction is that between mere intellectual intuition, i.e., self-reverting activity, which Fichte identifies as constituting the mere *possibility* of self-consciousness, *and* genuine (concrete) self-consciousness, i.e., the positing of the I as determinate (*Werke*, 1: 459). In contrast to the sheer self-positing expressed in the first principle of the *Wissenschaftslehre*, which never occurs unmixed but is arrived at only by abstraction, concrete self-consciousness requires a genuine otherness, an otherness more radical than the always immediately surpassed otherness of abstract self-positing; it requires that a not-I be brought forth. As the matter is expressed in the theoretical part of the *Grundlage*: "An I that posits itself as self-positing, or a *subject*, is impossible without an object brought forth in the manner described (the determination of the I, its reflection upon itself as determinate, is possible only on the condition that it bound itself by an opposite)" (*Werke*, 1: 218). This means: The I's reflection on itself, i.e., determinate self-consciousness, i.e., a determinate I as such, is possible only if a not-I is opposed to the I. The matter is even clearer in the *Zweite Einleitung*: Formulating the task of the *Wissenschaftslehre*, Fichte writes that it will be necessary to show "firstly, how the I is and may be for itself; then, that this being of itself for itself would be impossible, unless there also at once arose for it an existence outside itself" (*Werke*, 1: 458). In other words, opposition (negation) is required for determination; that is, the I can posit itself as determinate only in opposition to the not-I. Thus, for Fichte there is an intrinsic relation between genuine self-consciousness and serious otherness, and this relation has primarily to do with the possibility of determinateness in contrast to the total indeterminateness of the absolutely self-positing I of the first principle. This general connection which Fichte established between self-consciousness and serious otherness, the connecting of them through the concept of determination, remained decisive for Hegel.

On the other hand, the specific context of the connection was transformed when Hegel, following the lead of Schelling, replaced the Fichtean not-I with an object capable of reflection into itself, capable of unfolding into an objective subject-object. Regarding this development, see Marx, *Hegels Phänomenologie des Geistes*, 61ff.

19. "Unter mancherlei Folgerungen, die aus dem Gesagten fließen, kann diese herausgehoben werden, daß das Wissen nur als Wissenschaft oder als *System* wirklich ist und dargestellt werden kann" (*Phän.* 23).

20. Cf. *Phän.* 53, together with Werner Marx, *Reason and World* (The Hague: Martinus Nijhoff, 1971), 36.

21. It must be stressed that these considerations concern presentation *in general*, that is, they take no account of what is peculiar to an *initiatory* presentation or, therefore, of the specific way in which such a presentation would stand under the requirements here prescribed for presentation in general.

22. "Daß das Wahre nur als System wirklich, oder daß die Substanz wesentlich Subjekt ist, ist in der Vorstellung ausgedrückt, welche das Absolute als *Geist* ausspricht . . ." (*Phän.* 24).

23. Cf. Martin Heidegger, *Holzwege* (Frankfurt a.M.: Vittorio Klostermann, 1957), 120.

24. Cf. Marx, *Hegels Phänomenologie des Geistes*, 103f.

25. It is in terms of this "distance" that the problem of the form and, more specifically, of the language required of an initiatory presentation would need to be developed. The basis for such a development is provided by Hegel's deter-

mination of the form of speculative presentation, which is carried out in section 17 of the Preface and which is an extension of the considerations of language already given in section 6. The crucial point is that a speculative presentation is not the same as an initiatory presentation (cf. Marx, *Hegels Phänomenologie des Geistes,* 104); and thus the linguistic requirement under which the former stands cannot simply be carried over to the latter. In other words, it would be necessary to determine in precisely what measure an *initiatory* presentation stands under those requirements. The peculiar "distance" from the presented determines that measure, which may thus be posed (with respect to the single proposition as considered in section 6) as a general structural correspondence: To the extent that presentation is at a distance from the movement presented, so, to that extent the movement within the proposition will be referred to a knower outside the proposition rather than being actually the movement of the subject of the proposition.

5. IMAGE AND PHENOMENON

1. Edmund Husserl, *Cartesianische Meditationen,* vol. 1 of *Husserliana* (The Hague: Martinus Nijhoff, 1950), 54.
2. Husserl, *Ideen zu einer reinen Phänomenologie und phänomenologischen Philosophie,* Erstes Buch, vol. 3 of *Husserliana* (The Hague: Martinus Nijhoff, 1950), 52.
3. Martin Heidegger, *Sein und Zeit,* 34.
4. Husserl, *Logische Untersuchungen* (Tübingen: Max Niemeyer Verlag, 1968), I: x.
5. Ibid., II/1: 370–75 (§ 11).
6. Ibid., II/1: 424.
7. Ibid., II/1: 421–24.
8. Cf. ibid., II/1: 127–32; also 160–66.
9. Ibid., II/1: 422.
10. *Kritik der reinen Vernunft,* A 598/B 626.
11. In the Appendix in which the image-theory is criticized, Husserl makes explicit reference to Anselm's ontological proof, *Logische Untersuchungen,* II/1: 424.
12. *Die Geburt der Tragödie,* vol. III/1 of *Nietzsche Werke: Kritische Gesamtausgabe,* 22.
13. Husserl, *Die Pariser Vorträge,* vol. 1 of *Husserliana* (The Hague: Martinus Nijhoff, 1950), 18.
14. Cf. my *Phenomenology and the Return to Beginnings* (Pittsburgh: Duquesne University Press, 1973), 37f.

6. RESEARCH AND DECONSTRUCTION

1. Martin Heidegger, *Die Grundprobleme der Phänomenologie,* vol. 24 of *Gesamtausgabe* (Frankfurt a.M.: Vittorio Klostermann, 1975ff.), 3.
2. ". . . leave the last word to the things themselves and to work on them." Husserl, *Logische Untersuchungen,* I: x.
3. Husserl, *Philosophie als strenge Wissenschaft* (Frankfurt a.M.: Vittorio Klostermann, 1965), 71.
4. M. Merleau-Ponty, *Phénoménologie de la Perception* (Paris: Gallimard, 1945), 419.
5. Ibid., 375.
6. Ibid., 365.

7. Heidegger, *Logik: Die Frage nach der Wahrheit,* vol. 21 of *Gesamtausgabe,* 113–25.

8. Merleau-Ponty, *Phénoménologie de la Perception,* 377.

7. THE ORIGINS OF HEIDEGGER'S THOUGHT

1. The address is published in *Max Scheler im Gegenwartsgeschehen der Philosophie,* ed. P. Good (Bern: Francke Verlag, 1975).

2. *Sein und Zeit,* 164.

3. *Zur Sache des Denkens,* 71.

4. *Einführung in die Metaphysik* (Tübingen: Max Niemeyer Verlag, 1958), 29f.

8. WHERE DOES *BEING AND TIME* BEGIN?

1. *Sein und Zeit,* 153. Hereafter *SZ.*

2. *Sophist* 242c.

3. Ibid., 244a; *SZ* 1.

4. *Metaphysics,* IV, 2; VII, 1. Regarding the limits of the designation of this unity as a unity of analogy, see Joseph Owens, *The Doctrine of Being in the Aristotelian Metaphysics* (Toronto: Pontifical Institute for Medieval Studies, 1957), 59.

5. The issue here raised with respect to Hegel's thought is later elaborated and given fundamental importance in Heidegger's interpretation. Cf. "Hegels Begriff der Erfahrung," *Holzwege* (Frankfurt a.M.: Vittorio Klostermann, 1957), 141–43.

6. Cf. *SZ* 44–45. On the negative side, these limits have been worked out by Werner Marx, *Heidegger and the Tradition,* trans. Theodore Kisiel and Murray Greene (Evanston: Northwestern University Press, 1971), 85–100.

7. A marginal note from the "*Hüttenexemplar*" comments on the statement "it can be inferred only that 'Being' is not anything like a being." The note reads: "no! rather: by means of such conceptuality [*Begrifflichkeit*] nothing can be decided regarding Being." *Gesamtausgabe,* 2: 5. Presumably, the note means that from the indefinableness of Being one cannot even draw the inference that Being is not a being. Even this inference goes too far, which is to say that the indefinableness of Being proves to leave matters even more questionable than Heidegger's 1927 text allowed.

8. Cf. *Was Ist Metaphysik?* (Frankfurt a.M.: Vittorio Klostermann, 1960), 13f.

9. *SZ* 315f. The inappropriateness of taking that being (which we are) *as* an I (as a subject in the modern metaphysical sense) is an issue which Heidegger repeatedly takes up in the course of *Being and Time* in such a way that the issue gets clarified at progressively more fundamental levels in the course of the work (e.g., *SZ* 46, 114–17, esp. 315–23). Cf. F.-W. von Herrmann, *Subjekt und Dasein* (Frankfurt a.M.: Vittorio Klostermann, 1974), 15–43.

10. This connection is indicated in a general way by Harold Alderman, "Heidegger: The Necessity and Structure of the Question of Being," *Philosophy Today* 14 (1970): 143. However, the precise connection between the question of Being and Dasein as a questioning comportment to Being is not made explicit.

11. Descartes, *Principia Philosophiae,* I, Pr. 51; cf. *SZ* 92ff.

12. Fichte, *Grundlage der gesammten Wissenschaftslehre,* vol. 1 of *Werke,* 97.

13. See Fichte, *Erste Einleitung in die Wissenschaftslehre,* vol. 1 of *Werke,* 440f.; also *Zweite Einleitung,* ibid., 498–500.

14. *Vom Wesen der Wahrheit* (Frankfurt a.M.: Vittorio Klostermann, 1961), 27.

15. It should be noted, however, that as *Being and Time* proceeds to more original levels of questioning this problem of unity has repeatedly to be posed again, namely, in connection with the consideration of care, of death, and of temporality.

16. *Zur Sache des Denkens*, 61.

9. INTO THE CLEARING

1. *Sein und Zeit (SZ)*.

2. *Zur Sache des Denkens*, 61, 80.

3. The *Hüttenexemplar* of *SZ* contains two notes pertaining to this passage. The first, keyed to "gelichtet," reads: "'Αλήθεια—Offenheit—Lichtung, Licht, Leuchten." The other, keyed to the final "ist," reads: "aber nicht produziert." *Gesamtausgabe*, 2: 177.

4. *Logik, Gesamtausgabe*, 21: 114–25.

10. END(S)

1. *Sein und Zeit (SZ)*, 1. *Die Grundprobleme der Phänomenologie*, vol. 24 of *Gesamtausgabe*. Hereafter *GP*.

2. *Zur Sache des Denkens*, 61.

3. Ibid., 62.

4. Ibid., 63.

5. *Über den Humanismus* (Frankfurt a.M.: Vittorio Klostermann, 1947), 17.

11. HEIDEGGER/DERRIDA—PRESENCE

1. Held at the eighty-first meeting of the American Philosophical Association, Eastern Division, 30 December 1984. The other participants in the symposium were Edward S. Casey and Robert Bernasconi.

2. *Journal of Philosophy* 81, no. 10 (October 1984): 594–601.

3. Heidegger, *Nietzsche*, 1: 9.

4. "Speaking is of itself [*von sich aus*] a listening. It is a listening to the language that we speak. Thus speaking is, not at the same time but beforehand, a listening. In an inconspicuous way this listening to language precedes all other kinds of listening. Not only do we speak *the* language, we speak *from out of* it [Wir sprechen nicht nur *die* Sprache, wir sprechen *aus* ihr]." *Unterwegs zur Sprache* (Pfullingen: Verlag Günther Neske, 1959), 254.

5. *La Voix et le phénomène*, chap. 7.

6. Heidegger, *Nietzsche*, 1: 233.

7. Derrida, *La Dissemination* (Paris: Editions du seuil, 1972), 31f.

8. Ibid., 33.

9. Ibid., 31.

10. Cf. *Sein und Zeit*, 25ff.

11. "The relational character which these relationships of assigning possess, we take as one of *signifying* [*be-deuten*]. . . . The relational totality of this signifying we call *significance* [*Bedeutsamkeit*]." Ibid., 87. The more phenomenological formulation of the results in § 18 has usually been emphasized: Things can present themselves only from within a world whose structure (worldhood) is a referential totality. This formulation has the disadvantage of not underlining so forcefully the deconstructive character of the analysis.

12. *La Voix et le phénomène*, 75f.

13. Ibid.

14. "This arche-writing is at work at the origin of sense. Sense, being temporal in nature, as Husserl recognized, is never simply present; it is always already engaged in the 'movement' of the trace, that is, in the order of 'signification.' It has always already issued forth from itself into the 'expressive stratum' of lived experience." Ibid., 96.

15. *Marges de la philosophie* (Paris: Les Editions de Minuit, 1972), 35f. The issue is raised again near the end of "Ousia and Gramme": "What about presence then? We cannot easily think in the Latin word *presence* the movements of differentiation that are produced in the Heideggerian text. The task here is immense and difficult." Ibid., 75.

16. Ibid., 75.

17. *Die Grundprobleme der Phänomenologie*, 402–404.

18. *Marges de la philosophie*, 58.

19. *Sein und Zeit*, 151.

20. Martin Heidegger, *Parmenides*, vol. 54 of *Gesamtausgabe*, 118.

21. Ibid., 119.

22. Ibid., 118.

23. Ibid., 118, 125.

24. Ibid., 125.

25. The reference to ideality could, of course, be a reference to the ideality not only of the signified (meaning) but also of the signifier, i.e., of the text as something reproducible ad infinitum. The latter ideality is what most immediately allows one to refer to multiple copies of (for example) a printed text as copies of the *same* text.

26. Cf. Friedrich Nietzsche, *Zur Genealogie der Moral*, vol. VI/2 of *Werke: Kritische Gesamtausgabe*, 293.

27. Heidegger, *Parmenides*, 113.

28. Jacques Derrida, *Positions*, 18.

29. The note is keyed to section 5 ("Das Wesen der Wahrheit") and refers to the transition to section 6 ("Die Unwahrheit als die Verbergung"). It reads: "Zwischen 5. und 6. der Sprung in die (im Ereignis wesende) Kehre." *Wegmarken*, vol. 9 of *Gesamtausgabe*, 193.

12. REASON AND EK-SISTENCE

1. *Brief über den Humanismus*, in *Wegmarken*, vol. 9 of *Gesamtausgabe*, 349. Hereafter *HB*.

2. "Wo aber Gefahr ist, wächst/Das Rettende auch." Cited in "Die Frage nach der Technik," in *Vorträge und Aufsätze*, 36, 43; and in "Die Kehre," in *Die Technik und die Kehre* (Pfullingen: Günther Neske, 1962), 41.

3. *Die Grundprobleme der Phänomenologie*, *Gesamtausgabe*, 150.

4. Earlier editions do not contain the first part of the second sentence, which in those editions reads simply: "Aber sie denkt nicht den Unterschied beider."

5. "Thus in *Being and Time* (42) in the sentence cited [the 'essence' of Dasein lies in its existence] the word 'essence' was deliberately written in quotation marks. This indicates that 'essence' is now being determined neither from *esse essentiae* nor *esse existentiae* but rather from the ek-static character of Dasein [*aus dem Ek-statischen des Daseins*]. As ek-sisting, man sustains Da-sein in that he takes the *Da* as the clearing of Being into 'care'" (*HB* 327). "The question of the essence of truth finds its answer in the proposition [*Satz*]: *the essence of truth is the truth of essence*" ("Vom wesen der Wahrheit," in *Wegmarken*, 201).

13. MEANING ADRIFT

1. Heidegger, *Nietzsche*, 1: 233.
2. Nietzsche, *Götzen-Dämmerung*, 74f.
3. Ibid., 51.
4. "Geschichte eines Irrthums": The subtitle of the section "Wie die 'wahre Welt' endlich zur Fabel wurde."
5. This contrast derives from Plato's *Sophist*, from the same context as that from which Heidegger takes the passage with which *Being and Time* begins (244a). Cf. Heidegger, *Sein und Zeit*, 1, 2, 6.
6. This peculiar inclusion is outlined most directly in the following passage from "The End of Philosophy and the Task of Thinking": "No look [*Aussehen*] without light—Plato already knew this. But there is no light and no brightness without the clearing [*Lichtung*]." *Zur Sache des Denkens*, 74. In this text it is ἀλήθεια that is being thought as clearing.
A similar indication, but in direct reference to Husserl, is given in *Being and Time*: "Even the phenomenological 'intuition of essences' ['Wesenschau'] is grounded in existential understanding" (*Sein und Zeit*, 147).
7. Cf. *Sein und Zeit*, § 18.
8. Cf. ibid., §§ 28, 34.
9. Cf. *Zur Sache des Denkens*, 77.
10. *Parmenides*, Freiburger Vorlesung Wintersemester 1942/43, vol. 54 of *Gesamtausgabe*.
11. Ibid., 27.
12. Ibid., 31–32.
13. Cf. *Sein und Zeit*, § 33.

14. AT THE THRESHOLD OF METAPHYSICS

1. *Sophist* 244a, *Sein und Zeit* (SZ), 1.
2. *Wegmarken*, vol. 9 of *Gesamtausgabe*, 203–238. Hereafter *W*.
3. "Das Ende der Philosophie und die Aufgabe des Denkens," *Zur Sache des Denkens*, 61–80. Citation from 74. Hereafter *SD*.
4. The first German edition appeared in 1928. The second German edition of volume 1, to which the discussion of Heidegger was added, was published as *Platon: Seinswahrheit und Lebenswirklichkeit* by Walter de Gruyter in 1954. The second edition was translated into English by Hans Meyerhoff and published as *Plato: An Introduction* (New York: Pantheon Books, 1958); it was issued in a paperback edition by Harper and Row in 1964. Chapter 11 is entitled "Aletheia, a Discussion with Martin Heidegger."
5. *Plato: An Introduction*, trans. Hans Meyerhoff (New York: Harper and Row, 1964), 229.
6. *Platon*. Band I. Dritte durchgesehene und ergänzte Auflage (Berlin: Walter de Gruyter, 1964); *Plato I: An Introduction*, 2d ed., trans. Hans Meyerhoff (Princeton University Press, 1969; paperback edition 1973).
Robert Bernasconi has pointed out that with regard to Friedländer's criticisms of Heidegger there are significant differences between all the relevant editions. The first English edition (1958), though based on the second German edition (1954), adds the discussion of Hesiod's use of ἀλήθεια in reference to a person. In the third German edition (1964) the entire chapter on Heidegger is substantially revised. On it then is based the second English edition (1969), though the latter adds still further revisions. Hence, there are actually four different versions

of Friedländer's criticisms of Heidegger. Cf. Robert Bernasconi, *The Question of Language in Heidegger's History of Being* (Atlantic Highlands: Humanities Press, 1985), chap. 2.

7. *Plato: An Introduction*, 2d edition, with revisions, trans. Hans Meyerhoff (Princeton University Press, 1973), 229. Hereafter *F2*.

8. Cf. *Being and Logos*, 156.

9. *Parmenides*, vol. 54 of *Gesamtausgabe*. Hereafter *Parm*.

10. Cf. *Being and Logos*, chap. 5.

15. HADES

1. Martin Heidegger and Eugen Fink, *Heraklit* (Frankfurt a.M.: Vittorio Klostermann, 1970), 259. Hereafter *H*. The same issue is expressed more problematically by Heidegger in the course of the Heraclitus seminar: Heraclitus' thinking is not yet metaphysical, whereas our thinking is no longer metaphysical. Heidegger grants that the greater difficulty lies in determining the character of the "no longer metaphysical" (*H* 108, 123–25).

2. Diels-Kranz, *Die Fragmente der Vorsokratiker* (Zurich: Weidmann, 1968), 173.

3. John Burnet, *Early Greek Philosophy* (New York: Meridian Books, 1957), 136.

4. Kathleen Freeman, *Ancilla to the Pre-Socratic Philosophers* (Oxford: Basil Blackwell, 1956), 31.

5. Plutarch, "Concerning the Face which appears in the Orb of the Moon," trans. Harold Cherniss, 28, 943 D-E, in *Moralia*, vol. 12 (Loeb).

6. Cf. Cherniss' Introduction, ibid., esp. 24; also ibid., 203, note e.

7. Note that the descent to Hades enacted at the beginning of Plato's *Republic* occurs at the festival of Bendis, who is related to or even identical with Hecate, the goddess of the *dark* of the moon; one feature of that festival was to be a torchrace on horseback. Cf. my *Being and Logos*, 315.

8. Cf. Aristotle, *On Sense and Sensibles* 441a; *Metaphysics* 980a.

9. Cf. Karl Reinhardt, *Parmenides und die Geschichte der griechischen Philosophie* (Frankfurt a.M.: Vittorio Klostermann, 1959), 195; G. S. Kirk and J. E. Raven, *The Presocratic Philosophers* (Cambridge and London: Cambridge University Press, 1957), 211.

10. Cf. G. S. Kirk, *Heraclitus: The Cosmic Fragments* (Cambridge and London: Cambridge University Press, 1970), 3–13.

11. E.g., Frr. 1, 2, 17; 34, 51, 56, 72, 104.

12. Cf. *Oxford Classical Dictionary*, 484.

13. *Iliad* 15: 187ff.

14. *H*, 64–67, 72–73.

15. After Homer a connection is commonly made between Hades and λήθη. Cf. Simonides 184.6; Plato, *Republic* 621a.

16. *Odyssey* 11: 475f.

17. See the discussion of this fragment in *H*, 242–46. Note especially Fink's contention regarding the meaning of the final word of the fragment—"dass δοχεῖν hier nicht 'wähnen,' sondern 'vernehmen' bedeutet" ("that δοχεῖν here signifies not 'believe' but rather 'perceive'").

18. For review and criticism of the major interpretations, see Kirk, *Heraclitus*, 232–36.

19. Virtually the entire Heraclitus seminar is directed toward clarifying the sense of ἕν and its relation to τὰ πάντα from the various viewpoints from which Heraclitus regards it (as lightning, fire, sun, war, logos). See esp. 11–21, 28f., 36.

20. Cf. *H*, 51–54.

21. *On Sense and Sensibles*, 441a. This is the text, though not the context, in which Aristotle quotes Fr. 7. The quotation comes at 443a.

22. Cf. Aristotle, *On the Soul*, II. 9.

23. ὅσων ὄψις ἀκοὴ μάθησις, ταῦτα ἐγὼ προτιμέω (Fr. 55). The translation is adapted from Heidegger's which is defended in *H*, 224f.

24. Hesiod, *Theogony*, 756ff.

25. Diels, 22 A 16.

26. *H*, 52f.; cf. Aristotle, *On Sense and Sensibles*, 438b.

27. Cf. Heidegger, *Vorträge und Aufsätze*, 222–24.

Index

Absence: and image, 7, 33; essential, 37; and presence, 126–27, 135, 144; and possibilities, 127; and signification, 144; and Hades, 192–93
Absicht, 101
Absolute, 48, 49, 54
Abwesenheit, 135
Action, 157–58
Actuality: and spirit, 20, 52; and telos, 21; and subject/substance, 45–46; the true as, 51; and images, 70
Analogy, 104, 200
Ansatz, 119, 129
Anschauung, 142
Anwesenheit, 119, 135, 144
Anxiety, 121
Appearances, 163
Aquinas, 125
Archi-écriture, 144
Aristotle, 8, 14, 90, 102, 103, 104, 130, 140, 167, 171, 175, 191
Art, 95
Aufheben, 43
Aufhebung, 21
Ausarbeitung, 101
Aussehen, 172, 174, 203
Authenticity, 94

Bedeutsamkeit, 142
Bedeutung, 164
Befindlichkeit, 121
Befragte, 106
Being: meaning of, x, 87, 91, 101, 124–25, 133, 145, 150, 156, 170–71; question of, 24–25, 105, 108–109, 117, 124–25, 131, 145, 155, 175; as time, 87, 130, 157; as issue, 90; and *Sophist,* 100; as general concept, 104; as transcendental, 104; and analogy, 104; not a being, 105, 107, 200; preunderstanding of, 107–108; of beings, 107, 117, 136, 154, 156, 185; and clearing, 121, 125, 155–57; and phenomenology, 131; and production, 133; and presence, 142, 145, 150; truth of, 155–59; beyond of, 155–56
being(s): truth of, 5, 155–59, 174; qua being, 18, 25, 171; and Being, 25, 105, 136, 154, 155–56, 175, 185, 200; un-

perplexed about, 101; regional, 111; history of, 162
Being-in, 119–21
Being-in-the-world, 26, 118–24, 127, 147, 165
Bergen, 184
Bilden, 154
Bildlichkeit, 66
Bildung, 172
Bildungslosigkeit, 173
Body, 159, 185, 187

Care, 185, 202
Categories, 70
Cave, 20, 133, 174, 183, 185
Circle, 98, 118, 120, 155
Circularity, 106, 109
Circumspection, 125
Clearing: for self-showing, x; as space, 27, 155–56; and Being-in, 119–21; and light, 120, 177, 185, 203; displaces Being, 121; and Being-in-the-world, 127; and presence, 147; and truth, 174–75
Closure: ix, 18–23, 138, 141, 145, 150
Cogito, 54–56
Concealment, 93, 94, 148, 165–66, 171–74, 183–84, 189–93
Concern, 135
Consciousness: transcendental, 23; of self, 44, 61, 117; natural, 57; as intentional, 64, 67, 72; and "image-theory," 65; content of, 72; as subject, 132
Considerateness, 125
Content, 80, 81

Da, 114, 119, 147, 165, 202
Darstellung, 77
Dasein, 112–18; and death, 21–22; and truth, 94; questions Being, 109; as place, 109, 114; and its Being, 114; as no subject, 109, 117, 122
Death: as extreme possibility, 21, 97, 131; Scheler, Heidegger, Socrates, 86–87; and origin, 88; and disclosedness, 93; Being-toward, 93, 138; Heidegger's analysis of, 93; and Hades, 184; and soul, 187; and sleep, 191
Deconstruction: and *différance,* 24; phe-

206